DEMOGRAPHIC PROBLEMS
Controversy Over Population Control

Second Edition

RALPH THOMLINSON
California State University, Los Angeles

Dickenson Publishing Company, Inc.
Encino, California and Belmont, California

ISBN-0-8221-0166-1
Library of Congress Catalog Card Number: 75-7296

Printed in the United States of America
Printing (last digit): 9 8 7 6 5 4 3 2 1

Cover photo by William L. Thomlinson
Cover design by A. Marshall Licht

Dedication

To the man I would most like somehow to have given another twenty years of life:

Wolfgang Amadeus Mozart —
One of seven children, five of whom died within six months of birth;
Father of six children, only two of whom lived six months;
Himself a survivor of scarlet fever, smallpox, and lesser diseases,
Only to die at the age of thirty-five years and ten months
From a cause not diagnosable by the medical knowledge of his time;
Thus making his life demographically typical of most of man's history.

CONTENTS

List of Figures   viii

List of Tables   viii

Preface to the Second Edition   ix

Preface to the First Edition   xi

Part I: Why Population Problems Exist   1

1. What the Facts Are   2

The demographic equation.   What does the world's growth mean?
How did we get this way?   Can we control the causes?   What do
demographers recommend?   What do other people think?   Five
viewpoints.   A brief history of demography.   Becoming and working as a demographer.   Organization of this book.

2. Ways of Life   16

Causal explanations.   Malthus on population.   Current population
crisis.   Feeding the world's people.   Alleviating the food-supply
problem.   A vegetarian diet.   Industrializing underdeveloped areas.
Pollution and resource depletion.   Density and violence.   Education and literacy levels.   Ideal population size.   Diverging opinions.

Part II: World and National Growth   37

3. World Growth of Population   38

Gathering population information.   Measuring rates and changes.
Present world growth.   Causes of the increase.   Long-term growth
trends.   Regional variations.   Developing areas.   Estimates for
the future.   Methods of projection.   National and world
estimates.

4. The Countries of Eurasia   54

Europe.   The Soviet Union.   Asia.   The Near East.   The Indian
Subcontinent.   Southeast Asia.   Mainland China.   East Asia.

5. The Rest of the World   81

Oceania.   Africa.   The Arab countries.   Latin America.   Anglo
America.   United States future.   The world at large.   Implications
of these trends.

Part III: Family Planning Controversy   97

6. Birth Control: Background   98

Demographic determinants of fertility.   Social norms influencing
fertility.   Fecundity and sexual behavior.   Economic influences on
natality.   A summary of fertility motives.   Two high-fertility
American sects.   Sterility and subfecundity.   Ways to measure
fertility.   Small family systems.   United States natality trends.

7. Birth Control: Arguments   118

Traditional family planning methods.   The pill and the future.
Beyond family planning.   Freedom and civil liberties.   History of
birth limitation.   Values and preferences.   Receptivity to birth
control.   The number of children wanted.   Expectations and ideals.

8. Birth Control: Religion   136

The concept of a prevented birth.   Papal actions from 1958 to 1967.
The 1968 Encyclical "Humanae Vitae."   Support for the Encyclical.
Opposition to the Encyclical.   Who knows the unchanging truth?
Natural law and sexual relations.   Relevance of natural law to
fertility.   Demographic implications of "Humanae Vitae."   Behavior
of Catholic couples.   Prospects for Papal change.

Part IV: Disputes Over Deaths and Moves   153

9. Death Control   154

Ways to measure mortality.   Preindustrial mortality.   Prescientific
medicine.   Modern medical science and drugs.   Disease prevention.

World levels of mortality. Health laws and services. The cost of medical care. Mortality in different groups. Infant and maternal deaths.

10. **Migration Control   174**

The measurement of migration. Sources of data. Entry into the United States. The brain drain. Immigration restrictions. Current United States laws. Motives and directions. Adjustment and integration. Black migration. A look at the future.

Part V: Correlates and Remedies   191

11. **The Structure of Population   192**

Sex roles and ratios. Aging and younging. Minority groups. Regional characteristics. Marriage and divorce. Educational enrollment and attainment. College education. Achieving world literacy. Work and leisure. Women who work. Income and poverty.

12. **National Policies   215**

The demand for action. Zero population growth. International organizations. Types of policies. National programs. The developing nations. The problems of India. The struggle in China. Programs in other countries. United States government. Are antinatal programs succeeding? Perfect fertility control. Reducing growth toward zero. Conclusion.

Recommended Readings   235

Index of Names   237

Index of Subjects   241

List of Figures

Figure 1. The Demographic Transition   5
Figure 2. Birth and Death Rates by Continents, 1975   45
Figure 3. Immigration to the United States, 1821-1970   179
Figure 4. Population Pyramids for Sweden, United States, India, and
          Costa Rica   194

List of Tables

Table 1. Growth of World Population   44
Table 2. Projections of United States Population, 1980 to 2020   51
Table 3. Projected Population, 1970-2000, for Major World Regions   52
Table 4. Population, Vital Rates, Growth Rate, and Per Capita Gross
         National Product for 163 Countries, 1973   66-79
Table 5. Natural Increase and Net Immigration for the United States,
         1810-1973   89
Table 6. Natural Increase and Net Migration for Florida and California,
         1940-1973   91
Table 7. Motives Favoring Large or Small Families   104-105
Table 8. Births per 1,000 Population Per Year in Selected Countries,
         1955-1972   114-115
Table 9. Deaths per 1,000 Population Per Year in Selected Countries,
         1955-1972   162-163
Table 10. Expectation of Life at Various Ages for Selected Countries,
          1950-1971   164-166
Table 11. Selected Biological and Social Characteristics by State, United
          States, 1970   198-201
Table 12. Selected Economic Characteristics by State, United States,
          1970   208-211

Preface to the Second Edition

As a result of world changes that have taken place since the first edition of this book was published eight years ago, I have added two new chapters and enlarged all of the first-edition chapters. Nearly all of the original pages have been updated or rewritten to incorporate recent demographic events and discoveries.

Since the publication of the first edition I have had the good fortune to work overseas for four years, living in Bangkok, Thailand; Rabat, Morocco; Paris, France; and London, England. During 1969-1971 I was Demographic Advisor at the Institute of Population Studies at Chulalongkorn University, Evaluation Advisor to the Thailand National Family Planning Program, and Consultant to the 1970 Census of Thailand. During 1972-1973 I served as Research Advisor to the Center for Demographic Research and Study, Government of Morocco. In 1973-1974 I was Visiting Scholar at the National Institute for Demographic Study in Paris, France, and at the Population Investigation Committee of the London School of Economics, England. As part of this overseas work I visited research and teaching centers in the Philippines, Kenya, Korea, Taiwan, Malaysia, Singapore, Hong Kong, Greece, Australia, and Egypt. To my hosts in all of these places, I extend my gratitude for their courteous hospitality. Additional professional and vacation trips to more than 50 countries on all six continents surely must improve the cross-cultural scope of this book. That my four countries of residence were, respectively, Oriental and Buddhist, Arabic and Islamic or Moslem, French and Catholic, and British and Protestant undoubtedly contributes to the perspectives presented in the following pages. I thank the Population Council in New York and the University of North Carolina at Chapel Hill for providing the opportunity for these experiences. Four years of leaves of absence from California State University, Los Angeles, made all this travel possible; for such acceptance of a faculty member who spent so much time overseas, I am grateful.

Of the persons who contributed to the first edition, only one suffered also through the preparation of this revision. To Margaret Thomlinson I offer profound gratefulness for months of typing and years of forbearance.

I cannot forget also the capable assistance of Stephanie Browning and Janet Greenblatt and the encouragement of Dick Trudgen, all of Dickenson Publishing Company. Photographs at the beginning of each part of the book were taken by my son, William L. Thomlinson, all between 1970 and 1973.

Preface to the First Edition

IF it is true that, as the distinguished demographer Alfred J. Lotka said, the preface is written last, placed first, and read least, this is the one place where an author should be able to say whatever he pleases, secure in the knowledge that no one will find out. Still, it seems appropriate to state that this book is designed as a sociological analysis of selected population trends, problems, and controversies in the contemporary world and especially in the United States.

Since demography cross-cuts departmental segregation, I have attempted to place population phenomena in context by spelling out interconnections with related subjects to achieve what Kenneth Burke praised as "perspective by incongruity." Bibliographic references have two purposes: assistance to readers who want to learn more, and acknowledgment of help received. I have tried to emulate Odysseus by steering a safe course between the rock of Auguste Comte's "cerebral hygiene" (refraining from reading the works of others) and the whirlpool of Tom Lehrer's "Lobachevsky" (advice to aspiring scholars: plagiarize), while also avoiding too much paraphrase and periphrase.

Population facts can be examined fully only by statistical analysis, although reporting and interpreting may be done through prose and diagrams. Since numbers and tables tend to inspire sensations of ineptitude in many otherwise reasonable people, these necessary means of presentation are held to a minimum.

This book could never have been written without the knowledge created and disseminated by several hundred demographic researchers throughout the world, most of whom were industriously collecting and analyzing population information years before population problems were "discovered" by popular writers. Scholars at universities are acknowledged in footnotes, but others contributed anonymously through research organizations. Especially deserving of thanks are persons affiliated with the United Nations Population Branch, the United States Bureau of the Census and the National Center for Health Statistics, the nongovernmental Population Reference Bureau in Washington, and the Population Council in New York City.

Several persons contributed more directly to the manuscript. David Dressler, Don J. Hager, and Herman J. Loether read drafts and proffered advice; Margaret W. Thomlinson provided essential clerical assistance; Elsa R. Shafer prepared graphs; and the Dickenson editorial staff tempered my sometimes impassioned prose. I hope readers will appreciate their efforts as much as I do.

This street market in Katmandu, Nepal, attracts
wandering cattle and a few customers.

PART I. WHY POPULATION PROBLEMS EXIST

The world's first problem in the rest of the twentieth century is peace: to keep the nuclear cold war from heating up. The world's second problem is population: to keep the quantity of human life from unduly affecting the quality of human life.

> *(Bernard Berelson, "The World's Second Problem: Population," Oberlin Alumni Magazine, Vol. LXI, No. 1, January 1965, p. 4.)*

Unless man halts population growth, population growth will halt man.

> *(Joseph J. Spengler, "The Economist and the Population Question," Presidential Address at the Seventy-eighth Annual Meeting of the American Economics Association, American Economic Review, Vol. LVI, No. 1, March 1966, p. 17.)*

Chapter 1. What the Facts Are

POPULATION problems are those demographic conditions which are regarded as undesirable by a large number of people, and which evoke the feeling that something ought to be done to eliminate them or at least to diminish their harmful effects. The first need is to point out where the problems exist, their natures and extents, and their long-term and proximate causes. From such understanding we can strive for effective solutions, recognizing however that different kinds of people prefer different types of solutions, depending upon one's cultural background and value system. In fact, value judgments also play a part in defining and even causing social problems as well as preventing people from agreeing on how to attack them.

Population must be studied — historically, to learn how the problems arose; geographically, to ascertain their locations; and analytically, to comprehend their constituents. First we must know the relevant vocabulary. Two words are paramount: *population* and its rough synonym *demography* (with its derivative forms *demographic* and *demographer*). Population refers to the thing studied, demography to the specialty proper, and demographer to the specialist.

The study of population seeks to define the number and types of people in an area, their distribution throughout the area, the changes in population size and variety, and the factors contributing to such changes. *Number* means simply the total population; *types* refers to the classification of the total into such groupings as male or female, married or single, well-educated or poorly-educated, rich or poor, and so forth. Population distribution is indicated by variations in density, especially the clustering of people around urban centers as opposed to rural scattering.

The Demographic Equation

Changes are instituted by many factors, three of which are so important that they have come to be called the three fundamental demographic variables: fertility, mortality, and migration. A moment's reflection should suffice to realize that there are only three ways in which the number of people in an area can be altered: a birth may occur, a death may take place, or someone may enter or leave. Only some people migrate, but birth and death occur to us all. Before birth, there must be sexual intercourse; before death, often there is sickness and pain. Thus demography shares the classic ingredients of popular stories: sex and death.[1]

Expressed in a simple "balancing equation," these variables show how population growth occurs:

$$P_f = P_i + B - D + I - O$$

This equation states that for any period of time, the final population equals the initial population plus the births that occur during that period, minus the deaths in that interval, plus the persons who move in, minus the number who move out. For example,

$$Pop_{1976} = Pop_{1975} + Births_{1975-76} - Deaths_{1975-76}$$

$$+ \text{In-migrants}_{1975-76} - \text{Out-migrants}_{1975-76}$$

Substituting actual numbers for a utopian colony on Desola Island, we have:

$$84 = 76 + 10 - 4 + 5 - 3$$

This shows that Desola grew from 76 enthusiasts to 84 by having 10 babies born, 4 persons die, a new family of 5 move in, and 3 disgruntled colonists move out.

Population facts affect the quality of human existence today, and can affect, as well, our way of life for the rest of the century. Growth rates and characteristics go a long way toward determining whether a nation is among the "haves" or the "have-nots." Among the "have-not" peoples, who constitute a majority of mankind, the wounds and scars aggravated by demographic problems will at best require a long time to disappear; at worst, they will fail to heal at all, inhibiting improvements in the standard of living and preventing people from attaining their proportionate share of the world's goods and pleasures.

Like the weather, demographic problems receive a good deal of attention; also like the weather, their control is hard to achieve. This book discusses both the causes and some potential solutions for the chronic and sometimes painfully acute disruptions attributable in some places to rapid population growth. Particularly relevant are discrepancies between the increase in the number of people and the increases in the supplies of food, shelter, and the luxuries that nearly all people desire. But population growth is not inherently harmful, and one must first identify which parts of the world are troubled and which are not. Let us begin, then, with the question of whether the quantity of human beings is helping or hindering the quality of human life.

What Does the World's Growth Mean?

In 1975 the population of the world reached 4 billion. Throughout the entire history of the human species, there probably have been about 70 billion people.[2] Thus the persons alive in 1975 constituted about 6 percent of all the people who have ever lived. Put more simply, for every person alive today, there probably have been only some 15 or 16 predecessors in human history.

With the world's population now doubling in about 35 years — or quadrupling in the 70-year lifetime of an ordinary American — a number of consequences arise. Some of them are desirable: nineteenth-century United States was an example of a nation helped by rapid population growth. But today, most of the effects of rapid increase appear to be undesirable.

More people in a given land area implies more crowding. Cities grow denser, buildings are built taller, and there are longer waits in theaters and restaurants. If we double the population, we should double the number of physicians, law courts, gas stations, parking spaces, ball-point pens, and so forth. But some things cannot be doubled: there is only one Grand Canyon — and the Yosemite Valley is getting so crowded that a New York City apartment dweller was heard to express bewilderment at how the campers could enjoy living so close together.

More people generally create more pollution of water and air — although per capita consumption of natural resources and production of effluvia is at least as important a contributing factor. If there are to be twice as many people 35 years from now, they are sure to produce twice as much smog and chemical wastes — and probably will generate three or four times as much of these noxious products of human ingenuity. And if increasing proportions of the world's people come to live at the American standard of living, then they may produce many times more pollutants than at present, throwing away more cans and wrappers and using more nonreplaceable resources such as coal and iron and oil.

In trying to achieve a higher level of living, nations sometimes are held back by population increase, for much increased national production is absorbed by increased population. For example, if Generation One has 100 workers using 100 shovels, and Generation Two has 150 workers, then 50 additional shovels need to be supplied simply to maintain the status quo and keep the workers employed. Of course, 150 workers can shovel 50 percent more dirt than could 100, but they also consume 50 percent more food and other products.

How Did We Get This Way?

Logically, world population increase can result from either lowering the death rate or raising the birth rate or both. To look only at the birth rate is to see only one-half of the cause. Historically, death rates in most countries declined earlier and faster than birth rates, thereby creating a period of population increase.

Figure 1 portrays this recent historical discrepancy in declines of the two vital rates; the lightly-shaded area is designed to emphasize that irregularities exist and that this diagram is schematic rather than strictly representational. Through most of history, both birth rates and death rates were high, resulting in an approximate balance or zero growth. But beginning a few centuries ago, first in Northwest Europe and later in other parts of the world, death rates declined; as birth rates tended to maintain their previous level, there resulted an excess of births over deaths, causing the rapid growth in recent centuries. Later, birth rates began to fall, diminishing the surplus of births over deaths, until now, in the most modernized nations, growth is nearly at a standstill and seems likely to reach zero in the foreseeable future. This new balance is both more efficient and more pleasant than the old balance, as fewer women now have to go through the discomfort and danger of pregnancy to little or no avail. With the new balance, much less physical and emotional effort is expended in bearing and rearing each new generation. The three evolutionary stages illustrated in Figure 1 form the basis of transition theory, a widely accepted historical explanation developed by Thompson and Notestein.[3]

As an example, let us take a European country that had a traditional birth rate averaging about 50 per year per 1,000 persons and a death rate of about 40, and which has current rates of 20 and 10, respectively. The 30-point drop in the death rate can be split into thirds. The first third of the decline was caused by a rising level of living beginning in the seventeenth century, the second third by

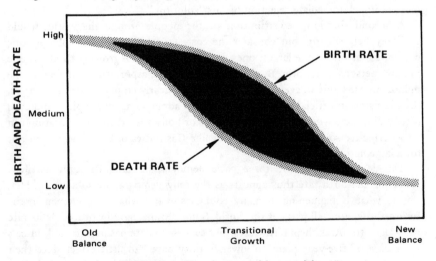

FIGURE 1. The demographic transition

5

improved sanitation (especially the widespread use of soap) beginning a century ago, and the final third by medical science beginning even more recently. For most of this period, the birth rate declined more slowly than the death rate — until the twentieth century, when the fertility decline speeded up. When, for instance, the birth rate had been reduced to 40 and the death rate was down to 20, the rate of increase was 20 (rather than the initial 10), which represents a growth of 2 percent a year (instead of 1 percent).

Some countries now are growing at more than 3 percent annually — a rate that may not seem very rapid unless one realizes that the maximum human performance is probably about 6 percent a year. The highest birth rate ever recorded throughout a generation is about 60. If no one died, the growth rate would be 6 percent. But as immortality is not a reasonable assumption, it seems more realistic to assume a death rate of 10 (the United States death rate has for years been fluctuating between 9 and 10), which results in an annual increase of 5 percent. Regarded in this light, the 3 and 3½ percent rates of some nations represent striking performances.

Can We Control the Causes?

One obvious solution to rapid population growth — and one that is quite feasible under present technology — is to raise the death rate until it equals the birth rate exactly. Although there are times when citizens suspect that their national leaders are trying to do this (through war, usually), humanitarian motives impel immediate rejection of this "solution."

A second solution, redistribution of the people around the world, would probably help slightly, but consider the cost. To examine the case of only one nation, albeit one of the largest ones, India's population is growing by about one million persons a month. But what means of transportation can carry one million Indians abroad every month (and return nearly empty)? For that matter, the immigration officials of no country would admit so many people — and even if they did, there would not be enough jobs or houses for them all. Migration can be an effective solution for a small area like Costa Rica or Puerto Rico, but not for a large nation the size of India.

This leaves, among the three basic demographic variables, only fertility. Lowering the birth rate thus appears as the only demographic solution. In fact, this is what is happening in many countries — and what may happen in the future throughout all parts of the world. Some nations have instituted deliberate campaigns to lower their birth rates, but success to date has been mixed. India's succession of five-year plans to lower fertility have had little effect since their beginning in 1951. On the other hand, the Japanese cut their birth rate in half in only 10 years (the most impressive fertility drop ever made by any nation). The success of such a program depends on many factors, only a few of which are understood.

In addition to those who advocate reduction of population increase are the persons who propose to leave population change alone and concentrate on increasing the production of food and other necessities. No one can oppose the idea of increasing the food supply, but if this were a feasible solution, then why have we not done so already? In fact, there are millions of undernourished people in the world today; if we cannot feed them properly now, how can we expect to feed 2 percent more people next year? The problem is essentially one of timing: certainly we can grow more food; but can we grow and equitably distribute twice as much food 35 years from now? And can we, similarly, produce twice as much housing, clothing, and so forth 35 years from now? Obviously, no one knows.

What Do Demographers Recommend?

To a demographer, these nondemographic solutions are not permanent: they just hold back the demographic tide for a while, like a finger in the dike. The popular view that agricultural, industrial, and transportational improvements will solve the problem of population growth is fallacious — and not just because of the need to increase production next year. Given a finite planet, an increasing population will ultimately overstretch the capacity of the planet to support its population.

Instead, most demographers are convinced that the only lasting adaptation is to lower the birth rate. Probably this must be done consciously and actively — which implies family planning or birth control. For national and world fertility to decline by voluntary action, ordinary people, even if illiterate, would have to come to understand the advantages to themselves personally of having fewer children than did their parents. That failing, it would be possible for governments to force people to limit family size, but there are obvious objections to such a Draconian step.

What Do Other People Think?

Public opinion polls report an increasing recognition of the seriousness of problems created by rapid population growth. This consciousness is reflected in newspapers: the number of inches in the annual index of *The New York Times* under the rubric "population" varied from 1 to 5 during 1950 through 1958, rose to 10 to 16 in 1959 through 1964, and thereafter rocketed to 26 in 1965 and 44 and 1970.[4] The number of annual entries in the *Readers Guide* under the

7

headings "Birth Control" and "Contraception" averaged 10 to 15 from 1915 through 1959, after which they zoomed to an average of 60 in the early 1960s and 100 in the late 1960s.[5] Possibly the greatest indicator of grass-roots popularity is the *Congressional Record*, the index of which devoted one inch or less to population annually throughout the 1950s but cited yearly entries averaging 6 inches in the 1960s, reaching 20 inches in 1969.[6] As multi-opinioned bumper stickers and even multi-opinioned television have now joined in recognizing population change as a force to be worried over and possibly manipulated, it is clear that concern over population growth is widespread and that solutions are open to debate.

Among the most basic concerns today is civil liberty, and population control has now entered this area. Should everyone be free to arrange the birth of his or her children whenever, and if ever, he or she wishes? Or should the federal government set and enforce restrictions on the freedom to conceive and bear children? Or is neither of these extremes reasonable, to be replaced by an intermediate alternative? Among the numerous possibilities is one suggested by the Women's Liberation movement whereby a woman would have freedom of control over her body and of the by-products of her body — to wit, fetuses. Some Roman Catholic authorities respond that fetuses are not subject to control by their female hosts, but have independent lives of their own and thus are entitled to all of the civil rights of living human beings. The argument is one of definition, whether a fetus is an independent living being or merely a protoplasmic blob in the mother's uterus. Whatever the solution to the fetal-entity conundrum, the birth rate in most nations will wend its way downward, and the death and migration rates will tend to persist more or less unchanged.

Curiously, Americans have never been exposed either to rigid restrictions on fertility and other population behavior, or to complete freedom from such regulations. Americans never have been required to have a specified number of children during a specified time period; nor have they ever been permitted to determine their reproductive behavior without governmental interference regarding the sale and use of contraceptives (nowhere does the American government permit the sale of contraceptives without hindrance). Advocates of one position or another want to portray the advantageous consequences of adopting their demographic ways (or to decry the disadvantages of following some other proposal) of living and trying to thrive in one or another country.

Five Viewpoints

Beliefs concerning population growth vary widely — as they have for many years. Some people hold positions reminiscent of Malthus, Marx, Catholic teaching, or other classic statements. Added to these continuing incarnations of

8

classic ideas are positions developed more recently. Five points of view tend to dominate today, as described by The Population Council in 1974.[7]

"At one end of the spectrum population growth is seen as a major crisis now facing mankind, perhaps the major crisis overshadowing all other issues." The key word is "crisis," appearing again and again in brochures distributed by public-spirited organizations crying out that population must be stabilized, that rapid growth prevents adequate food consumption and elevation of living standards, that zero growth should be achieved as soon as possible, that no one should have more than two children, or that the environment can be saved only if we retard population growth. This declaration of impending doom usually is advanced by a nondemographer who suddenly discovers that population is a major problem. Demographers live with this concern and ordinarily adjust to it gradually during their course of study; scholars in other disciplines, however, sometimes appear to have a sudden insight that population increase can generate severe problems. Some persons seem almost to experience a religious conversion. "This position has the attractiveness of clarity and simplicity — both the villainous cause and noble end are sharply identified, and in some formulations so are the means of solution, however severe — and that in itself, as in earlier historic crusades, is enough to gain adherence and fuel efforts."

A less clarion position is held by the "population establishment": rapid growth is undesirable, but it is not the source of all of mankind's ills. It should not be accepted as God-given, but its retardation should be encouraged by national policies. Advocates of this position divide into two camps concerning the means to achieve this agreed-on end. The long-run-oriented demographers believe that the only real solution is to increase educational levels, the status of women, levels of income, and to otherwise modernize the nation. Opposed are those who argue that significant short-run benefits can be derived from supplying birth control information and supplies to all who desire them, thereby preventing the birth of now-unwanted children.

Superficially moderate, but not so classified by scholars familiar with the facts of population change, are persons who hold that "population is a nonproblem — either irrelevant in that social change will automatically take care of adverse demographic trends, or trivial as compared to such issues as peace, poverty, racism, civil rights." This view slightly resembles that of the long-run demographic school in its advocacy that social and economic development will "naturally" bring down fertility and, hence, overall growth. But it differs in declaring the villain to be, variously, improper organization of society, technological depredations against nature, undue consumption of natural resources by the unduly affluent residents of "overdeveloped" countries, urban sprawl and the demographic denudation of the rural countryside, inequities in the distribution of income, or failure to follow traditional rules of morality.

A fourth stance claims that "population growth is positively good": density is too low, we need more soldiers, we need more people to run our factories, and more people buy more commodities and thereby elevate industrial productivity. People can flow into empty lands, people sustain economic vitality, people make the nation bigger and therefore stronger. In this view, countries win wars by throwing more soldiers into the field than the enemy can muster; and if the war is lost, the peace can be won in the classic Chinese fashion of interbreeding with the conquerors so that the victorious invaders eventually become absorbed into the defeated population.

The last position is concerned less with growth itself than with the meaning of ill-guided attempts to reduce growth: "growth is a false issue, and probably deliberately so. By this view, increasingly heard in Latin America and Africa in recent years, the population movement operates as, and probably is meant as, a neo-colonialist approach by the rich countries to hold down the poor countries in their own selfish interest." This interpretation is popular with black activists in the United States: "in its extreme form, this becomes the argument of 'genocide', especially as applied to its implications for differential fertility by ethnic and class groups." Abroad, the United States often is seen as a powerful but not necessarily benign influence, whose motives are suspicious. American efforts to lower fertility in developing nations sometimes is seen as offering greater benefit to the United States than to the receiving nation: by decreasing fertility elsewhere, the United States maintains its numerical superiority and hence its national power. Also, insofar as the United States offers welfare assistance to the poor people of developing countries, the fewer of them there are, the less money the Americans need to spend.

A Brief History of Demography

Questions concerning population have interested statesmen and scholars throughout history. In the fourth century B.C., Plato specified the ideal population of a city-state and prescribed measures to control fertility and migration. Benjamin Franklin was so concerned about the balance between resources and population growth that in 1755 he published a pamphlet entitled *Observations Concerning the Increase of Mankind.*

But until the nineteenth century, interest in population remained general, and there was little systematic investigation of the factors influencing the number of births, deaths, and migrants — nor was there much research into the relation of these three basic demographic factors to social and economic conditions and to human welfare. In fact, the word *population* did not come into significant use in the English language until the seventeenth century, and the term *demography* first appeared in 1855.

The title Father of Demography probably belongs to John Graunt, an

Englishman who in 1662 published a pamphlet called *Natural and Political Observations Made Upon the Bills of Mortality*. Unlike earlier scholars who had approached the study of population philosophically, Graunt was a believer in raw facts. He analyzed parish records of christenings, marriages, and burials, and he was the first to observe a number of important demographic phenomena, including the excess of male births over female births and the excess of deaths over births in large towns of those times.

This new science of "political arithmetic" received increasing attention during the century following Graunt, during which there were several important advances in knowledge and research techniques, including the construction of the first "life table" of mortality by Edmund Halley (of comet fame). Yet it was not until 1798 that the next major development in demography occurred, when Thomas Robert Malthus published his famous work, *An Essay on the Principle of Population*. Malthus's interest in population theory stemmed from a controversy that was popular in the aftermath of the French Revolution: whether or not man and society were capable of perfection. Malthus argued that they were not — because the human capacity to reproduce was greater than the ability to increase the means of subsistence — and that throughout history, therefore, population has always been held to the limit imposed by subsistence. This essay stirred tremendous interest in the "population question" throughout Europe, and as a result, Malthus is intimately associated with the origins of population theory. Such has been his prominence in intellectual history that his *Essay* is often listed as one of the one hundred most influential books in the history of the Western world.

Due in part to this stimulus provided by Malthus and other writers, the nineteenth century was a time when population theory was introduced into other social and economic theories, including, for example, the writings of John Stuart Mill and Karl Marx. Two major developments which occurred during the nineteenth century also added to the impact of demography. First, the growing popularity of life insurance encouraged advances in the measurement and analysis of mortality. Second, the increasing scope and reliability of the two basic sources of demographic data — censuses and vital statistics registration systems — provided a tremendous increase in the quantity of accurate data, thereby permitting a greater range of demographic research.

In the present century, increasing attention has come to be devoted to nearly all aspects of demography, from the mathematical to the policy-oriented. Formal demography attempts to explain the logical interrelationships among the various patterns of fertility, mortality, and migration; some researchers carry this to the extent of building mathematical models and simulating regional populations using computers. From the early interest of Graunt and other pioneer students of demography in mortality, the primary emphasis has now shifted to fertility — especially the childbearing practices of persons of different social and economic classes. This interest and concern reached a high level during the depression of the 1930s, when birth rates dropped nearly to what was defined as the "replacement level" of the adult generation by their children. The increase in fertility that immediately followed World War II — the "baby boom" — further stimulated investigation into the determinants of fertility behavior. The change after 1957 to an uninterrupted decline in fertility has continued to stimulate research.

The 1970s marked the entrance of this technically oriented subject into the area of national policy through the efforts of such organizations as Zero Population Growth. The Commission on Population Growth and the American Future was appointed by the President and Congress of the United States to study long-term national population trends, to estimate probable repercussions of these trends, and to recommend solutions to resultant problems. The Commission's final report in 1972 suggested a national policy welcoming and planning eventual stabilization of population growth in the United States. Whether such stabilization is to be sought after or achieved — as well as how to select the means toward achieving or avoiding stabilization — is for the demographers of the present to discuss and for the demographers of the near future to decide upon.

Becoming and Working as a Demographer

If there is enough disputation and factual information on a subject to write a book about it, then presumably people work at it. Population is no exception. Demographers deal with population statistics and their interpretation, and they work in various occupations: many are college professors, others work for federal or local government agencies, some are employed by research foundations or businesses, and a few have the good fortune to go overseas as consultants to other nations. Their primary function is not always demographic, for demography forms an underpinning of many other subjects; many specialists in other fields believe that population is one of the "givens" of their work.

Demographers have many functions, collecting data by supervising field interviews, putting this information through computers to be systematized for analysis, and evaluating and explaining the meaning of such statistical findings. Usually a demographer is qualified also to work as a sociologist, economist, statistician, or other specialist; some even combine demography with more distant fields such as medicine, anthropology, or public health.

To be a journeyman demographer calls for a Bachelor of Arts or even a Master of Arts degree plus several years of experience working with population statistics; full qualification normally requires a Ph.D. With only the baccalaureate, one is likely to be a technician.

12

Some demographers develop narrow specialties which fit them uniquely for certain posts, such as measuring the migration toward the suburban fringe or evaluating the effectiveness of birth control programs. Others are broadly knowledgeable, able to change from one specialty to another. The complete demographer is a Doctor of Philosophy who has done research on all of the three basic variables of fertility, mortality, and migration, and who is reasonably competent at data collection, statistical analysis, and oral and written presentation of results to peers and outsiders. Few demographers possess all of these attributes to a high degree, but many can perform each of these tasks satisfactorily albeit not brilliantly.

People who wish to be identified with demography join professional organizations in that field. In the United States the most complete list of demographers is the membership roster of the Population Association of America, which in October 1974 included 2,504 persons. Some members are best described as "interested in demography," so that the actual number of *bona fide* demographers is appreciably smaller. By whatever criterion, demographers and quasi-demographers are increasing more rapidly than the general population, for P.A.A. membership twelve years earlier was only 660.

The international association of demographers is the I.U.S.S.P. — the International Union for the Scientific Study of Population — which included 1,209 members as of December 31, 1973. The five countries contributing the most members are: United States, 332; France, 80; United Kingdom, 54; India, 53; and Italy, 46. Undesirable though it may be that any one nation should contribute one-fourth of the world total, there is no question from this and other evidence that the United States is the world leader in demographic research and personnel. Partly for this reason, English is the dominant language of demographic research, with French second, and all other tongues far behind.

Organization of This Book

Now that the most prominent demographic questions have been raised and several halting answers offered, the remainder of this book will explore more thoroughly the existence, causes, and cures for many demographic ills. But the problems and controversies should not be overemphasized here, for much of the book will be devoted to non-problems — that is, population facts and how they came to be facts.

Nevertheless, Chapter 2 briefly and broadly portrays population in relation to social problems affecting many of our activities. Two major problem areas concern the standard of living. First is food — the prime necessity for life. That people must be fed is obvious; but how the food supply is to be increased to keep up with population increase is far from obvious. Second is the satisfaction of the desire for luxuries — comfortable housing, automobiles, electric appliances, and other materialistic products best supplied by industrialization.

Chapter 3 turns to the numbers of people in the world, the condition most popularly viewed as the major world demographic problem. Actually, however, the greatest threat arises not from sheer quantity of people but rather from the rate and amount of increase in that quantity. Natural increase — the surplus of births over deaths — is adding vastly to the amount of people inhabiting the world. Throughout most of history, population grew slowly or not at all and sometimes even declined; but during the last few hundred years the tendency has been toward a large increase — a trend which has been augmented decade by decade. This shift from a gradual rise in humanity's numbers in eras before the industrial revolution to the present rapid acceleration is called the *population explosion* — a term chosen to indicate both the rapidity of growth and the possibly disastrous implications thereof. While there are many persons who doubt the validity of the term "explosion," population specialists agree that world population is increasing faster than it ever did before. Exploration of the causes and consequences of this shift in speed of growth, and what, if anything, can or should be done about it is the primary objective of this book.

In Chapters 4 and 5, discussion of population size and growth is addressed to continents and countries. Because the presentation of bare population statistics does not ensure understanding, these two chapters include geographic, anthropological, and economic information (albeit minimal) about the resident populations, to provide a context for comprehension of what is now occurring or may occur in the immediate future in these nations.

Chapters 6 through 10 are devoted to the three crucial factors — births, deaths, and migration — explaining why population increase does or does not take place, and how quickly. Because nearly all national increases occur through an excess of births over deaths, and because the most controversial issue in population today is that of control over the birth rate, fertility is discussed first and most extensively, in Chapters 6, 7, and 8. The other biological way to change population numbers, mortality, is joined with its obverse, longevity, in Chapter 9. The third of the three variables forming the heart of demography is migration; Chapter 10 analyzes movement into and out of countries, regions, and cities.

These three basic variables are interrelated with other demographic variables, the most important of which are discussed in Chapter 11. The age and sex composition of a population is fundamental to all demographic phenomena. Similarly, the racial, linguistic, family, educational, occupational, and other make-up of population are both responsible for, and responsive to, multifarious nondemographic trends in social and cultural change.

What to do about population forms the nucleus of Chapter 12. Various ideals and theories regarding population size, growth, and quality lead to recommendations concerning what to do about population trends and the present and prospective problems arising from them. Rulers and administrators use some of these recommendations to enact a variety of national policies attempting to alter demographic trends.

NOTES

[1] Goran Ohlin, quoted in T. H. Hollingsworth, *Historical Demography* (London: Sources of Hisotry, 1969), p. 11.

[2] Nathan Keyfitz, "How Many People Have Lived on the Earth?," *Demography*, Vol. III, No. 2, 1966, pp. 581-582.

[3] Warren S. Thompson, "Recent Trends in World Population," *American Journal of Sociology*, Vol. XXXIV, No. 6, May 1929, pp. 959-975; and Frank W. Notestein *et al., The Future Population of Europe and the Soviet Union* (Geneva: League of Nations, 1944).

[4] Phyllis Tilson Piotrow, *World Population Crisis: The United States Response* (New York: Praeger, 1973), p. 22.

[5] *Ibid.*, p. 21.

[6] *Ibid.*, p. 104.

[7] The Population Council, "The President's Report," *Annual Report: 1973*, New York, 1974, pp. 20-26 (all quotations in this section are from this source).

Chapter 2. Ways of Life

DEMOGRAPHY is not a narrow discipline; it is related to many fields of study. Demography is a service discipline — that is, its facts and theories are basic to every social science for description, causal analysis, and prediction. The stock of human beings is the raw material out of which human lives and interrelationships stem; as a result, population is fundamental to almost every problem besetting mankind.

Consequent upon demographic breadth is the fact that acquisition of accurate quantitative information about the population in a given place and time is only an initial, although essential, step toward the more important objective of discovering the motivations and consequences of demographic behavior. Understanding population conduct is aided by accepting the pertinent advice traditionally given to fledgling newspaper reporters: state who, what, when, where, why, and so what.

The complexity of population factors is such that one may not look at only one hypothesis at a time or seek explanation for population growth in oversimplified "urges" such as the reproductive instinct. Such particularism is more to be found in after-the-fact explanations than in actual demographic behavior. In recent years the Japanese, faced with larger families than they apparently wanted, responded to the stimulus of rapid growth in almost every known demographic manner, each taking his own route: "Within a brief period they quickly postponed marriage, embraced contraception, began sterilization, utilized abortions, and migrated outward."[1] They also adopted nondemographic responses: increasing industrial productivity, increasing the food supply, and raising the standard of living. The moral of this story is that if several weapons are available, people tend to use them all.

With life expectancy varying from 74 years in Sweden to about 35 years in several African nations; with literacy ranging from 99 percent in Scandinavia to about 5 percent in Ethiopia; and with the per capita gross national product rising as high as $4,700 in the United States and remaining below $100 in many African and a few Asian countries — the world's opportunities and goods are so unevenly divided as to threaten peace and harmony and to spur meliorists into action to improve the human existence, especially in underdeveloped areas.

Causal Explanations

Explanations of the ways in which populations and their constituent parts remain the same or grow have been put forth by many writers in ancient, medieval, and modern times. For instance, the sixteenth-century Benedictine monk François Rabelais had one of his characters in *Gargantua and Pantagruel* speak of the effects of alcohol and intellectual activity: the former leads to "dissipation of the generative seed" (though moderate drinking is helpful: "Master Priapus was the son of Bacchus and Benus"), the latter to impotence ("That is why Pallas, the goddess of wisdom and protectress of scholars, is said to be a virgin"). Other sources supply evidence that this nonsense was widely believed — and is still accepted by some people. Another very popular generalization was advanced by, among others, James Steuart, who believed that eating meat lowered fecundity:

> Were the people of England to come more into the use of living upon bread, and give over consuming so much animal food, inhabitants would certainly increase, and many rich grass fields would be thrown into tillage. Were the French to give over eating so much bread, the Dutch so much fish, the Flemish so much garden stuff, and the Germans so much sauerkraut, and all take to the English diet of pork, beef, and mutton, their respective numbers would soon decay.[2]

This fallacious reasoning lives on in the specious scientizing of such men as Josué de Castro, a contemporary physician who grossly overstates the influence of certain dietary elements (especially protein) on fertility.

Long before Malthus was born and long after he died, other scholars and policy-makers accepted that part of Malthusian reasoning that has come to be called the dismal theorem of economics: since the major checks on population growth are disease and famine, then regardless of how bounteous is the natural environment or how advanced the technology, population will inevitably continue to increase to a certain maximum, after which sickness and starvation will curb further growth. The third-century Christian priest Tertullian wrote that the strongest witness of the blessings of catastrophes is "the vast population of the earth to which we are a burden, and she scarcely can provide for our needs; as our demands grow greater, our complaints against nature's inadequacy are heard by all. The scourges of pestilence, famine, wars, and earthquakes have come to be regarded as a blessing to overcrowded nations, sinse they serve to prune away the luxuriant growth of the human race."[3] Not to be outdone by the pessimism of early writers, modern economists have evolved a corollary known as the utterly dismal theorem: since the major checks on population growth are disease and starvation, then any technological or social improvement will ultimately increase the sum of human misery through permitting a larger number of people to live their lives suffering from undernourishment and chronic illness.

Many motives besides a desire for intellectual understanding inspired such rationalizations of existing situations and attempts at theorizing — and since the inspiration was more often practical than intellectual, the so-called theories were frequently little more than policy recommendations. Another deterrent to successful theoretical explanation was the paucity of accurate statistical information from which to generalize and through which to test hypotheses. But by the eighteenth century, data were forthcoming, and when Cantillon, Godwin, Wallace, and Condorcet wrote with heated convictions about population problems, the Reverend Thomas Robert Malthus was motivated to reply in a thin volume published in 1798, factually documenting his arguments in subsequent revisions of this thickening best-seller.

Malthus on Population

Before the appearance of Malthus's famous *Essay on Population*, useful demographic theory was virtually nonexistent; with this book, demography as a scholarly subject came of age. The sixth edition of 1826 was a detailed, organized compilation of existing statistics, bound together as systematically as could be expected for those times by analyses of causes and results. Malthus's book immediately attracted and continues to attract an amount of attention rarely equaled in the history of scholarly publishing, and the *Essay* has been included in most listings of "greatest" and "most influential" writings. The book plunged its author at once into heated controversy, figuring prominently in political, economic, and moral disputations from its publication to the present time.

Malthus's accomplishments were less a product of originality than of synthesis. As biographer James Bonar wrote, Malthus "got most of his phrases, and even many of his thoughts, from his predecessors; but he treated them as his predecessors were unable to do; he saw them in their connection, perspective, and wide bearings."[4] That Malthus should get the credit for thus developing other men's ideas is quite fitting, for as Alfred North Whitehead said, "We give credit not to the first man to have an idea but to the first one to take it seriously."

The direction of Malthus's book is indicated by the title of the definitive edition of 1826: "An Essay on the Principle of Population, or a View of Its Past and Present Effects on Human Happiness, with An Inquiry into Our Prospects Respecting the Future Removal or Mitigation of the Evils which It Occasions." The heart of his doctrine lies in two propositions: "(1) Population is necessarily limited by the means of subsistence. (2) Population invariably increases where the means of subsistence increase, unless prevented by some very powerful and obvious checks."[5]

China, which in Malthus's time was the largest nation on earth (as it is today), illustrates the operation of these propositions. Malthus reported the Chinese population as "immense," cited Adam Smith's supposition that it was stationary, and proffered his own view that "it certainly seems very little probable that the population of China is fast increasing."[6] According to propositions one and two, China's population grew to the maximum supportable by having nearly the entire labor force engaged in food production. This "natural tendency" of the population to increase was reduced sharply in times of drought, flood, war, or pestilence — after which it gradually returned to its previous maximum.[7] Thus China, as other nations, was described as experiencing a zig-zag pattern of slow growth up to a limit, sudden decline, slow increase to the same limit, another abrupt decline, and so forth — an interpretation of demographic history which has supporters to this day, if one does not take the maximum limit too literally.[8]

Malthus made many telling points, but because of his neglect of the possibility of improved agricultural methods, widespread industrialization, faster transportation, and extensive use of birth control devices, his theory lost favor after his death in 1834. Malthus lacked the modern appreciation of change, conceiving of the world in essentially static terms and assuming that the social, economic, moral, and technological conditions of his day would also be the conditions of the future.

But Malthusian doctrine seems to contain more strengths than weaknesses, for twentieth-century scholars and politicians alike have revived Malthus to the extent that all post-Malthusian theories are classified as neo-, pro-, anti-, semi-, or quasi-Malthusian, and a few writers go so far as to attach these prefixes to theories antedating Malthus. Thirty years before President Johnson's 1964 declaration of "war on poverty," a group of Englishmen formed a Malthusian League having the motto "A Crusade against Poverty" and claiming that "prophylactic intercourse alone and unaided is fully sufficient to eliminate poverty." Although passersby might have noticed angry rumblings from the parson's grave (for Malthus could not tolerate contraception), these words agree in spirit if not in method with Malthusian principles.

The English cleric influenced research as well as action programs. During an illness Alfred Russell Wallace, the co-founder of evolution theory, read Malthus's remark that the various checks to population growth tend to eliminate the least fit: 'Vaguely thinking over the enormous and constant destruction this implied, it occurred to me to ask the question, 'Why do some die and some live?' . . . Then it suddenly flashed upon me that this self-acting process would improve the race. . . . Then at once I seemed to see the whole effect of this."[9] Charles Darwin also credits Malthus with the phrase "struggle for survival" and the inspiration for Darwin's thought; but Malthus should not be considered the originator of the notion of evolution, for being mainly interested in population and economics, he did not take the idea seriously enough to follow it to its scholarly conclusions.

Current Population Crisis

That any one book should prove so viable testifies to the continuing significance of population concerns. The future of the world depends to a large extent on solving the problems of the population explosion.

Aside from practical considerations is the matter of esthetic values. Population growth accelerates dissipation of resources and intensifies scarcity. Recent demographic growth is megalomaniac, being dominated too much by dinosaurism and too little by esthetic values; the countryside is chewed up, and blind and pointless urban blight is accentuated.[10]

In Japan land is so limited that venerated cemeteries are being dug up to make room for modern buildings and superhighways. Graves are reclaimed with due ceremony and the remains are resettled in cells inside high-rise "apartments for the dead." The superior of one ten-story "Thousand and One Tower" said he "felt sorry for the dead, some buried in ancestral plots for more than 300 years. But we figured the dead would understand our difficulties and the changing times." As for the living, "the people who want to rest here after they die are mostly city folks used to living in small crowded houses."[11]

Humanity creates its own culture, and in so doing alters the environment it inhabits and also the rhythm of its own reproduction and demise. Consequently, the number of people has increased explosively during the past three centuries and today continues to gain at an increased rate. Short-run prospects of unabated demographic acceleration include augmented political unrest and exacerbated threats to world peace; long-run extrapolation of present rates of expansion indicate that they cannot possibly continue, for people would eventually run out of standing room and even breathing space.

Feeding the World's People

The most important issue raised by population increase is food. For people living in a nation whose major food problem seems to be how to eat as much as they want and not get fat, it is difficult to realize that residents of many regions are faced with exactly the opposite problem: how to get enough food to keep from starving. Compared with the 3,000-plus calories per day customary to Americans and western Europeans and the 2,500 calories needed for good health, inhabitants of many African and Asian nations average fewer than 2,000 calories daily — and these are the very people whose diet is poorest in balance. Caloric requirements are not identical for all people, for they increase according to body weight, decrease with age, increase in cold climates, and increase for women who are pregnant or lactating.[12]

Diet-deficient areas include most of Central America and the Caribbean, the northern part of South America, all of Africa, and all of Asia except Japan and Israel. So badly-off are some of these countries that when an American economics professor returning from five years in India was asked: "I would like a simple yes or no answer. No long lecture. Is India going to make it or not?," the best he could do was to reply: "India is one-sixth of the human race. Is the human race going to make it?" and then write a five-page article ending with "It depends."[13]

Much hope is placed in the "green revolution" fathered by Norman E. Borlaug, the 1970 Nobel Peace Prize winner and the developer of "miracle" wheat. Such high-yield grains plus the increased use of chemical fertilizers have raised food production. But if food supply is to keep pace with the increasing people supply, still more improvement is needed.

Insufficient quantity and variety of food occasionally kill people. But it is not death through famine that is the greatest problem; rather, it is the malnourished person's chronic fatigue and his susceptibility to disease. Relatively few people actually die of starvation, but huge numbers are weakened from too little food — or from too little protein and too few vitamins and minerals. Often these persons cannot manage an effective day's work, and when they are struck by disease, they are sicker than would be a well-fed person. They lack the general bodily resistance, the strength to fight off disease, so that an ailment that a sound body can thrust aside in a week may linger for a month — or kill. A 1971 report by the Pan American Health Organization on deaths of children under age five disclosed that malnutrition directly caused only 8 percent of the deaths, but that it was a contributory cause in another 46 percent. That is, it played a role in 54 percent of all childhood deaths (under five), but in most cases its effect was through aggravation of a disease — and at that, a disease which might not have killed a well-nourished child.

Perhaps half of the people of the world are insufficiently nourished as regards both quantity and variety. Some observers assert that enough food is produced, and that the problem is one of distribution; however, evidence supports the contention that there is not enough food produced in the world today. And if population succeeds in doubling every third of a century, the food supply must be doubled also just to maintain its per capita level. To reach a reasonably adequate nutritional level, the world's food production would have to double between 1975 and 2000, a faster production increase than the 2 percent a year now achieved. Thus throughout the 1960s, increased food production almost exactly equaled increases in population, permitting no improvement in nutrition. Some agricultural regions had an even smaller production increase than this disappointing world average, and unfortunately these laggard areas were frequently among the ones experiencing the fastest population growth, thereby aggravating existing inequalities in per capita food supply.

Alleviating the Food-Supply Problem

Each region should be able to supply enough food for its inhabitants. However, as long as some areas have an insufficiency while others have a surplus, there is an immediate prospect of loading food into cargo ships and sending it to where it is most needed. But the question arises, just where will the food do the most good? Because no nation has enough surplus food to distribute it to all who ask, selection is necessary. One approach is to send a little food to every nation in need. Another approach is to select the neediest nations and send them as much food as they require; if any food is left over, it can then be sent to nations whose distress is not quite so pressing. But the decision remains: which nations should get priority? Two Americans — William Paddock, an agronomist, and his brother Paul, a Foreign Service official — suggest solving the problem by the concept of *triage*.[14]

Originally, triage was developed by military doctors to assign priorities in treating wounded soldiers. Ideally, of course, each casualty should receive full attention, but often there are so many wounded soldiers that doctors and paramedical personnel have time only to attent to a minority of the wounded, the rest being left for tomorrow. Often there are not enough beds, bandages, salves, and serums. And as war is inherently callous, it should not come as a surprise that treatment may be ordered in an unfeeling and practical fashion. Triage divides the wounded into three classes: first are those so badly injured that they have no chance for survival, for which medical treatment would only drag out life or relieve pain; second are those who can recover without treatment, although probably faster and less painfully if given medical aid; and third are those who would die without care but whose lives can be saved by treatment. It is this third group that receives the attention of the medical corpsmen and physicians.

By analogy, the Paddocks recommend that the United States, the Food and Agriculture Organization, and other food-distributing agencies might supply food first to those agriculturally-wounded nations whose citizens might die without foreign aid but may live because of it. Probably few persons would object to giving them priority, and one can easily rationalize that residents of class two countries are not really starving; but it is heartrending to deny food to class one. How can we consign a nation of people to this "hopeless" category, so far "behind the eight ball" agriculturally that, in the Paddocks' judgment, "to send food to them is to throw sand in the ocean"?[15]

Regardless of what the assistance agencies do, the problem is caused by an unfavorable ratio between population and food supply. And the problem will not be solved until each region of the world produces enough food for its people. Other difficulties, such as income disequities, exacerbate this problem, but they are not basic causes.

In his Presidential Address before the 1965 meeting of the American Economic Association, Joseph Spengler took a centuries-long view: "The future of the food problem may be stated simply. Suppose we increase world output 700 percent by doubling crop and acreage and quadrupling yields. World population would catch up with this increase in about 107 years, given an annual growth rate of 2 percent, and in about 140 years, given a 1.5 percent rate."[16] As the 1973 world growth rate was 2 percent, the implication is clear.

The quantity of food produced is only a part of the problem; not only agriculture but also transportation, politics, economics, and sociology are germane. To assure everyone the necessary caloric, vitamin, and mineral intake would require expansion of transportation facilities, greater ease of crossing national boundaries, reorganization of land tenure, raising the minimum income to the point where everyone could afford to buy what food is available, and persuading people to eat the less desirable foods.

Americans are prone to assume that mechanization of agriculture will automatically raise production. But the truth is that mechanization raises production per man-hour and per dollar while actually lowering production per acre. If it is maximum total production we want rather than maximum profits, then it would be better to reconvert to hand cultivation with its provision for tender loving care for each plant.[17] Fertilization, irrigation, pesticides, and use of hybrid and more efficient crops also are recommended, but unfortunately most of the world's farmers cannot afford to buy commercial fertilizer, water pumps, sprays, and new plants and animals — although this situation is correctable with enough subsidy. Irrigation suggests another problem: water is coming into short supply as more people make more per capita use of it. Inexpensive desalination of ocean water seems just a question of time, but natural scientists hint that thus tampering with the balance of nature may add more problems than it solves.

Rapid reorganization of the present wasteful systems of land ownership and marketing would require almost superhuman efforts, for legal and social change almost always proceed slowly. And raising the real income of the impoverished is no easier.

We might almost as easily abandon farms and develop new systems of aquaculture — farming the ocean — a promising source of vast quantities of additional food, if only men can agree which nations have jurisdiction where. Yet the prospects of aquafarming can easily be overstated. Ponds, rivers, and lakes can be stocked with fish, and ocean shorelines can be farmed systematically for fish and algae. But most water surface — and by far most of the water depth — is open sea, which is far less capable of producing edible products. Growing food in vats of water — hydroponics — is another possibility, but it is very expensive and profligate in its use of water. In the face of existing threats to water supply, it seems inadvisable to expend water in this way.

Increasing food from the oceans will require some sort of international cooperation, which has been lacking for centuries but has developed into a crisis-level problem only recently. The traditional doctrine that the seas are free to everyone was enunciated by Hugo de Groot in 1609 on the principle that oceans are limitless, cannot be enclosed, and therefore cannot be the possession of anyone. But national leaders were not willing to allow foreign powers close to their shores, and in the eighteenth century an agreement was made that each nation's jurisdiction extended three miles out from the coastline (because three miles was the range of the largest cannon of the time). In 1945 the United States extended this principle by claiming to own the petroleum resources on and under its continental shelf, which extends in places as much as several hundred miles from the shore. In the 1950s other nations claimed territorial privileges, including exclusive rights to fish and transportation routes, extending variously 12, 50, or even 200 miles out to sea. The United Nations attempted to make such nationalistic claims consistent through conferences in 1958, 1960, and 1974, but maritime laws remain a jumble of arguments and counterclaims, as fishermen and national governments argue acrimoniously over catches. As in other matters, each country seems to want the most it can get, expecting the other nations to compromise. Until some sort of international law of the sea is agreed upon, unilateral manifestos and two-nation agreements will continue to make rational development of ocean resources nearly impossible, as each country rushes to grab all the food it can with little or no effort at conservation or seeding for future generations.

A Vegetarian Diet

Vegetarianism appears to be the best way to support a large and dense population, as is illustrated in China. It is remarkable that between one-fifth and one-quarter of all the world's people are supported by the land area in a single country, especially as that country has had until quite recently almost no industry. As Trewartha points out, the support of vast rural populations at high densities is unique to the rimlands of South and East Asia.[18] So how do they do it?

The explanation lies in the manner in which each civilization orders its human and natural resources and organizes its territory. The cultures of China and most other southeastern Asian societies are based on vegetable products. The diet is vegetarian, cloth is woven from vegetable fibers, tools are made from plant products, and houses are wooden. Such dependence on the vegetable kingdom affects the appearance of the landscape and determines the upper limit of population that the land can keep alive. People who live largely on a diet of grains, vegetables, tubers, fruits, and nuts are capable of much greater densities than those whose food intake is balanced between vegetable and animal products. A valley planted in rice or wheat produces five to ten times more food than if the same area were devoted to pastureland for edible animals. It is for this reason that the vegetarian diet typical of the Far East has enabled the build-up of large and dense populations. Vegetarianism also seems to provide a one-way route to population growth, for once an agricultural population has reached the high density level permitted by a strictly vegetarian intake, it cannot turn back; and though it might be gastronomically interesting to add beef and ham to the weekly fare, it is not possible to teach the land to produce enough animal products to feed the numbers of people that already inhabit the region. Thus an agricultural economy which has maximized its density by maintaining a non-animal diet can add to its consumption of animal protein only by importing food from outside areas.

Vegetarian cultures did not adopt vegetarianism in order to maximize their populations. No one knows why they adopted this dietary practice, for all we can do is reject the most obvious hypotheses. As Buddhism is the dominant religion in East and South Asia, it is tempting to lunge at a religious explanation. In fact, however, vegetarian habits preceded Buddhism. Moreover, the Buddhist exhortation to respect life does not necessarily imply a corollary prohibition of eating milk, cheese, and eggs; it depends on which branch of Buddhism one follows. There is no evidence that any quality in the physical environment of this part of the world encourages a vegetarian diet. Neither population growth nor density provides an explanation, for the historical fact is that the population surge was produced by the vegetarian diet, and not the reverse. Se we are left with the pseudo-explanation that oriental cultures favored vegetarianism — for unknown reasons.

The cause is past, but the moral remains: if we want to support larger numbers of people, one way to do this is to reduce consumption of meat and dairy products. To feed ever-increasing populations, world leaders may be compelled to encourage or even compel people to eat more grains and vegetables and less meat, eggs, and milk. If food prices continue their present tendencies, persuasion may not be necessary, for rising prices may induce the next generation to change from meatless Tuesday to meat only on Wednesday.

Recommendations concerning food production, processing, and distribution too frequently presuppose that the problem is simply one of instituting agricultural and technological improvements. People resist changes regarding the ways farms are run, the way food is sold and bought, and what is eaten. The social and psychological factors affecting receptivity to unfamiliar food is a highly emotional subject. During World War II, shortages of certain foods in the United States were accompanied by an abundance of other foods that people did not care to eat. To some people, corn is for animals, not humans; to others, milk is considered bad for the stomach; in other cases the lower class or caste connotations of certain foods make them unsuitable ("nigger food" or "po' white food" in the South); and so on. Food preferences are much more culturally determined than is commonly believed, being for most of us a matter of eating what we like, liking what we are accustomed to, and categorically rejecting some nourishing substances.

Industrializing Underdeveloped Areas

If dietary preferences are among the best examples of resistance to innovation, the standard of living provides a marked contrast. Few peoples anywhere resist chrome-encrusted Chevrolets and cowboy movies on television; the real complaint against American materialism seems largely that Americans have so much more of it than the have-nots. Unfortunately for these desires, producing transistor radios and automatic pistols requires raw materials, capital, and technological skill. In the two-thirds of the world that is underdeveloped (Japan is the only fully industrialized non-Western country), capital to buy factory machines and workers with the knowledge to operate them are scarce. Foreign capital and personnel are difficult to obtain, so the underdeveloped nations must do their own developing – a progress slowed by high agrarian density and rapid population growth.

When the food intake averages 1,800 calories a day, it is difficult for leaders to decide to channel money away from the purchase of food and into the purchase of turret lathes, however desirable in the long run. And when the number of these hungry mouths grows by 2 or 3 percent annually, the economy has to grow by that percentage just to keep up, thus absorbing much if not all of the hard-won gain in the gross national product. The arithmetic is simple: the more people, the more food and clothing and shelter they must have to subsist. Where, then, comes the financial or other surplus for investment in technological equipment and the school buildings and books necessary to train the labor force needed to operate and service this equipment? Ironically, in these densely populated regions there is often actual labor shortage, created by large proportions of people too young to work, poor health among adults, taboos on certain work for certain groups, and low educational standards.

In such nations as India, Morocco, Brazil, Colombia, and Ghana, more than 10 percent of the gross national product is absorbed merely in keeping income per person from declining.[19] To increase per capita income, still more would be required. But as these countries have little prospect of so dramatically augmenting their production, a more effective route to increased personal incomes would be the reduction of fertility. So important is this that an economist with extensive experience in impoverished nations has written explicitly that "no country has ever modernized, or reached an advanced level economically, with sustained high fertility."[20]

Pollution and Resource Depletion

High fertility means more people, each of whom turns into a resource-exhauster and polluter as soon as he or she becomes old enough to know how to consume and litter. But numbers of people are not enough, for the developed nations have learned how to supply their citizens with enough materials to pollute at a higher rate than inhabitants of underdeveloped areas. Every person who drives an American car is pushing around a ton of metal and hundreds of pounds of other raw materials, burning gallons of petroleum products and using miles of cement and bitumen. The better one's standard of living, the more of the world's resources one squanders. For this reason, the United States and other rich nations have been accused of expending more than their share of the world's resources.

In a provocative essay, Paul Ehrlich has an Indian Ambassador to the United Nations present a "25 Indians and a dog" speech, in which he argues that Americans consume so much more of the world's goods than do Indians that the birth of one American baby is "a greater disaster for the world than that of 25 Indian babies," adding pejoratively that an average American family dog is fed more animal protein in a week than the average Indian person gets in a month.[21] Less inflammatory but more telling is Lincoln and Alice Day's documentation of the great drain on world resources by Americans, especially rich Americans.[22] Viewed in this light, each new baby may be a blessing to its parents, but to the rest of the world it represents a tiny, long-lasting capsule of catastrophe.

In its diatribe against the global disaster implied by present population growth trends, the Club of Rome made four basic points about the earth's capacity to absorb pollutants. First, pollutants seem to be increasing exponentially. Second, we do not know what the upepr limits of these pollutants might be because scientists have not yet figured out how much we can disturb the natural ecological balance of the planet without serious perturbation — "how much CO_2 or thermal pollution can be released without causing irreversible changes in the earth's climate, or how much radioactivity, lead, mercury, or pesticide can be absorbed by plants, fish, or human beings before the vital processes are severely interrupted." Third, the existence of natural delays in ecological processes makes difficult both the assessment of long-term effects and the estimation of the control measures needed; if we underestimate the controls

27

that we need, we may inadvertently reach the upper limits of pollution. Finally, many pollutants travel well, so that harmful effects occur at great distances from their places of generation; some pollutants thus become distributed throughout the world, regardless of their points of origin. [23]

Contamination began almost with the first human village, although application of the full force of our abilities had to await high densities and the development of modern chemicals. By spraying the pesticide DDT and then eating the plants so sprayed, Americans have managed to lodge in their body tissues an average of 10 parts DDT per million. As DDT is a suspected carcinogen, and as the Federal Food and Drug Administration forbids the sale of food containing carcinogens, it follows that Americans are not fit for human consumption.

Waste disposal is a problem of growing immensity, which began with our assumed arboreal ancestors. "The trees offered a built-in sanitation and refuse system. Whatever was discarded, it all fell neatly to the ground — excreta, nutshells, pods, hair-droppings." When someone died, the body released its handhold, "slumped off, fell, and disappeared. On the ground below, the humble scavengers and the processes of decay soon dissipated all such materials and returned them to the soil." [24] Twentieth-century disposal habits do not seem significantly improved, as Walt Kelly pointed out in a famous Pogo cartoon: "We have met the enemy, and he is us."

Water and air are especially damaged. Air is contaminated by factory and auto exhausts, water by the use of our streams and lakes as repositories for industrial effluvia. As both water and air suffer from such treatment, so do those who consume them. "Till taught by pain, men really know not what good water's worth." [25]

If there is such a thing as an ultimate typology of pollution and resource depletion, Barry Commoner has prepared it in the form of four laws of ecology: 1) "everything is connected to everything else," 2) "everything must go somewhere," 3) "nature knows best," and 4) "there is no such thing as a free lunch." [26]

Density and Violence

To increasing pollution is added another liability that may be associated with high population density: aggressiveness. The hypothesis that overpopulation and high density lead to tensions, crime, violence, and perhaps war is becoming popular with certain biologists. For years we have been told that aggressive behavior is inherent in man — an inescapable part of his basic nature. [27] Now some scientists argue that aggression is environmentally caused, resulting from painful frustrations induced by lack of food, sex, or space. Perhaps the truth lies in a combination of the two viewpoints: some aggression may be biologically caused, some socially caused. As yet, no one knows.

Research on laboratory animals has led to some fascinating findings. Calhoun's experimentation on rats over many years points clearly to deteriorating social relations as density increases. Some males become highly aggressive, attacking other males, nests of babies, and pregnant females more or less indiscriminantly. Others become passive, avoiding all social interaction. Female rats become lackadaisical about infant care and experience a higher proportion of spontaneous abortions. [28] But one cannot generalize to other creatures, for Chauvin points out that the reactions to ultra-high density vary greatly from species to species. [29] Certainly it is not wise to infer that human beings would have the same reactions as rodents.

For this reason, some scientists have tried to test the density-aggression hypothesis for man by examining crime rates and the incidence of other antisocial behavior in areas of markedly different densities. Unfortunately, however, the effect of density cannot be isolated from the effects of the many other environmental influences that inevitably are present in a nonlaboratory setting, and the only reasonable response to such studies is skepticism.

One psychologist suggests that the cause is not density at all but rather the absolute number of people that one has contact with. In the view of Jonathan Freedman, the sheer number of individuals with which a person interacts has a substantial influence on his personality and behavior. [30] Both density and numbers have logical rationales, but until further research is completed, all we can do is consider the rival hypotheses. Perhaps eventually someone will discover that both theories are valid — to supplement or even replace the hypothesized role of instinct.

Education and Literacy Levels

There is no dispute, however, about another consequence of population growth: the difficulty of raising educational attainment and reducing illiteracy. The prevailing low levels of literacy and schooling in underdeveloped nations is disturbing. But to improve these conditions requires teachers, paper, and places for instruction. And when a country has trouble feeding or housing all of its people, leaders are tempted to devote the national budget to the immediate needs for food and shelter and put off until tomorrow the allocation to build schools, buy books, and pay teachers' salaries.

Two types of persons must be provided for: the ones in school and those potentially able to attend. The government of Thailand has decided to raise its level of compulsory, free public education from four years to seven years. In order to do this, it must jump two hurdles: first it needs to send a larger proportion of 5-to-14-year-old children to school; second, it must accommodate a larger number of 5-to-14-year-old children. A country with zero population growth would only have to solve the first problem; but as Thailand's population is increasing by 3 percent a year, the educational planners must be prepared to have 3 percent of their accomplishments absorbed by the population increase; only after that can they hope to improve the general level of educational attendance and eventual attainment. [31]

The increases in pupils flowing from each of these two sources have been calculated by Gavin Jones. For illustration, Jones assumed that a high-fertility country increases the proportion of its children aged 5 to 14 who attend school from 40 percent to 95 percent in 30 years. If fertility continues high throughout the 30 years, then the enrollment rate would increase by 517 percent (and what developing nation could afford the cost of such an increase?); if fertility declines slowly, the pupils increase by only 292 percent; finally, a rapid fertility reduction means that the department of education would have to contend with only 200 percent more pupils. [32] As even this latter growth of the student bodies would be difficult to manage (even if they got the money, where would they find that many competent teachers?), it is obvious that the faster a high-fertility nation reduces its birth rate, the more feasible will be the improvement in educational standards so badly sought in most countries.

Without universal literacy and moderate education, it is difficult to establish the skilled labor force needed to staff factories, produce and repair machinery, and otherwise modernize a nation. Educational deficiencies can cripple national efforts to raise the standard of living; indeed, one of the most common impediments to industrialization is the lack of an educated labor force in a country with an excess of illiterate manpower. Obviously the benefit is there for the taking; the riddle is how a developing country can channel enough national effort into education today to raise its level of living tomorrow.

Ideal Population Size

Overpopulation and its opposite, underpopulation, both imply the existence of an ideal or optimum population. But demographers are increasingly reluctant to compute an optimum, partly because of the difficulty of agreeing on criteria (social welfare, military strength, gracious living, or industrial production?), partly because the optimum twenty or fifty years in the future might well be different (and much of the point of ascertaining the optimum is to have something toward which to direct policy), and partly because size is frequently less important than direction and rate of growth. Despite this inability to identify an ideal size, demographers generally feel competent to state that some countries are definitely too large or too small in population, and of course it is the "too large" category that is more common and which receives more attention.

The most optimistic scholars refuse to worry about overpopulation on the presumption that if there is sufficient need, technological improvements will be developed to meet the threatened crisis — necessity is the mother of invention. On the other hand, an ounce of prevention is worth a pound of cure. The humanitarian action of preventing distress is preferable to the Samaritan readiness to help the afflicted afterwards. One may be disposed to ask why the world should support larger numbers of people at a low standard of living — or why we should permit population growth to contribute to continuance of low living levels.

Most nations are raising their per capita gross national product, but such improvement is not always possible. Nigeria, for example, had its GNP per person decrease during the 1960s. Even those developing nations that are increasing their per capita GNP are not improving it as fast as most of the developed countries. Thus the existing gap in living levels between the rich and the poor nations may widen instead of narrowing. The cause is two-fold: first, the gross national product results from the operation of a complicated economic, industrial, and agricultural network, with intermittent interference from war or civil disturbance; second, increases in GNP inexorably are counterbalanced by increases in population. Thus a slow growth of GNP per capita may be caused by a poor economic-industrial system, or the growth may be canceled out by having the population grow as fast as the GNP. To improve an unsatisfactory situation, a country can either improve its mechanisms for productivity or reduce population growth — or both.

Diverging Opinions

Population ramifications are both practical and theoretical, harmful and beneficial. Leaders have the choice of advocating demographically conflicting aims: for example, national military prowess and the gross national product may be augmented by an increasing population, but this very growth may accelerate depletion of raw materials, retard accumulation of capital, and hinder improvement in per capita income. Thus, depending on one's point of view and one's conception of problem priorities, the growth of population may be regarded as either a contributor or an obstacle to economic and social betterment.

Some authorities argue that rapid population increase constitutes the world's foremost problem, exceeding in importance even the threat of atomic warfare. Witness four forceful statements despairing the imbalance of natural resources and population growth; for similes, these natural scientists chose cancer, rabbits, maggots, and nuclear bombs — compelling imagery indeed. First is a former director of the Rockefeller Foundation medical division: "There is an alarming parallel between the growth of a cancer in the body of an organism and the growth of human population in the earth's ecological economy."[33] Another leading physician also fears an adverse outcome: "The number one problem facing man today and tomorrow is overpopulation and starvation. . . . If we breed like rabbits, in the long run we have to live and die like rabbits."[34] A California Institute of Technology biochemist supplies the sobering thought that: "A substantial fraction of humanity today is behaving as if . . . it would not rest content until the earth is covered completely and to a considerable depth with a writhing mass of human beings, much as a dead cow is covered with a pulsating mass of maggots."[35] A despondent atomic physicist completes the list: "The population bomb is as great a threat to mankind as the nuclear bomb. Fortunately, its fuse is longer."[36] Apropos of such unbridled rhetoric, T. W. Schultz remarks "how indebted we are to talent from the exact sciences for revealing to us the ominous scarcity of natural resources . . . axioms explicit and exact, concepts clear and identifiable, and the connections rigorous and precise."[37]

In the eyes of demographers, the people of the world are now facing one of the most serious threats to peace and, indeed, life in the history of man. Neglect or disparagement of the gravity of demographic trends and their consequences may lead to an untoward dénouement and conceivably even to catastrophe. On the other hand, if men inform themselves about the genesis and possible consummations of population change, they may be able to take action to bring about a more favorable outcome. After all, men have faced grave problems before and have demonstrated themselves to be flexible and often ingenious in averting potential disaster.

In the past, old demographic problems often have been solved by creating new ones. Men have alleviated the tragedy of early death only to introduce the unanticipated consequence of rapid and massive population increase and a resultant demand for unprecedented quantities of food, clothing, shelter, and various quasi-necessities. While growth pains might be eliminated by increasing the death rate or by suddenly decreasing the birth rate, both of these actions would in turn introduce additional difficulties — as the former solution is inhumane and the latter opposed to many prevalent ethical and religious injunctions (not to mention the problem of a suddenly aging population that might result from precipitous fertility decreases).

The population explosion is coming to rank with the nuclear bomb as man's greatest threat — an ironic pairing in that the two potential evils are superficially opposite in effect.

NOTES

[1] Kingsley Davis, "The Theory of Change and Response in Modern Demographic History," *Population Index*, Vol. XXIX, No. 4, October 1963, pp. 345-366.

[2] James Steuart, *An Inquiry into the Principles of Political Science* (London: 1767).

[3] Quintus Septimius Florens Tertullianus, *De Anima*, c. 200-230 A.D.

[4] James Bonar, *Malthus and His Works* (New York: Macmillan, 1924), pp. 32-33.

[5] Thomas Robert Malthus, *An Essay on the Principle of Population* (London: 1826), p. 14.

[6] Malthus, *An Essay on the Principle of Population*, first edition, 1798 (New York: The Modern Library, 1960), pp. 24-25.

[7] *Ibid.*, pp. 205-219.

[8] Leo A. Orleans, *Every Fifth Child: The Population of China* (London: Eyre Methuen, 1972), p. 37.

[9] Alfred Russel Wallace, *My Life* (London: Chapman and Hall, 1905), Vol. I, p. 362.

[10] Joseph J. Spengler, "The Aesthetics of Population," *Population Bulletin*, Vol. XIII, No. 4, June 1957, pp. 69-73.

[11] Associated Press story from Tokyo, published in Bangkok *Post*, August 14, 1969, p. 7.

[12] J. Carpenter, "Man's Dietary Needs," in Joseph Hutchinson (ed.), *Population and Food Supply* (London: Cambridge University Press, 1969), p. 68.

[13] Robert R. R. Brooks, "Can India Make It?," *Saturday Review*, August 9, 1969, pp. 12-16.

[14] William Paddock and Paul Paddock, *Famine — 1975!* (Boston: Little Brown, 1967), p. 206.

[15] *Ibid.*, p. 207.

[16] Joseph J. Spengler, "The Economist and the Population Question," *American Economic Review*, Vol. LVI, No. 1, March 1966, p. 19.

[17] Fred Cottrell, *Energy and Society* (New York: McGraw-Hill Book Co., 1953), pp. 134-135.

[18] Glenn T. Trewartha, *The Less Developed Realm: A Geography of Its Population* (New York: Wiley, 1972), p. 268.

[19] George C. Zaidan, "Population Growth and Economic Development," *Studies in Family Planning*, Vol. I, No. 42, May 1969, p. 5.

[20] Gavin W. Jones, "The Economic Effect of Declining Fertility in Less Developed Countries," The Population Council, New York, 1969, p. 27.

[21] Paul Ehrlich, "Eco-Catastrophe," in Michael E. Adelstein and Jean G. Pival (eds.), *Ecocide and Population* (New York: St. Martin's Press, 1972), p. 36.

[22] Lincoln H. Day and Alice Taylor Day, *Too Many Americans* (Boston: Houghton Mifflin, 1964).

[23] Donella H. Meadows, Dennis L. Meadows, Jorgen Randers, and William W. Behrens III, *The Limits to Growth* (New York: New American Library, 1972), pp. 78-93.

[24] George R. Stewart, *Not So Rich as You Think* (Boston: Houghton Mifflin, 1967), p. 9.

[25] Lord Byron (George Gordon), *Don Juan*, 1819-1824.

[26] Barry Commoner, "The Closing Circle," *The New Yorker* September 25, 1971, pp. 60, 68, 70, and 76.

[27] Konrad Lorenz, *On Aggression* (New York: Harcourt, Brace and World, 1963).

[28] John B. Calhoun, "Population Density and Social Pathology," *Scientific American*, Vol. CCVI, No. 2, February 1962, pp. 139-148.

[29] Rémy Chauvin, "Vues de démographie animale," *Population*, Vol. XXVIII, No. 2, March-April 1973, pp. 253-258.

[30] Jonathan L. Freedman, "The Effects of Population Density on Humans," in James T. Fawcett (ed.), *Psychological Perspectives on Population* (New York: Basic Books, 1973), pp. 209-238.

[31] Ralph Thomlinson, *Thailand's Population: Facts, Trends, Problems, and Policies* (Bangkok: Thai Watana Panich Press Co., 1971; republished in Winston-Salem, North Carolina: Wake Forest University, 1972), pp. 83-84.

[32] Gavin W. Jones, "Effect of Population Change on the Attainment of Educational Goals in the Developing Countries," in Roger Revelle (ed.), *Rapid Population Growth: Consequences and Policy Implications* (Baltimore: Johns Hopkins Press, 1971), p. 339.

[33] Allen Gregg, "Hidden Hunger at the Summit," *Population Bulletin*, Vol. XI, No. 5, August 1955, p. 74; quoted in Harold J. Barnett, "Population Change and Resources: Malthusianism and Conservation," in National Bureau of Economic Research, *Demographics and Economic Change in Developed Countries* (Princeton: Princeton University Press, 1960), pp. 423-451.

[34] A. J. Carlson, "Science Versus Life," *Journal of the American Medical Association*, Vol. CLVII, April 16, 1955, pp. 1437-1441.

[35] Harrison Brown, *The Challenge of Man's Future* (New York: The Viking Press, 1954), p. 221.

[36] Quoted in Robert C. Cook, "The Population Bomb," *Bulletin of the Atomic Scientists*, Vol. XII, No. 8, October 1956, p. 296.

[37] Theodore W. Schultz, "Comment" on Barnett, "Population Change and Resources," *op. cit.*, p. 454.

Squatter shacks adjoin modern apartments in
overcrowded Hong Kong.

This aboriginal Meo village in northern Thailand
has ample space.

PART II. WORLD AND NATIONAL GROWTH

Somewhere in the world there is a woman giving birth every minute. What we have to do is find that woman, and stop her.

(Anonymous)

The period of gestation here is three months.

(Dominican Republic official)

Chapter 3.   World Growth of Population

POPULATION arithmetic is sometimes simple and sometimes complicated. At its simplest, the number of people is measured by merely counting heads, and changes are found by adding births and subtracting deaths — the difference being the growth or decline of world population. But confining oneself to this basic method limits generalization and prediction; hence demographers make complex analyses of various factors contributing to changes in the numbers of births and deaths, from which they may estimate the likelihood that present rates will continue or alter. Therefore, this chapter begins with the discovery and analysis of the simple facts of present totals plus births minus deaths, and then examines the interwoven threads of human behavior, which give life to population statistics.

Gathering Population Information

Facts concerning population are derived from a number of sources, the principal ones being censuses, registration systems, and sample surveys. Various other data sources also contribute to demographic knowledge: archives, unofficial historical descriptions, studies of housing and farms, health records, and even such recondite material as can be found in excavations of ancient communities and the inscriptions on tombstones and family Bibles; these only contribute marginally, however, to the centrally-important statistics that have been obtained over the last few centuries from censuses and registration systems, and in the present century from sample surveys.

A census is the observation and recording of the number of people in a country. Everyone is counted, and usually information is obtained about age, education attained, occupation, marital status, housing accommodations, income, and similar properties of the people. Because taking a complete census is quite expensive, censuses are normally separated by intervals of about ten years; also because of the expense, only major governmental units can afford to conduct censuses. Huge numbers of interviewers must be hired, many forms must be printed, and much transportation must be undertaken. After the data are gathered, they must be checked for accuracy and completeness, compiled into tables, and printed.

Originally intended in most countries to provide the rulers with information about potential sources of tax revenue or about manpower available for military service, censuses now have been transformed into scientific instruments carefully separated from exploitative uses. No longer are censuses arms of the tax collectors or the military; indeed, census information about individuals is now regarded as secret information, not to be disclosed even to other government agencies.

Modern censuses attain high levels of accuracy and coverage. Special studies designed to evaluate censuses reveal that those taken in highly literate, industrial nations generally contain errors of 2 to 3 percent; the percentage varies from country to country, from year to year, and from region to region within a given country. Older censuses everywhere and recent censuses in underdeveloped nations often contain gross inaccuracies and omissions, even exceeding 10 percent, and usually it is necessary to interpret their results with informed caution.

The number of countries that take censuses is increasing. In the decade 1965-1974, some 89 percent of all countries and territories took censuses. In 1955-1964, this percentage was 79. A more meaningful way of looking at these statistics is that the percentage that did not take censuses was cut from 21 to 11 — a reduction by almost one-half. This remarkable improvement was created mostly by the thirteen African nations that took censuses for the first time in the period around 1970.[1]

A census is the best instrument for learning the number, distribution, and characteristics of the people residing in any stipulated area. But it is a poor instrument for measuring change, for it provides a static portrait, correct for a given moment in time. Changes can be detected and measured only by comparing the results of two censuses covering exactly the same territory. Implicit in this procedure is the liability of having to wait until after the second census to learn anything about the rate of change since the earlier census.

Complementing the census is the registration system, which is not as useful as a census in providing a one-moment snapshot, but which is far more valuable for supplying detailed measures of growth or diminution of population, region by region, and period by period. A registration system records the occurrence of births, deaths, marriages, divorces, and whatever other events are chosen for inclusion — for example, moves to other dwellings, onset of and recovery from major illnesses, or entrance into and release from military service — for any given time interval, but usually a month or a year.

Like censuses, most registration systems were originated for nondemographic purposes, most often to keep records of christenings and funerals, to provide evidence for inheritance of property, or to supply proof of identity and citizenship of each individual. Unlike censuses, most registration systems have maintained all or part of these legal objectives, while adding demographic functions as well. As with censuses, registration systems vary greatly in completeness from country to country, generally increasing their accuracy through time, and generally providing reasonably complete coverage in modern countries having high literacy and high levels of living. Finally, registration systems resemble censuses also in that they are too expensive to be maintained by nongovernmental means.

Partly because of the expense of these first two methods of obtaining data, and partly because our knowledge of sampling has grown so considerably in the present century, government as well as private statisticians are turning with increasing frequency to sample surveys as sources of information. Also, sampling is coming to be used within censuses as a means to reducing costs. Demographic sample surveys do not differ methodologically from other sample surveys (except that the sample size tends to be larger in population surveys), the requirement being to obtain a representative sample through probabilistic, randomized procedures. Because they take less time and money to conduct, sample surveys can be made more frequently than censuses. In addition, they sometimes contain more questions — or more penetrating ones — than either censuses or registration systems can handle.

Possibly the world's best example of a demographic sample survey is the Current Population Survey which the United States Bureau of the Census has been conducting since 1942. Every month, interviewers ask questions (which change frequently) of some 58,000 households across the nation. Results are published in several series of "Current Population Reports" on school enrollment, unemployment, intention to purchase major appliances, and similar topics. Many other countries maintain similar national sample surveys.

So popular is opinion sampling becoming in industrialized nations that it would be difficult to find an American newspaper reader who had not heard of the Gallup Poll. Developing countries also are beginning to use sample surveys, even in situations where the interviewer must ford a stream, hack down underbrush to make a path, fight off vicious dogs, or ride an elephant.[2]

Measuring Rates and Changes

Once collected, statistics must be analyzed if they are to be meaningful. The most obvious tools are the familiar percentages, proportions, and rates with which so many other types of data are analyzed. Rates for births, deaths, and moves will be discussed in Chapters 6, 9, and 10, respectively. In addition, more complicated measures have been devised, some of which also are mentioned in later chapters.

Like other social researchers, demographers make extensive use of the means, medians, variances, confidence levels and limits, and other impedimenta of basic statistics. Because population data involve especially large numbers of cases, they are particularly suited to analysis by computers. Simulation models are also being used. And because population is inherently related to territory, maps and graphs are essential.

For statements about the future, demographers use a special set of techniques which are summarized later in this chapter. Finally, we have also developed research techniques especially designed to help understand population trends in countries where complete data are unavailable; these techniques, however, are too complicated to be presented here.

Present World Growth

From a literal reading of available census and registration results, plus what sometimes are little more than informed guesses in the cases of countries with incomplete data, demographers estimate that the world population is about four billion people, of whom almost three-fifths live in a single continent – Asia. At its present global rate of increase of approximately 70 million annually (enough to populate a new nation larger than Great Britain and one-third the size of the United States), the world will double its present population by the end of the century. If any facts can give us pause, certainly these should.

A quick and easy way to assess historical growth is to note how long it took to reach each billion of population. The world's people first totaled one billion about 1820 and thereafter rose to two billion around 1930, three billion in 1960, and four billion in 1975. Thus after requiring hundreds of thousands of years to achieve the first billion, the people of the world added another billion in little more than a century and then two more billion in the last 45 years. The five- and six-billion marks are expected to be reached by about 1985 and 1995 respectively.

Clearly this rapidity of increase cannot proceed for more than a few years without creating drastic dislocations. The speed-up in world growth since the middle of the twentieth century was described by Robert C. Cook, director of the Population Reference Bureau, as "one of the most omnious developments of our time." Julian Huxley admonishes us that "the human population is probably the gravest problem of our time." Indeed there is substantial agreement among authorities on demography that uncontrolled human increase is a luxury the world can no longer afford.

Not only is this high velocity of growth a serious challenge to the world, but it presents an especially formidable and grievous problem to those countries having high densities, low incomes, depressed living standards, and a sometimes desperate desire for economic development. In such areas present population growth rates of 2 and 3 percent a year – and in some nations even more – are crippling

41

handicaps compelling heroic efforts even to maintain existing economic levels, let alone to raise them.

Causes of the Increase

The primary reason for these increases is easy to find: there has been an historically unprecedented decline in mortality in the developed nations, and a recently increasing decline in the underdeveloped areas. Reasons for lowering of the death rate include improved agriculture and transportation, the development of industrialization, advances in preventive and curative medicine, and various other factors raising the level of living. On the other hand, fertility has not experienced the same rapid drop; in fact, in some areas it is hardly declining at all. The result is an increase in the quantity of people walking on the earth. Since agreement exists regarding the desirability of lowering the death rate still further, the birth rate, for the first time in human history, is becoming the principal dynamic force in world numbers — and consequently the principal problematic factor for demographic policy-makers.

This demographic transition has to date followed a standard sequence in all countries. From an early condition of balance, the greater rapidity of the mortality decline over the fertility decline creates a transitional growth stage, which may finally end when birth and death rates are once more approximately equal. The shift from the old balance to the new one (assuming it is ever reached) generally requires a century or two, although recently a few nations — Japan, in particular — have shown signs of completing this transition in a few decades. One should not take this balance idea too literally; the equality is approximate, as illustrated by a letter to Alfred Tennyson concerning his lines "Every minute dies a man/every minute one is born," written by Charles Babbage, the man who made the greatest contribution to the development of computing machines:

> I need hardly point out to you that this calculation would tend to keep the sum total of the world's population in a state of perpetual equipoise, whereas it is a well-known fact that the said sum is constantly on the increase. I would therefore take the liberty of suggesting that in the next edition of your excellent poem the erroneous calculation to which I refer should be corrected as follows:
>
> Every moment dies a man
> And one and a sixteenth is born.

I may add that the exact figures are 1.067, but something must, of course, be conceded to the laws of nature.[3]

In the past, ravages of disease kept mortality and fertility in balance with each other — and also with the natural resources on which life depends. In recent times, epochal medical and other advances have conquered many of our former major killers, with the revolutionary result of greatly augmenting our numbers. The present falling birth rate shows signs of an eventual equality with a now low death rate, but until that equipoise is attained, the world will continue to multiply several times in the lifetimes of our children, thereby precipitating a chain of economic and social crises that may or may not be controlled.

Long-Term Growth Trends

The unusualness of the recent acceleration of world population growth is documented in Table 1. Note that the growth rate that Malthus feared remained in his lifetime only .5 percent a year; what, then, would he think of our present rate exceeding 2 percent? All figures in the table are presented with only one or two digits (plus some zeroes as place-holders) to avoid conveying a false impression of accuracy. The first four figures are most flatteringly described as informed guesses, but since 1650 there has been a gradual improvement in our knowledge, and the twentieth-century statistics are fairly well known. That is to say, the first digit is certainly correct, and the second is a close approximation; 3.6, for example, means that the population is three and a half million or somewhat more, and 3.9 signifies a population of four million or a bit less. The earliest statistics in the table, however, are based on the principle of "the population must have been about this much."

The "Years to double" column helps to bring the percentages to life: for many persons, .8 percent is hard to visualize, but it is easy to understand that 90 years from your birth, there will be twice as many people in the world. Even more meaningful is the idea that 33 years from now, when most college students will be in their 50s, the present population will be doubled if current growth rates continue unchanged. And if a 20-year-old lives another 66 years to reach age 86, the present population of some four billion will be quadrupled to 16 billion or so unless there is a change in birth and death rates. The utility of the doubling notion lies in the ease with which we can visualize two (or four) times as many persons in our home town or neighborhood shopping center — and the quick fright that this double vision engenders.

The present rate of world population growth of approximately 2 percent annually results from an estimated world birth rate of 35 persons per 1,000 population per year and estimated world death rate of 15. The 100-120 million babies that probably will be born during the next 12 months should exceed the 45-50 million deaths to result in a natural increase of 55-70 million persons.

TABLE 1

GROWTH OF WORLD POPULATION

Year	Population	Percent increase per year since the previous date	Years to double since the previous date
10,000 B.C.	1-10 million	Negligible	Many thousand
5,000 B.C.	5-20 million	Negligible	Many thousand
0	200 million	Negligible	Many thousand
1300 A.D.	400 million	Negligible	Many thousand
1650	.5 billion	.1	1000
1700	.6 billion	.2	300
1750	.7 billion	.3	230
1800	.9 billion	.4	180
1850	1.2 billion	.5	140
1900	1.6 billion	.6	120
1950	2.4 billion	.8	90
1970	3.6 billion	2.1	33
1975	4.0 billion	2.1	33

Source: Compiled from A.M. Carr-Saunders, *World Population* (Oxford: The Clarendon Press, 1936), p. 42; United Nations, *Demographic Yearbook,* New York, 1948-1973; and Bernard Berelson et al, "World Population: Status Report 1974," *Reports on Population/ Family Planning,* No. 15, January 1974, p. 3.

It is unfortunate that these basic facts are not precisely known, but the truth of the matter is that the world's population has never been completely counted nor thoroughly covered by statistical systems registering births, deaths, and moves. Thus, although most of the world's people are periodically counted and about 90 percent of all human beings have been enumerated at some time since 1950, there are still major gaps in demographic knowledge. Despite these deficiencies, population statistics are in general among the most accurate measurements taken with respect to human beings. Most industrial countries have well-developed census and registration systems yielding data reaching a precision of 97 or 98 percent. Additionally, a few peasant-agricultural nations have surprisingly competent organizations devoted to collecting and analyzing data. Other countries are less fortunate, notably China. The deficiencies in world

44

demographic knowledge are due to three facts: some nations cannot afford censuses and registration systems; there is a shortage of qualified research personnel; and some governments give little importance to counting their inhabitants.

Regional Variations

World averages mask considerable regional variations. Continental birth rates vary from Europe's 15 persons per year per 1,000 population to Africa's 45. As for death rates, the continental variations range from about 10 in Europe, Anglo America, and Oceania to around 20 in Africa. These statistics are consistent with the historical fact that the western European nations were first to experience the demographic transition from the old balance to the new. The high rates for both fertility and mortality in Africa are indicative of the lag of that continent in entering the transition cycle. Intercontinental variations in birth and death rates and hence in natural increase are shown in Figure 2. The residual natural increase is not identical to the overall rate of growth, which may be slightly larger or smaller than natural increase because of migration.

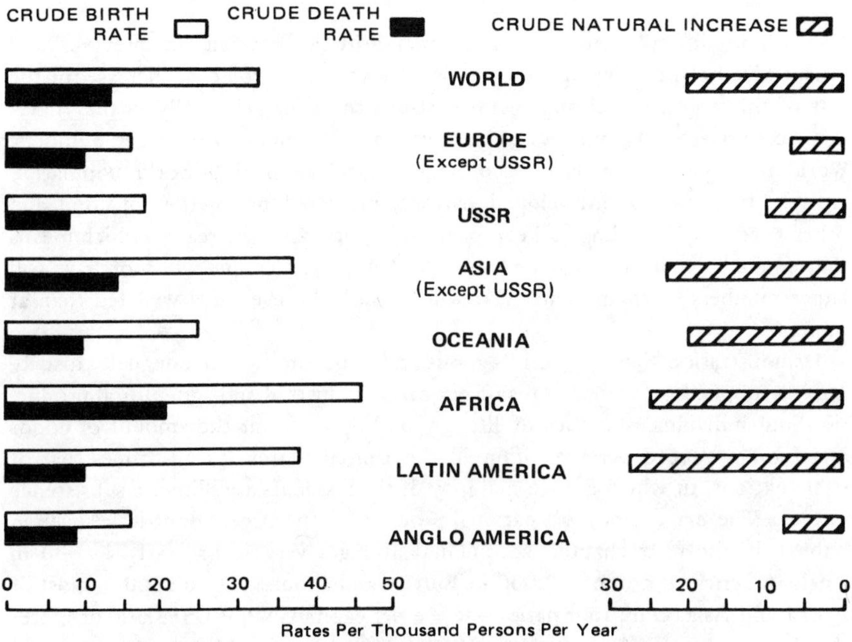

FIGURE 2. Birth and death rates by continents, 1975

45

Combining growth rates and density of settlement yields a four-part typology based on rapid or slow growth and high or low density. Each type has its own problems. Regions of low density and slow growth (Anglo America, temperate Latin America, the Soviet Union, and Australia) have little population pressure, yet subtle and important problems do subsist — for example, in the geographic regrouping and concentrating of population resulting from migration. Regions of low density and rapid growth (Africa, the Near East, and most of Latin America) experience increasing surpluses of people for whom jobs and other economic provision must be made, and disorders connected with urbanization are acute. The problems of areas of high density and slow growth (nearly all of Europe) are quite different and possibly transitory: given their low birth rates, maintenance of adequate living levels depends on continuing efficient use of resources. The most troubled areas, of course, are those of high density and rapid growth; and as they contain half of the world's people, their troubles are, in a sense, everyone's troubles. In most of Asia, existing levels of poverty present a severe challenge to human ingenuity, a problem made all the more baffling by the gigantic increases of population arriving annually.

Developing Areas

A prime difficulty in the transitional growth between the previous and prospective balances lies in the circumstance that the projected increase for the rest of the twentieth century seems destined to occur principally in the "have-not" countries — the very ones least capable of coping with larger numbers. World food production is on the verge of lagging behind world population growth. In some underdeveloped nations, increased production of food and other necessities is failing to keep pace with population increases, which means that countries that now contain millions of underfed people will soon have still larger numbers of inhabitants who will possibly be even less well fed than at present.

Demonstration that the world's goods and opportunities are unequally distributed is supplied by comparisons of per capita industrial and agricultural production and individual statistics of literacy and occupation: the amount of goods and food produced per inhabitant in the United States is many times that of some nations, in which a huge majority of the residents are illiterate subsistence farmers. The per capita gross national product for the larger countries is given in Table 4 in the next chapter; continental averages vary from nearly $5,000 in Anglo America to around $2,000 in Europe and about $100 to $300 in most of Africa and Asia. Only four nations have a per capita GNP of US$3,500 or more: the United States, $4,760; Sweden, $4,040; Kuwait, $3,760; and Canada,

$3,700. In general, the nations with the lowest levels of living are experiencing the fastest population growth.

Living levels in the poorer areas are often retrogressing; in the opinion of three California Institute of Technology scientists, "the evidence suggests rather strongly that in most underdeveloped countries the lot of the average individual has worsened appreciably in the last half century. People have become more poorly fed. There are fewer available goods per person. And practically every attempt to improve the situation has been nullified by the relentless pressure of population growth."[4] What happens in the future will be partly a result of direct action to improve material welfare and partly a consequence of demographic trends.

The world's demographic future seems to rest mostly with the underdeveloped countries. The underdeveloped areas have far more opportunity and therefore more choice to alter their population future than do industrialized regions. This reasoning can best be seen by examining the two variables contributing the most to demographic tendencies: fertility and mortality. In an industrialized nation having birth and death rates of, say, 15 and 10 per 1,000 population per year, the death rate is already almost as low as it can be made given current ability to curb deaths, and it is unlikely to be raised; as for the birth rate, it cannot be decreased by very much, and there is little incentive to raise the rate to 30 or 40. Thus both mortality and natality are likely to remain approximately at existing levels, with possible variations in the rates amounting to perhaps 5 for fertility and 2 for mortality. A contrasting situation is presented in underdeveloped nations having birth and death rates of, say, 40 and 20 respectively. Clearly the birth rate has a great deal of room for decline, and the death rate invites improvement; again, raising either is unlikely. Thus the underdeveloped nations have the potential to cut their death rates by 10 and their natality rates by 25 or 30 — a sharp contrast to the relative inflexibility of rates in modernized areas. The new balance, once achieved, carries an implicit semi-static quality as nations strive to keep past accomplishments and slowly add new ones. The question before underdeveloped countries and hence before the world at large is how rapidly their birth and death rates will decrease — or whether they will decline at all in the immediate future.

The success or failure of underdeveloped areas in trying to raise their levels of living will profoundly influence both human welfare and the distribution of national power. At present the overriding political issue is whether the free or Communist bloc will dominate, and one factor in this struggle is which side will receive the allegiance of uncommitted nations — a decision that cannot help being affected by the extent to which underdeveloped nations are frustrated or delayed in their efforts to advance their gross national products and the comfort and well-being of their citizens.

Estimates for the Future

Where we go from here is a perennial question. The demand for knowledge about future population size and properties is not only persistent but increasing. Military leaders want to estimate national strength, of which manpower still forms an essential though probably decreasingly significant part. Other government agencies need estimates of those segments of the citizenry that fall within their purview — the aged under social security, for example. Business and industrial concerns want to project sales figures. Colleges and public schools must plan for future enrollments.

Another reason for making population estimates is to further knowledge. For instance, we may compute the probable size and composition of the population of France if the Second World War had not caused so many deaths; by comparing the actual composition with this theoretical one, demographers can draw inferences about the effects of the war that could not be made without the hypothetical comparison group. Detailed component estimates making use of births, deaths, and migration projections are preferable to simple totals. Often social scientists are more interested in knowing about the demographic and other causative processes than about the results.

Because of the potential dangers consequent upon the present dramatic world population increase, informed citizens join political leaders in wondering whether the future will provide demographic catastrophe or pleasant equilibrium. The answer, of course, must await the passage of time, and until then, concerned persons must rely on fallible statisticians.

Demographers know that they cannot foresee the future; but people keep asking them for predictions in order to know how many schools to build or how many baby buggies to hope to sell, and so demographers sometimes respond by making estimates of future population. But if experts cannot predict the arrival of a war, a stock market decline, the breaking of the record for the mile run, an earthquake, or the cost of living increase for next year, then it should not be surprising to learn that demographers do no better in foretelling the population seven or seventeen years in advance. "The future is not always seen as through a glass darkly, but sometimes as through a brick wall."[5]

Preparation of a population estimate demands discipline, "historical perspective, current information, and a sense of humor."[6] Although the ability to not take oneself too seriously may be the most important ingredient of estimation, it is also essential to know the base population from which to begin, plus some means of assessing the most probable rate of growth or decline. In developing countries, both the base and the increment are difficult to ascertain; but in developed nations, the census provides a satisfactory starting figure, leaving only the percentage growth as a quandary. Extrication, however, is available in the form of multiple estimates: the statistician states two, three, or more contingencies and then traces the demographic outcome of each.

Although such statements of "If A then Q, but if B then R" leave future-seekers uncertain, that is the best that an honest demographer can do. No one knows what will be the birth or death rate three or six years from now. So what better procedure than to say that if you believe that during the next ten years the birth rate will stay the same or decline by one-fourth or decrease by one-eighth, or that the death rate will remain constant or decline by one-twelfth, then the resultant population will increase by X or Y or Z percent or decrease by J or K percent. In this way the reader is offered the choice of believing in alternative A, B, or C (or, in the example above, nine other possibilities), according to his impression of which forces are most likely to affect the three demographic variables, and to what extent. Thus the demographer presents a set of choices, each dependent on an exactly specified set of conditions; among these possibilities, the user may choose the prospect that seems most likely to occur — and, therefore, its corollary population projection.

Methods of Projection

Projections are made in several ways, the simplest of which is to plot the population growth of the known past and then to continue that line. If, for example, the population of a country from 1900 to 1970 can be represented by a straight line that gradually rises, then we are inclined to extend a dotted straight line into the future. If the historical growth takes the form of a parabola, then we are tempted to continue the parabola into the future. For 10 years or so this procedure may not be too bad, but after 50 years the dotted portion of the parabola may take on a form that becomes unrealistic even on cursory inspection. The problem, basically, is that the population growth of 1900-1970 was a reflection of (and also a cause of) the circumstances of life in those years, whereas the population growth of 1970-1990 or 1970-2020 very likely will be a function of new and differing conditions of national life; hence there is no justification for extrapolating the past rate of growth without change.

For this reason demographers prefer component projections based not on rigid continuation of past trends, but on stated expectations for the future. For instance, if the crude birth rate (CBR) is now 38, the crude death rate (CDR) 19, and net migration zero, a demographer might prepare a projection that assumes that these three figures will remain the same for the next ten years. Or, if he believes that fertility and mortality will drop, he may calculate the population that would result from a reduction of the CBR in ten years to 34 (at a constant rate over the ten years, or at an increasing rate of decline, or something else) and a reduction of the CDR to 17. A third possibility might be to assume that the new family planning and malaria programs will be highly effective, causing the rates to decline in ten years to 27 and 11, respectively. Additionally, he may assume that net migration will be plus 1,000 in the first year of the estimation period, plus 1,300 in the second year, and so forth. In this way a demographer can make several estimates instead of one — and this, in fact, is what is generally done. Also, demographers prefer to work not with the overall crude vital rates, but rather with the age-sex-specific rates, from which they can project the size of each five-year age-sex group separately — a procedure much more likely to result in a meaningful estimation. It becomes evident even from this simplified description of procedures that projecting future population requires both good judgment and considerable arithmetic — and because of the latter, computers are often used.

National and World Estimates

The United States Bureau of the Census has prepared and revised several sets of these conditional projections, called Series A, Series B, Series C, and so forth. Because mortality and migration change so little, the differences between the projections are based entirely on changes in fertility. In all the projections, mortality is assumed to decline slightly, and net migration is fixed at 400,000 every year. In the latest report, Series A and B were discarded because their fertility-decline assumptions were too conservative to be meaningful to anyone who has observed the phenomenal but unpredictable fertility reduction of the 1970s. That left Series C through F. Series C assumes that the average woman will have in her lifetime 2.8 children; Series D assumes 2.5; Series E assumes 2.11 (approximately the replacement or zero-growth level); and Series F assumes 1.8 (less than replacement, or a decreasing population never anticipated until very recently).[7] As Table 2 shows, the population at the end of the century is projected to be in the range of 250 to 300 million. Even if the women have an average of only 1.8 babies, the projected population for the year 2020 still reaches 264 million.

One of the best sets of international projections was published by the United Nations Population Division in 1973.[8] Three projections through the end of the century were offered for each of eight major world regions, the high and low estimates being intended to represent the upper and lower extremes of plausibility, and the medium estimate being the most likely in the opinion of the United Nations demographers. Many countries prepared their own estimates and the United Nations staff copied the results, but in other cases the staff prepared their own estimates. As a result, the underlying assumptions differ considerably from country to country and are too numerous to list here. In general, mortality

TABLE 2

PROJECTIONS OF UNITED STATES POPULATION, 1980 TO 2020

Year (July 1)	Projected population (in millions)			
	Series C	Series D	Series E	Series F
1980	231	229	224	222
1990	266	259	247	239
2000	300	286	264	251
2010	344	318	282	259
2020	392	351	298	265

Source: U.S. Bureau of the Census, "Projections of the Population of the United States, by Age and Sex: 1972 to 2020," *Current Population Reports,* Series P-25, No. 493, December 1972, p. 1.

was assumed to decrease slowly toward (but for most countries, not reaching) a limit implying a life expectancy at birth of 74 years. Fertility was nowhere assumed to increase, but there was considerable variation in the rapidity with which it was assumed to decrease. Net migration assumptions varied so as to reach a world total of zero; generally, migration contributed little to the projections.

Results of the medium variant are shown in Table 3. For the world, the CBR is assumed to decline from 34 in 1965-70 to 25 in 1995-2000, the CDR from 14 to 8, and the crude rate of natural increase (CRNI) from 20 to 17. Thus the United Nations experts expect the decline in fertility to be almost equaled by the mortality decline, thereby maintaining nearly as great a rate of increase at the end of the century as at the beginning of the estimation period.

No one knows, of course, how close these projections will be to the realities of A.D. 2000, but whichever of the three projections comes closest, the United Nations estimates imply that each of the world's eight regions will increase through the end of the century. Unfortunately, the regions that will probably grow the most rapidly are the very regions that are least able to cope, economically and otherwise, with rising numbers of people.

Especially foreboding is the implied rise of population in the less developed regions: the proportion of the world's population residing in developing areas was slightly less than 70 percent in 1970; but a set of projections published by Frejka in 1973 indicate that by the end of the century, that proportion "will certainly not be less than 75 percent and might even be close to 80 percent."[9] By mid-twenty-first century, "the proportion in the less developed regions is likely to be between 80 and 90 percent."[10] That may be the ceiling of this

51

TABLE 3

PROJECTED POPULATION, 1970-2000, FOR MAJOR WORLD REGIONS

Region	Projected population (in millions)			
	1970	1980	1990	2000
World Total	3,632	4,457	5,438	6,494
More developed regions[a]	1,090	1,210	1,336	1,454
Less developed regions[b]	2,542	3,247	4,102	5,040
East Asia[c]	930	1,095	1,266	1,424
South Asia[d]	1,125	1,486	1,912	2,354
U.S.S.R.	242	270	302	330
Europe	462	497	533	568
Africa	344	457	616	818
Anglo America	227	261	299	333
Latin America	283	377	500	652
Oceania	19	24	30	35

[a]Including Europe, the U.S.S.R., Anglo America, Japan, Temperate South America, Australia, and New Zealand.
[b]Including East Asia less Japan, South Asia, Africa, Latin America less Temperate South America, and Oceania less Australia and New Zealand.
[c]Mainly China, Mongolia, Korea, Japan, Taiwan, and Hong Kong.
[d]Mainly Philippines, Indonesia, Vietnam, Thailand, Malaysia, Burma, Bangladesh, India, Pakistan, Iran, Afghanistan, Iraq, Saudi Arabia, Israel, and Turkey.

Source: Adapted from United Nations Department of Economic and Social Affairs, *The Determinants and Consequences of Population Trends,* Population Studies No. 50, New York, 1973, p. 564.

percentage, for it is possible that by that time, all countries might have reduced their growth rates to, or nearly to, zero.

But in the meantime, some countries may double their populations by the end of this century. Asia alone may reach three and a half billion people by the year 2000 — approximately equaling the total world population in 1970. Whether any of these conditions will come to pass is not known, of course, and family planning programs in many nations are seeking to ensure that this rapid growth will not become reality.

NOTES

[1] Bernard Berelson *et al.*, "World Population: Status Report 1974," *Reports on Population/Family Planning*, No. 15, January 1974, p. 34.

[2] Visid Prachuabmoh, Ralph Tomlinson, Lincoln Polissar, *et al.*, *The Methodology of the Longitudinal Study of Social, Economic, and Demographic Change* (Bangkok: Institute of Population Studies, Chulalongkorn University, Research Report No. 6, 1971), pp. 13 and 26-27.

[3] Philip Morrison and Emily Morrison, "Introduction" to Charles Babbage, *Calculating Engines: Selected Writings* (New York: Dover Publications, 1961), p. xxiii.

[4] Harrison Brown, James Bonner, and John Weir, *The Next Hundred Years* (New York: the Viking Press, 1957), p. 48.

[5] W. Duane Evans and Marvin Hoffenberg, "The Nature and Uses of Inter-industry-Relations Data and Methods," in Conference on Research in Income and Wealth, *Input-Output Analysis: An Appraisal* (Princeton: Princeton University Press, 1955), p. 104.

[6] Peter A. Morrison, "Demographic Information for Cities: A Manual for Estimating and Projecting Local Population Characteristics," The Rand Corporation, Santa Monica, California, 1971, p. 44.

[7] U. S. Bureau of the Census, "Projections of the Population of the United States, by Age and Sex: 1972 to 2020," *Current Population Reports*, Series P-25, No. 493, December 1972.

[8] United Nations Department of Economic and Social Affairs, *The Determinants and Consequences of Population Trends*, Population Studies No. 50, New York, 1973, pp. 563-570.

[9] Tomas Frejka, *The Future of Population Growth: Alternative Paths to Equilibrium* (New York: Wiley, 1973), p. 71.

[10] *Ibid.*, p. 73.

Chapter 4. The Countries of Eurasia

POPULATION size, vital rates, and densities vary from region to region and nation to nation; the heaviest clustering occurs in eastern China, Japan, India, and parts of Europe. Not only is China by far the most populous nation in the world, but Asia's second nation, India, is larger in population than most continents, and its annual increment is greater than the entire population of Sweden. At the other extreme, almost three-fourths of the world's countries have populations smaller than metropolitan New York.

Turning from size to rate of increase, the highest rates are found in Latin America, where some nations are now growing at a rate which if unchanged will double the national population in 25 years. Such enormous growth poses severe problems for national planners striving to raise living levels. At the opposite end of the scale are several countries growing at annual rates of less than one-half of 1 percent, thus requiring more than a century to double. East and West Germany are almost static and hence pose relatively few demographic problems to national planners. Of the world's 200 babies born per minute, 140 draw their first breaths in Asia — a fact that spawns many problems for these already swollen lands, for every new baby is another mouth to feed, another body to clothe and shelter, another brain to educate, and in sum, another individual requiring land, air, water, employment, medical care, police protection, other amenities of life, and, if he is lucky enough to live so long, care for the aged.

Population statistics for 1973 are provided in Table 4 for all members of the United Nations as well as all geopolitical entities larger than 200,000 persons. This table is produced annually by the Population Reference Bureau, a non-governmental research organization in Washington, D.C., using data collected by national census and registration systems, supplemented in certain cases by estimates and corrections made by United Nations and other experts. For certain countries, data of any kind are hard to come by. In cases where estimates of vital rates and growth rates were unavailable at the time this table was compiled, the desired numbers were replaced by dashes; such is the case regarding Lebanon, North and South Vietnam, and several other nations. For the majority of countries, reasonably accurate figures are presented. In European nations and in Canada, United States, Australia, and New Zealand, birth and death rates are quoted in decimals, reflecting the superior accuracy of their data-collection systems.

For Africa generally and for some parts of Asia, figures should not be assumed to be precise: for example, a birth rate of 43 might be interpreted to mean "between 40 and 45." The least accurate column in this table is the gross national product per capita; in common with other averages, it is doubly susceptible to mistakes because both the productivity and the base population are included. But even in this column, although residents of a country with a per capita GNP of $140 are not demonstrably better off than those of a nation that achieves $120, differences of 100 dollars are meaningful.

These qualifications notwithstanding, Table 4 contains as good a distillation of current demographic knowledge as is usually needed. Even if a birth rate of 32 really signifies "in the low 30s," it is unquestionably larger than a death rate of 18 or 27 (meaning "in the high 20s"). And for industrialized nations, the rates sometimes become so accurate that a death rate of 11.2 can be guaranteed greater than one of 11.1.

Europe

Europe was the first continent to show explosive increases in numbers — and the first to fear a decrease. By and large, Europe is at the end of the traditional growth cycle and is not likely to give rise to another population upsurge of the magnitude seen from the seventeenth to twentieth centuries. Since other continents are now experiencing this abrupt increase, Europe probably will become a decreasing part of the world's total population. The three largest European nations — West Germany, the United Kingdom, and Italy — were in 1973 the eleventh, twelfth, and thirteenth most populous countries in the world, positions that before the end of the century may be yielded to the Philippines, Mexico, and Thailand, thus leaving Europe without a representative among the largest nations.

Europeans represented a fifth of the world in 1650. Today, thanks to three centuries of substantial natural increases and colonization of other areas, Europeans and their descendants living in other continents constitute about a third of the world's people. The prominence of Europe in world political, economic, and scientific history overshadows the fact that the continent's 475 million inhabitants amount only to about 15 percent of the world total — and by the year 2000 this percentage may be 9 or 10. However, the influence of European population growth is not confined to the continent itself; Europeans have colonized and profoundly affected the peoples and cultures of many other lands. Moreover, the industrial revolution as well as the demographic explosion originated in Europe: mortality was cut by distribution of industrial goods, public sanitation, and modern medicine; and fertility decreases were made possible by plastic, rubber, and chemical products. Therefore, the demographic impact of

Europe has been considerable, despite its being territorially the smallest continent. Europeans were the first people to free themselves from the vagaries of nature, thus paving the way to lower mortality, higher living levels, and increased population control.

Current rates of growth vary somewhat, but aside from Albania, no European country is doubling in less than one-half of a century, and East Germany is even losing population. Densities fluctuate from about 900 persons per square mile in the Netherlands — the densest country in the world — to around 30 in Norway, and are fairly uniform and rather high in central Europe and England.

Age pyramids (see Figure 3 in Chapter 11) of most European nations have altered in shape: the traditional hierarchy of many children, moderate numbers of adults, and very few aged has yielded to an age structure in which the number of persons at each age is nearly as great as those at the next younger age, as improvements in health enable more and more people to live complete biological lives, passing through the entire cycle from childhood through adolescence and adulthood to middle and old age. Thus the dependency load is altering from a large number of children and few aged to a moderate number of the young and many retired persons, a demographic circumstance having profound effects on the labor force and pension and education systems.

Nonetheless Europe is enjoying the greatest prosperity in its history.

Developing countries with high population densities would do well to take a close look at Western Europe. It is the most densely populated of the major regions of the world. Yet, because it has gone through the vital revolution as well as the industrial and agricultural revolutions, Western Europe has been able to shed the shackles of poverty. That Europe had time on its side, plus the opportunity to send 67 million persons overseas, merely emphasizes the urgency for today's developing regions to complete their demographic transitions from high to low rates of births as well as deaths.[1]

The Soviet Union

Bridging Europe and Asia is the U.S.S.R., comprising some 250 million residents, growing at a rate of 1 percent annually, appreciably slower than the world at large. Russian census-taking has the usual history of incomplete and inaccurate enumerations: local counts in the eleventh and twelfth centuries; partial enumerations by the Tatars in 1256 and 1273; abortive attempts at national censuses in 1646, 1678, and 1710; enumerations confined to tax-paying men on several occasions between 1718 and 1856; the first general census in 1897; an unsuccessful attempt at a second national census in 1920 under V. I. Lenin; and complete censuses in 1926, 1939, 1959, and 1970.[2] Divorce of census-taking from politics is not as complete as demographers would like: a census conducted in 1937 was suppressed and officially disclaimed, supposedly because it contained serious methodological errors; Western observers were inclined to view the "methodological errors" as being essentially a failure to indicate the desired number of inhabitants.[3]

A half century ago the new socialist government embarked on an ambitious program of national economic planning and development designed to strengthen the nation and improve living conditions. These efforts have been generally successful in both respects. Demographically, the death rate declined from about 35 per 1,000 per year at the opening of the century to its present low of 8, a figure among the lowest in the world and below the United States' 9½ (although the lower proportion of Soviet population in the older and hence more death-prone ages is at least partially responsible for this excellent showing). Similarly, the birth rate has been cut sharply during the same period, from about 45 to the present 18. Life expectancy at birth rose from 32 years in 1897 to over 70 at present — certainly a commendable accomplishment in this fundamental index of survival.

In the near future, life expectancy will probably approach 75 years, although the death rate will probably not decline, as health and antimortality improvements are counterbalanced by an aging population. This expected combination of lowered fertility and relatively constant mortality may slow the rate of increase, although the total population certainly should surpass 300 million before the close of the century.

Asia

The largest continent, containing 57 percent of the world population, is growing rapidly, threatening to increase its majority. Within this huge region are found some of the world's most extreme conditions of crowding and sparseness, richness and poverty, modernity and traditionalism. The fastest growing nations are doubling in 20 years; the slowest, Japan, is doubling in about 60 years — a marked change from the rapid Japanese growth rate in the 1950s.

The demographic history of Asia has been marked by lulls and spurts governed not by variations in the birth rate but by unusually wide fluctuations in the death rate arising from spasmodically recurrent wars, famines, and epidemics. Populations grew irregularly as long eras of slow increase alternated with eras of stagnation and periods of rapid decline following an epidemic, famine, or conquest. The Asian countries' ancient civilizations, colonial status, rising nationalism, and in some cases declarations of political independence evoke fundamental questions of national and international demographic policy. These countries are in varying stages of the transition to the new balance. In most cases the decline in mortality has begun but is not yet completed, and the decline of fertility is only just starting.

Asia's situation is not analogous to that of Europe during its industrial and demographic revolutions. Europe's modernism arose internally, spontaneously, and early, giving Europeans a temporary monopoly over virgin industrial resources and expanding world markets. Also Europe began her period of rapid population growth at a time when the world's population was still fairly small and density levels were relatively low; for these reasons, the surplus could be dissipated in emigration to newly discovered and often sparsely settled territories. By contrast Asia entered her stage of accelerated growth far less propitiously, being confronted with an already vast and dense population and an inauspicious political and religious climate. Various folkways and mores operate to deter tranquil expansion: the extended family prevails, creation and nurture of a son is often a religious and familial obligation, and early marriage predominates.

The Near East

The southwestern corner of Asia is a land of archaeological fascination, dotted with remnants of ancient civilizations whose former riches contrast strongly with present-day poverty. This important trading area, of heterogeneous and conflicting religious and ethnic groups, commands a central position at the edges of three continents. Moslems predominate, and Arabic is the principal language. Incessant wars of ambiguous outcome constantly alter the distribution of political power and impede progress. Illiteracy is high, agricultural pursuits dominant, and industrial production inadequate. Statistical data are fragmentary for many of these countries, and frequent border changes obscure long-term population trends. The largest nations are Turkey and Iran, at 39 and 31 million respectively.

Turkey's role in the Near East resembles that of Japan in the Far East. Determined to transform an antiquated agrarian culture into a modern industrial one by central fiat, Turkey's drastic internal reforms since 1923 under Kemal Ataturk and more recent leaders have pushed forward modernization with reasonable speed — though not so fast as Japan in recent years. The population-resources ratio in Turkey is favorable, and it would not be wise to predict that Turkey will experience Japan's population increase problems — nor their unprecedentedly rapid solution of them, though the traditionally pronatalist slant of Turkish law is slowly shifting in response to the now-increasing popular approval of family planning.

The small new nation of Israel is demographically interesting as a violation of the rule that countries grow by natural increase rather than by migration. From its founding in 1948 through 1963, there were added 911,000 Jewish residents through net migration as compared with 486,000 through excess of births over deaths; thus 65 percent of national growth during the first 15 years was contributed by migration. Israel is also unusual for its exceptionally low death rate of 7 per 1,000 people per year, which results partly from the youth of the citizenry (33 percent of the residents were under age 15 in 1973), partly from a high standard of living, and partly from the excellence of Israel's health services (for example, the per capita supply of physicians is almost twice as great as that of the United States). Life expectancy at birth reaches 70-75 years. Whether such favorable conditions improve will depend in part on the quantity and character of future immigrants. And since an estimated 45 percent of the world Jewish population of 14 million is resident in the United States, the Israeli way of life may be importantly affected by the magnitude of American-Jewish emigration to Israel as well as its continued financial support.

The Indian Subcontinent

In south central Asia are located the three large countries of India, Bangladesh, and Pakistan, which together with Sri Lanka, Nepal, Bhutan, and Sikkim constitute a cultural and geographical subcontinent. In this tongue-shaped peninsula sprang forth one of the world's most ancient concentrations of human population. The earliest period for which a population estimate exists is the reign of Emperor Asoka in the third century B.C., when (according to twentieth-century conjecture) there probably were between 100 and 140 million inhabitants — a number that seems not to have changed greatly until the beginning of modern times in the seventeenth century.[4] Of course, the population must have fluctuated, rising in times of peace and agricultural plenty and falling in times of war, epidemic, and food scarcity in accordance with the usual demographic history of pre-industrial humankind.

The population of India in mid-1973 was 600 million. At its present growth of a million persons a month, by 1985 India will probably contain 800 million people, a number that may be difficult to support even with full exploitation of India's fertile soil and agriculturally favorable climate. In this single country are now gathered more people than inhabit all of Europe (excluding the Soviet Union) or all of the United States and the U.S.S.R. combined.

Responsibility for this size and growth rests, as it does nearly everywhere, on the difference between the birth and death rates. From a rough equipoise of around 45 per 1,000 people per year in the first years of this century, the two rates have diverged until the death rate is now down to about 17 while the birth rate remains at about 40. Almost all Indian women marry early, almost all have children, norms and values encourage large families, and few couples actually practice family planning; a study of one section of India revealed that the median ages of mothers at the birth of their first and last children were 21 and

40 years respectively, as compared with 24 and 29 in the United States.[5] With this median child-bearing span of 19 years, it is no wonder that Indian women produce many offspring. In fact, were it not for several forces tending to reduce fertility — low levels of living impairing the biological capacity to bear children, high mortality making many women widows while still young enough to procreate, the Hindu custom forbidding widows to remarry, taboos on sexual relations on numerous religious holidays, and a rise in age at marriage from about 13 to nearly 20 — the birth rate might be still higher and the rate of national increase correspondingly more rapid. Consequent upon this high fertility is a large proportion of the population in the youth-dependent ages and a tremendous pressure upon school facilities. There are 250 million children under age 15, many not in school.

Average per capita income is barely more than $100. Although two-thirds of the labor force is agricultural, India nevertheless imports millions of tons of food annually, and per capita consumption of food is less than 2,000 calories daily. Density exceeds 400 persons per square mile (greater than New York State) despite the prevailing rural pattern of habitation (the population is 80 percent rural). Thus the population per acre of arable land is high enough to put considerable pressure on the ability to feed and otherwise supply the needs of the populace. Since this already huge, densely settled, and rapidly growing nation burdened with high youth dependency and extensive unemployment is reducing its death rate, population will continue to grow rapidly even if fertility is reduced appreciably, thus presenting a picture so bleak that some people are even wary of the humanitarian action of curbing mortality.

India and its neighbors form an Indian culture sphere. Bangladesh (East Pakistan until 1971) is the eighth populous country in the world, and Pakistan is ninth. These three countries, together with Sri Lanka (Ceylon), Nepal, and smaller Indian-culture nations, form a subcontinent containing about 770 million persons, or almost the population of China.

Bangladesh and Pakistan are India's alter egos, notwithstanding differences implicit in the Hinduism of India and the Islamic commitment of Bangladesh and Pakistan. The 1947 partition of the Indian culture sphere could just as easily have resulted in one, two, or three nations; it did, in fact, create two countries, one of which was so divided geographically and culturally that it eventually split into two. The result is one gigantic nation and two large nations that recognize traditional resemblances yet distrust each other profoundly because of religious and military disagreements — not to mention pressure of the rapid population growth on land and resources.

After the 1971 re-partition, Bangladesh got most of the people and Pakistan got the industry and most of the land. Bangladesh is one of the highest-density countries in the world — and one of the most frequently beset by disasters. In 1970 the area suffered the second-worst tidal wave catastrophe in human history, killing an estimated quarter of a million persons. Yet so accustomed to the recurrent disasters are the coastal residents that a Moslem fatalist said, "If they die in a cyclone, they are mourned, but the mourners grieve the loss without cursing the storm."

Both Pakistan and Bangladesh are traditional, male-dominated societies, having pervasive illiteracy, low income, extremely high fertility, high infant mortality, and large proportions of children. In short, these countries resemble India demographically, much as the United States resembles the Soviet Union demographically — and they have about as much good fellowship toward each other.

Southeast Asia

Southeast Asia, which extends from Burma through Indochina to the islands of the Philippines and Indonesia, is growing at about the same rate as India and its neighbors, but it differs in that the anticipated increment will be imposed upon a less dense pattern of existing settlement. For reasons that are not fully known, densities in Southeast Asia are lower than those in either South Asia (the Indian subcontinent) or East Asia (mostly China and Japan). The average density in Southeast Asia is only one-third that of China or India, and a mere one-sixth that of Japan. The region is catching up, however, as its rate of growth is higher than that of either East or South Asia.

Death rates are still fairly high, and prospective reductions offer the probability of an accelerating rate of natural increase. When that happens, these underdeveloped economies will be confronted with a pressing compulsion to expand industrially or territorially or both in order to avoid lowering the present rudimentary standard of living.

Easily the largest nation in Southeast Asia is Indonesia, which at 132 million is the fifth largest nation in the world. Indonesia consists of a group of islands extending 3,000 miles from east to west and 1,000 miles from north to south; the major islands are Borneo, Java, and Sumatra. Indonesia's birth rate is around 45 per 1,000 per year, its death rate has dropped to 20, and its rate of population increase is rapid, but overall density is not so great as to constitute a major problem. However, the population is very unevenly distributed throughout the islands; Java is particularly heavily populated, having more than 1,000 persons per square mile, and Javanese land is of necessity intensively cultivated. On the other hand, Sumatra and Borneo are mainly jungle. Thus little excess Javanese population can be resettled on these less dense islands — although authorities have persuaded a few Javanese to move to Sumatra. The core island, Java, supports about 65 percent of the country's people on only 8 percent of the land area. Three-fourths of all Indonesians make their living from subsistence agriculture while consuming a meagre average of 2,000 calories a day. The largest ethnic group is Malay, with infusions of Chinese, Indians, and Eurasians. Nine-tenths of Indonesians are Moslems, the rest being Hindus, Christians, and Buddhists. Cultural variations in the archipelago are profound: modern Djakarta's teeming streets contrast with the primitive byways of the head-hunters of New Guinea; Islam, Hinduism, and Christianity are all represented; and dozens of languages and hundreds of dialects are spoken.

The sixteenth and seventeenth largest nations in the world are the Philippines and Thailand, at 42 and 40 million population, respectively. As both countries are growing at more than 3 percent a year, each must either reduce its natural increase or approach 100 million before the century ends.[6] Because of their high fertility, both nations have young age structures, with 40 to 45 percent of the population under age 15. Educational levels are low but rising, families with six or ten children are not unusual, and most people are farmers. Both countries are dominated by one large metropolis, with neither nation having a second city of competitive size or prominence. Lest the impression be given that these two nations are identical — although their inhabitants do have similar facial features and physiques — it should be pointed out that the Thai are Buddhist, whereas the Filipinos are predominantly Roman Catholic, and that their cultural heritages and histories are about as disparate as any two countries' can be.

Like Indonesia, the Philippines is an archipelagic nation consisting of a dozen major islands and some 7,000 minor ones. Also like Indonesia, its culture and population are heterogeneous. Most Filipinos are of Malay descent, but the sixteenth-century Spanish conquest left a heritage of Catholicism, and the 1898 American invasion made English a major language. Walking on a Manila street, one hears English, Spanish, Tagalog (the official language), and numerous local languages carried to the capital by migrants from various islands; many Filipinos speak several languages fluently. Coastal strips tend to be densely settled, but many island areas are thinly populated.

In comparison, Thailand is far more homogeneous. Except for Bangkok, most of Thailand is populated by people with similar physical features, agricultural occupations, low incomes, little education, Buddhist faith, and proficiency only in the Thai language. In the cities reside perhaps three million Chinese and a quarter million Indians and Pakistanis; about a million Malay-speaking Moslems live in the southernmost provinces, and isolated northern jungle areas harbor Karen, Meo, and other Hill Tribes.[7] Each of these minorities, however, is clustered geographically, leaving the bulk of the country occupied solely by the Thais themselves.

Mainland China

The giant of Asia, as of the world, is mainland China, a monster nation of 800 million people on their way to becoming a billion by 1990. Apparently the

Chinese were always numerous, though population changes in the area that has come to be labeled China have been cyclical rather than linear — that is, they have fluctuated instead of maintaining a regular growth. In the peaceful order of a new dynasty, population increased through an excess of births over deaths; but as time passed, the increased density gradually intensified the struggle for existence until the eventual famine, pestilence, revolution, or war broke out, thus abruptly reducing population size and pressure and instituting a new phase of the cycle of slow increase and sudden decline. Some cycles continued several decades, while others lasted several centuries, but in either case the long-run trend consisted of a zig-zag gradual increase having extended but slow upward zigs and brief but rapid downward zags.[8] Unfortunately even in modern times it is not possible to make demographic statements about China with much precision — and yet what happens to China's population is of great importance. "The most inexplicable aspect of Chinese studies is the neglect of the Chinese population. The most inexplicable aspect of population studies is the neglect of China and the Chinese."[9]

With these qualifications, we can report a few facts: the birth rate is probably in the vicinity of 30 or 35 per 1,000 per year, and the death rate appears to be about 15. Density is approximately 150 persons per square mile, but there are large variations from region to region, as a result of which the government has been evacuating millions of people out of the thickly-settled river valleys and littorals and relocating them in the interior provinces. About 85 percent of the population is rural; still, barely enough food is produced. Youth dependency exerts a tremendous drag on the productive working ages, since children below the age of 15 comprise nearly 40 percent of the total population (as compared with an average of 25 percent in industrial nations). The immensity and rapidity of growth of China's population are deterrents to the economic aspirations and political ambitions of Communist leaders, a fact which they seem to acknowledge in spite of ideological "party lines" contending that Communist organization can handle any number of people.

East Asia

Taiwan, or Formosa, an island off the Chinese coast, now shelters the Republic of China. The country is growing fairly rapidly, with a density already exceeding 1,000 persons per square mile, making it even more dense than Japan and one of the densest in the world, despite its mountainous terrain. Both birth and death rates are lower than in mainland China, and the rate of growth is doubling the population in 35 years. Both Chinas are faced with growth and density problems, which both governments are coming to face to the extent of instituting national policies of population control.

At the mouth of the Canton River in southeast China is the British colony of Hong Kong, in which are crowded 4.5 million inhabitants at an almost intolerable density of about 10,000 persons per square mile. In parts of North Point the density exceeds one million persons per square mile. The colony is presently doubling its population in about 30 years, although its rate of growth is slowing, having "moved swiftly in demographic transition."[10]

Several East Asian countries experienced dramatic fertility declines during the 1960 decade. The city-state of Hong Kong lowered its birth rate by more than 15 points, and Taiwan and South Korea lowered theirs by more than 10. As death rates declined slowly, the net rates of growth declined from about 3 percent annually to little more than 2 percent. Family planning officials credit these declines to their programs, but it is not clear whether the fertility reduction truly was induced by program efforts or instead by the social changes accompanying modernization — or, more likely, partly by each. The answer is important with the possibility that these East Asian nations might serve as bellwethers for other Asian countries, if leaders can only determine which actions are most likely to produce a similarly dramatic fertility reduction in their own jurisdictions.

Japan, the sixth largest country in the world in 1973, is unique in the rapidity with which its birth rate was brought down to a controlled level. Faced with a high density amounting to over 600 inhabitants per square mile and a burgeoning population, the Japanese, beginning in 1948, instituted an ambitious program of industrialization and fertility control, borrowing deliberately and selectively those elements of Western culture which could be most painlessly and advantageously interwoven into the traditional Japanese pattern of culture. As the first Asian nation to begin modernization, Japan had a greater opportunity for industrial expansion and market exploitation — and hence manageable population enlargement. In this way modern Japan is more akin to Europe and Anglo America than to continental Asia, while remaining a country of intensive hand agriculture and awesome pressure of population on land. Japan's birth and death rates of 19 and 7 per thousand, respectively, have slowed population growth to the point of doubling in only about 60 years. Because of this relatively slow growth, the nation is expected to drop to about tenth largest in the world by the end of the century.

Japan is alone among Asian lands in being no longer predominantly agricultural; the only Asian nation that has become modern, literate, urban, industrial, and demographically mature, Japan has far more in common economically, technologically, and demographically with the Occident that with the Orient. This circumstance has made Japan a symbol of hope and suggests that non-Western nations may have an alternative to demographic doom.

In the Asian continent as a whole, the prevailing high natality rates show little decline. Although several Asian nations are introducing programs encouraging family limitation, the rapid reduction of death rates through concerted attacks on communicable diseases seems unlikely to be matched in the near future by equivalent reductions of natality. And so the Asian population continues to grow.

The Eurasian land mass is a heterogeneous collection of countries with widely varying demographic prospects for the remainder of the twentieth century. The nations of northwest and central Europe will make small gains in population, and southern and eastern Europe should grow moderately. But the huge Asian population is due for a gigantic increase to approximately four billion — nearly twice its present quantity — by the year 2000.

TABLE 4

POPULATION, VITAL RATES, GROWTH RATE, AND PER CAPITA
GROSS NATIONAL PRODUCT, FOR 163 COUNTRIES, 1973

Continent, region, and country	Rank in population size	Population mid-year 1973 (in millions)	Birth rate	Death rate	Annual rate of growth (percent)	Number of years to double	Gross national product per capita, 1970 (U.S. dollars)
WORLD	—	3,860	33	13	2.0	35	—
AFRICA	—	374	46	21	2.5	28	—
Northern Africa	—	*95*	*44*	*17*	*2.7*	*26*	—
Algeria	39	15.5	50	17	3.3	21	300
Egypt	19	36.9	37	16	2.1	33	210
Libya	115	2.1	46	16	3.1	23	1,770
Morocco	36	17.4	50	16	3.4	21	230
Sudan	37	17.4	49	18	3.1	23	120
Tunisia	78	5.6	38	16	2.2	32	250
Western Africa	—	*110*	*49*	*24*	*2.5*	*28*	—
Cape Verde Islands*	151	0.3	39	14	2.5	28	160
Dahomey	105	2.9	51	26	2.6	27	90
Gambia	146	0.4	42	23	1.9	37	120
Ghana	55	9.9	47	18	2.9	24	310

TABLE 4 (Continued)

POPULATION, VITAL RATES, GROWTH RATE, AND PER CAPITA GROSS NATIONAL PRODUCT, FOR 163 COUNTRIES, 1973

Continent, region, and country	Rank in population size	Population mid-year 1973 (in millions)	Birth rate	Death rate	Annual rate of growth (percent)	Number of years to double	Gross national product per capita, 1970 (U.S. dollars)
Guinea	88	4.2	47	25	2.3	30	120
Ivory Coast	86	4.6	46	23	2.4	29	310
Liberia	123	1.2	50	23	2.7	26	240
Mali	79	5.5	50	27	2.3	30	70
Mauritania	122	1.3	44	23	2.1	33	140
Niger	90	4.2	52	23	2.9	24	90
Nigeria	10	59.6	50	25	2.6	27	120
Portuguese Guinea*	138	0.6	41	30	1.1	63	250
Senegal	89	4.2	46	22	2.4	29	230
Sierra Leone	106	2.8	45	22	2.3	30	190
Togo	117	2.0	51	26	2.5	28	140
Upper Volta	74	5.7	49	29	2.0	35	60
Eastern Africa	—	*106*	*47*	*22*	*2.5*	*28*	—
Burundi	94	3.9	48	25	2.3	30	60

TABLE 4 (Continued)

POPULATION, VITAL RATES, GROWTH RATE, AND PER CAPITA GROSS NATIONAL PRODUCT, FOR 163 COUNTRIES, 1973

Continent, region, and country	Rank in population size	Population mid-year 1973 (in millions)	Birth rate	Death rate	Annual rate of growth (percent)	Number of years to double	Gross national product per capita, 1970 (U.S. dollars)
Comoro Islands*	153	0.3	–	–	–	–	140
Ethiopia	25	26.8	46	25	2.1	33	80
Kenya	48	12.0	48	18	3.0	23	150
Malagasy Republic	66	7.5	46	25	2.1	33	130
Malawi	83	4.8	49	25	2.5	28	80
Mauritius	132	0.9	25	8	1.7	41	240
Mozambique*	63	8.2	43	23	2.1	33	240
Reunion*	141	0.5	30	8	2.2	32	800
Rhodesia	75	5.6	48	14	3.4	21	280
Rwanda	93	3.9	52	23	2.9	24	60
Somalia	102	3.0	46	24	2.2	32	70
Tanzania	44	14.3	47	22	2.6	27	100
Uganda	58	9.3	43	18	2.6	27	130
Zambia	85	4.7	50	21	2.9	24	400

68

TABLE 4 (Continued)

POPULATION, VITAL RATES, GROWTH RATE, AND PER CAPITA GROSS NATIONAL PRODUCT, FOR 163 COUNTRIES, 1973

Continent, region, and country	Rank in population size	Population mid-year 1973 (in millions)	Birth rate	Death rate	Annual rate of growth (percent)	Number of years to double	Gross national product per capita, 1970 (U.S. dollars)
Middle Africa	—	*38*	*44*	*24*	*2.1*	*33*	—
Angola	73	6.1	50	30	2.1	33	300
Cameroon	71	6.2	43	23	2.0	35	180
Central African Republic	119	1.6	46	25	2.1	33	140
Chad	91	4.0	48	25	2.3	30	80
Congo	127	1.0	44	23	2.1	33	300
Equatorial Guinea	152	0.3	35	22	1.4	50	210
Gabon	140	0.5	33	25	0.8	87	630
Zaire	34	18.7	44	23	2.1	33	90
Southern Africa	—	*25*	*41*	*18*	*2.4*	*29*	—
Botswana	135	0.7	44	23	2.2	32	110
Lesotho	124	1.1	39	21	1.8	39	90
South Africa	30	21.7	41	17	2.4	29	760
Namibia*	136	0.7	44	25	2.0	35	760
Swaziland	142	0.5	52	24	2.8	25	180

69

TABLE 4 (Continued)

POPULATION, VITAL RATES, GROWTH RATE, AND PER CAPITA
GROSS NATIONAL PRODUCT, FOR 163 COUNTRIES, 1973

Continent, region, and country	Rank in population size	Population mid-year 1973 (in millions)	Birth rate	Death rate	Annual rate of growth (percent)	Number of years to double	Gross national product per capita, 1970 (U.S. dollars)
ASIA	—	2,204	37	14	2.3	30	—
Southwest Asia	—	84	44	16	2.8	25	—
Bahrain	156	0.2	50	19	3.1	23	550
Cyprus	139	0.6	23	8	0.9	77	950
Gaza*	143	0.5	44	8	3.6	19	—
Iraq	52	10.8	49	15	3.4	21	320
Israel	97	3.1	28	7	2.4	29	1,960
Jordan	109	2.6	48	16	3.3	21	250
Kuwait	130	0.9	43	7	9.8	7	3,760
Lebanon	98	3.1	—	—	—	—	590
Oman	134	0.7	50	19	3.1	23	350
Qatar	162	0.1	50	19	3.1	23	1,730
Saudi Arabia	62	8.4	50	23	2.8	25	440
Syria	68	6.8	48	15	3.3	21	290

70

TABLE 4 (Continued)

POPULATION, VITAL RATES, GROWTH RATE, AND PER CAPITA
GROSS NATIONAL PRODUCT, FOR 163 COUNTRIES, 1973

Continent, region, and country	Rank in population size	Population mid-year 1973 (in millions)	Birth rate	Death rate	Annual rate of growth (percent)	Number of years to double	Gross national product per capita, 1970 (U.S. dollars)
Turkey	18	38.6	40	15	2.5	28	310
United Arab Emirates	163	0.1	50	19	3.1	23	2,390
Yemen Arab Republic	72	6.2	50	23	2.8	25	80
Yemen, People's Republic	121	1.4	50	21	2.9	24	120
Middle South Asia	–	*828*	*44*	*17*	*2.6*	*27*	–
Afghanistan	35	18.3	51	27	2.4	29	80
Bangladesh	8	83.4	–	–	–	–	–
Bhutan	131	0.9	–	–	2.2	32	70
India	2	600.4	42	17	2.5	28	110
Iran	23	31.1	45	17	2.8	25	380
Maldive Islands	161	0.1	46	23	2.3	31	100
Nepal	49	12.0	45	23	2.2	32	80
Pakistan	9	68.3	51	18	3.3	21	100
Sikkim	157	0.2	48	29	1.9	37	80

TABLE 4 (Continued)

POPULATION, VITAL RATES, GROWTH RATE, AND PER CAPITA GROSS NATIONAL PRODUCT, FOR 163 COUNTRIES, 1973

Continent, region, and country	Rank in population size	Population mid-year 1973 (in millions)	Birth rate	Death rate	Annual rate of growth (percent)	Number of years to double	Gross national product per capita, 1970 (U.S. dollars)
Sri Lanka (Ceylon)	45	13.5	30	8	2.2	32	110
Southeast Asia	—	*313*	*43*	*15*	*2.8*	*25*	—
Burma	24	29.8	40	17	2.3	30	80
Indonesia	5	132.5	47	19	2.9	24	80
Irian, West*	129	1.0	—	—	—	—	80
Khmer (Cambodia)	65	7.8	45	16	3.0	23	130
Laos	96	3.2	42	17	2.5	28	120
Malaysia	51	11.8	38	11	2.7	26	380
Philippines	16	42.2	45	12	3.3	21	210
Portuguese Timor*	158	0.6	43	25	1.8	39	110
Singapore	110	2.3	23	5	2.2	32	920
Thailand	17	39.9	43	10	3.3	21	200
Vietnam, North	28	22.5	—	—	—	—	100
Vietnam, South	33	19.1	—	—	—	—	200

TABLE 4 (Continued)

POPULATION, VITAL RATES, GROWTH RATE, AND PER CAPITA
GROSS NATIONAL PRODUCT, FOR 163 COUNTRIES, 1973

Continent, region, and country	Rank in population size	Population mid-year 1973 (in millions)	Birth rate	Death rate	Annual rate of growth (percent)	Number of years to double	Gross national product per capita, 1970 (U.S. dollars)
East Asia	—	*978*	*29*	*12*	*1.7*	*41*	—
China	1	799.3	30	13	1.7	41	160
Hong Kong	87	4.5	20	5	2.4	29	970
Japan	6	107.3	19	7	1.2	58	1,920
Ryukyu Islands*	128	1.0	22	5	1.7	41	1,050
Korea, North	40	15.1	39	11	2.8	25	330
Korea, South	20	34.5	31	11	2.0	35	250
Macau*	154	0.3	—	—	—	—	150
Mongolia	120	1.4	42	11	3.1	23	460
Taiwan	41	15.0	27	5	2.2	32	390
NORTH AMERICA	—	233	16	9	0.8	87	—
Canada	29	22.5	15.7	7.3	1.2	58	3,700
United States	4	210.3	15.6	9.4	0.8	87	4,760

TABLE 4 (Continued)

POPULATION, VITAL RATES, GROWTH RATE, AND PER CAPITA
GROSS NATIONAL PRODUCT, FOR 163 COUNTRIES, 1973

Continent, region, and country	Rank in population size	Population mid-year 1973 (in millions)	Birth rate	Death rate	Annual rate of growth (percent)	Number of years to double	Gross national product per capita, 1970 (U.S. dollars)
LATIN AMERICA	—	308	38	10	2.8	25	—
Middle America	—	75	*43*	*11*	*3.2*	*22*	—
Costa Rica	116	2.0	34	7	2.7	26	560
El Salvador	95	3.8	42	10	3.2	22	300
Guatemala	76	5.6	43	17	2.6	27	360
Honduras	103	3.0	49	17	3.2	22	280
Mexico	13	56.2	43	10	3.3	21	670
Nicaragua	112	2.2	46	17	2.9	24	430
Panama	118	1.6	37	9	2.8	25	730
Caribbean	—	*27*	*33*	*11*	*2.2*	*32*	—
Bahamas	155	0.2	28	6	4.6	16	2,300
Barbados	150	0.3	22	9	0.8	87	570
Cuba	60	8.9	27	8	1.9	37	530
Dominican Republic	84	4.8	49	15	3.4	21	350

74

TABLE 4 (Continued)

POPULATION, VITAL RATES, GROWTH RATE, AND PER CAPITA GROSS NATIONAL PRODUCT, FOR 163 COUNTRIES, 1973

Continent, region, and country	Rank in population size	Population mid-year 1973 (in millions)	Birth rate	Death rate	Annual rate of growth (percent)	Number of years to double	Gross national product per capita, 1970 (U.S. dollars)
Guadeloupe*	145	0.4	30	8	2.2	32	760
Haiti	77	5.6	44	20	2.4	29	110
Jamaica	114	2.1	35	7	1.5	47	670
Martinique*	147	0.4	27	8	1.6	44	910
Netherlands Antilles	159	0.2	23	6	1.7	41	1,380
Puerto Rico*	104	2.9	25	7	1.4	50	1,650
Trinidad and Tobago	125	1.1	24	7	1.1	63	860
Tropical South America	—	*165*	*40*	*10*	*3.0*	*23*	—
Bolivia	81	5.0	44	19	2.4	29	180
Brazil	7	101.3	38	10	2.8	25	420
Colombia	27	23.7	45	11	3.4	21	340
Ecuador	69	6.7	45	11	3.4	21	290
Guyana	133	0.8	36	8	2.8	25	370
Peru	43	14.9	42	11	3.1	23	450

75

TABLE 4 (Continued)

POPULATION, VITAL RATES, GROWTH RATE, AND PER CAPITA GROSS NATIONAL PRODUCT, FOR 163 COUNTRIES, 1973

Continent, region, and country	Rank in population size	Population mid-year 1973 (in millions)	Birth rate	Death rate	Annual rate of growth (percent)	Number of years to double	Gross national product per capita, 1970 (U.S. dollars)
Surinam*	144	0.4	41	7	3.2	22	530
Venezuela	50	11.9	41	8	3.4	21	980
Temperate South America	—	*41*	*25*	*9*	*1.7*	*41*	—
Argentina	26	25.3	22	9	1.5	47	1,160
Chile	53	10.4	26	9	1.7	41	720
Paraguay	107	2.7	45	11	3.4	21	260
Uruguay	100	3.0	23	9	1.4	50	820
EUROPE	—	472	16	10	0.7	99	—
Northern Europe	—	*82*	*15*	*11*	*0.4*	*175*	—
Denmark	80	5.1	15.8	10.2	0.5	139	3,190
Finland	82	4.8	12.7	9.6	0.3	231	2,390
Iceland	160	0.2	19.7	7.3	1.2	58	2,170
Ireland	99	3.0	22.4	11.2	0.5	139	1,360
Norway	92	4.0	16.6	10.0	0.7	99	2,860

TABLE 4 (Continued)

POPULATION, VITAL RATES, GROWTH RATE, AND PER CAPITA
GROSS NATIONAL PRODUCT, FOR 163 COUNTRIES, 1973

Continent, region, and country	Rank in population size	Population mid-year 1973 (in millions)	Birth rate	Death rate	Annual rate of growth (percent)	Number of years to double	Gross national product per capita, 1970 (U.S. dollars)
Sweden	64	8.2	13.8	10.4	0.3	231	4,040
United Kingdom	12	57.0	14.9	11.9	0.3	231	2,270
Western Europe	–	*151*	*14*	*11*	*0.4*	*175*	–
Austria	67	7.5	13.8	12.6	0.1	700	2,010
Belgium	57	9.8	13.8	12.0	0.2	347	2,720
France	15	52.3	16.9	10.6	0.6	117	3,100
Germany, West	11	59.4	11.5	11.7	0.0	–	2,930
Berlin, West*	113	2.1	9.1	19.0	-1.0	–	–
Luxembourg	148	0.4	11.8	11.9	0.0	–	2,890
Netherlands	46	13.4	16.1	8.5	0.8	87	2,430
Switzerland	70	6.5	14.4	8.7	1.0	70	3,320
Eastern Europe	–	*107*	*17*	*10*	*0.7*	*99*	–
Bulgaria	61	8.7	15.3	9.8	0.6	117	760
Czechoslovakia	42	15.0	16.5	11.5	0.5	139	2,230

TABLE 4 (Continued)

POPULATION, VITAL RATES, GROWTH RATE, AND PER CAPITA
GROSS NATIONAL PRODUCT, FOR 163 COUNTRIES, 1973

Continent, region, and country	Rank in population size	Population mid-year 1973 (in millions)	Birth rate	Death rate	Annual rate of growth (percent)	Number of years to double	Gross national product per capita, 1970 (U.S. dollars)
Germany, East	38	16.3	11.7	13.7	-0.2	—	2,490
Berlin, East*	126	1.1	13.4	16.2	-0.3	—	—
Hungary	54	10.4	14.7	11.4	0.3	231	1,600
Poland	22	34.0	17.4	8.0	0.9	77	1,400
Romania	32	21.0	19.6	9.5	1.0	70	930
Southern Europe	—	*132*	*18*	*9*	*0.9*	*77*	—
Albania	111	2.3	35.3	7.5	2.8	25	600
Greece	59	9.1	15.9	8.3	0.8	87	1,090
Italy	14	54.9	16.8	9.6	0.7	99	1,760
Malta	149	0.3	16.8	9.1	-0.1	—	810
Portugal	56	9.8	21.3	11.1	1.0	70	660
Spain	21	34.2	19.4	8.2	1.1	63	1,020
Yugoslavia	31	21.2	18.2	9.1	0.9	77	650

TABLE 4 (Continued)

POPULATION, VITAL RATES, GROWTH RATE, AND PER CAPITA
GROSS NATIONAL PRODUCT, FOR 163 COUNTRIES, 1973

Continent, region, and country	Rank in population size	Population mid-year 1973 (in millions)	Birth rate	Death rate	Annual rate of growth (percent)	Number of years to double	Gross national product per capita, 1970 (U.S. dollars)
U.S.S.R.	*3*	*250*	*17.8*	*8.2*	*1.0*	*70*	*1,790*
OCEANIA	–	21	25	10	2.0	35	–
Australia	47	13.3	20.5	8.5	1.9	37	2,820
Fiji	137	0.6	30	5	1.8	39	430
New Zealand	101	3.0	22.1	8.5	1.7	41	2,700
Papua - New Guinea*	108	2.6	42	18	2.4	29	300

*Nonsovereign country.

Source: Population Reference Bureau, "1973 World Population Data Sheet: Population Information for 163 Countries," Washington, D.C., 1973.

NOTES

[1] Dorothy L. Nortman, *The Population Problem* (New York: National Educational Television, 1965), p. 24.

[2] M. V. Putkha, "Population Census Methods in the U.S.S.R.," *Bulletin de l'Institut International de Statistique*, Vol. XXXVI, Part 2 (Stockholm: 1957) pp. 190-197.

[3] Michael K. Roof, "The Russian Population Enigma Reconsidered," *Population Studies*, Vol. XIV, No. 1, July 1960, p. 3.

[4] Kingsley Davis, *The Population of India and Pakistan* (Princeton: Princeton University Press, 1951), p. 24.

[5] Andrew Collver, "The Family Cycle in India and the United States," *American Sociological Review*, Vol. XXVIII, No. 1, February 1963, pp. 86-96.

[6] Ralph Thomlinson, *Thailand's Population: Facts, Trends, Problems, and Policies* (Bangkok: Thai Watana Panich Press Co., 1971; republished in Winston-Salem, North Carolina: Wake Forest University, 1972), p. 81.

[7] *Ibid.*, pp. 33-35.

[8] Ta Chen, "Population in Modern China," *American Journal of Sociology*, Vol. LII, No. 1, Part 2, July 1946, p. 4.

[9] Irene B. Taeuber, "China's Population: An Approach to Research," *Social Science Research Council Items*, Vol. XVIII, No. 2, June 1964, pp. 13-19.

[10] Irene B. Taeuber, "Chinese Populations in Transition: The City-States," *Population Index*, Vol. XXXVIII, No. 1, January 1972, pp. 3-34.

Chapter 5.   The Rest of the World

FROM the largest single land mass in the world, Eurasia, the focus of inquiry shifts to the islands of Oceania, the resurgent nations of Africa, and the two continents of the Western Hemisphere.

Oceania

The smallest continent, Oceania, has a total of about 21 million persons in Australia, New Zealand, and the numerous south sea islands of Melanesia and Micronesia. Included among these Pacific islands are Samoa, the Solomons, Fiji, Guam, New Guinea, Tahiti, and Easter Island. "All of the populations are increasing rapidly and will continue to do so unless there is some radical change in the levels of either mortality or fertility, or far more emigration than has yet occurred."[1]

New Zealand has justifiably achieved the reputation — shared with the Scandinavian nations — of having one of the world's most enviable records for health care, low mortality, and high longevity. Expectation of life at birth is well over 70 years, and although the native Maori did not share in all of these benefits, even their life expectancy of 60 years is higher than that of similar groups. This is a considerable improvement on Maori life expectancy around 1900, which was merely 35 years; indeed, in the influenza epidemic of 1886-1896, it dipped to 20-22 years — not unusual among indigenous populations in various nations.[2]

At 13 million population in 1973, Australia is growing fairly rapidly, but there seems plenty of spare room in its more hospitable sections. In fact, Australia appears to be one of those rare nations that can actually be described — although not without some argument — as underpopulated. It is also, along with the United States, Canada, Israel, Argentina, and Brazil, one of the major destinations for international migrants. In 1973 Australia received 105,000 immigrants — the lowest figure in a decade, but still nearly double the 59,000 births.

Oceania's population undoubtedly will be kept small by the collection of deserts and wastelands comprising the bulk of Australia. This least-populated continent is also the least dense large area in the world aside from Antarctica and

Greenland, having only five persons per square mile — a figure that can easily be misinterpreted if one forgets the forbidding character of Australia's interior.

Africa

Africa's one-third of a billion inhabitants, constituting about 9 percent of the world's people, are divided among a number of small nations, only four exceeding 20 million in population: Nigeria, Egypt, Ethiopia, and South Africa. For long a dark mystery demographically as in other ways, Africa's thick jungles and wide deserts are only now becoming accessible to census-takers. To four sovereign states at the end of World War II have been added dozens more in the surge toward independence since 1960. Africa is growing slightly faster than the world as a whole, a striking contrast with previous times, for the African population had remained almost constant for several hundred years before 1900. Today's growth is based entirely on natural increase, and both the estimated birth rate of 45 and death rate of about 20 per 1,000 are the highest of any continent; if this situation continues, the African population will double by the end of the century.

Africa would be easier to describe if it were two continents, for the countries bordering on the Mediterranean Sea are vastly different from the rest of the continent. North Africa is predominantly white, Arabic, and Moslem, whereas tropical and southern Africa is black and of mixed religions. So large is this difference that most of the discussion of North Africa will be deferred to the following section on the Arab countries.

Except for the vast drought area called the Sahara, habitation is spread throughout the continent. Unlike parts of Asia and most of Latin America, Africa is not bordered by a high-density belt around its perimeter. The most densely-settled locality is probably the riverine development along the entire length of the Nile in Egypt. Flying over Egypt, as elsewhere on the periphery of the Sahara Desert, one has the impression that the land is either empty or full of people, with no in-between condition. Geographer Glenn Trewartha describes the African density pattern as irrational: more than in most parts of the world, low-density areas are often lightly inhabited because of historical accidents rather than environmental hardships, and dense clusters do not necessarily imply a benevolent environment. Within black Africa, "the present patterns of population-density inequalities do not consistently reflect the qualities and potentialities of the physical resource base."[3] Partly because tropical Africa is divided into young and economically weak countries having changeable and vague boundaries, "the mix of factors making for the present patchwork of empty and crowded regions varies from place to place; among them should be included the following: water availability, soil quality, the incidence of tsetse fly infestation, defense considerations, intensity of slave raiding, the scourge of warfare, and the varying abilities of different peoples in ordering their political and economic affairs."[4]

Nigeria is nearly twice as large as any other country in Africa. This west central country is growing rapidly, and its 60 million population in 1973 appears likely to burgeon to 85 million by 1985. The birth rate of about 50 per 1,000 causes a very high youth dependency. The literacy rate is about 20 percent. The densest clusters of people are the Ibo in the east, the Yoruba in the west, and the Moslems in the north.

The second most populous African country is Egypt, in the northeast corner of the continent. Ninety-six percent of the country is uninhabitable desert; this fact, contrasting sharply with an average density of 2,000 persons per square mile in the Nile valley and delta, and combined with a national increase of about 2 percent a year, presents a set of demographic obstacles severely challenging the economic and social melioration of extreme poverty. Mortality has declined considerably, and unless the high fertility rate follows suit, Egypt's 1973 population of 37 million may surpass 50 million by 1985. The government has begun programs of industrialization, improved agriculture, public works (such as the Aswan High Dam providing hydroelectric power), and advocacy of birth control.

The only other country in the continent exceeding 25 million population is Ethiopia, on the eastern edge of Africa. Since no complete census of Ethiopia has ever been taken, demographic knowledge is scant, although the population is probably increasing at about 2 percent annually. The very low standards of living and public health keep mortality high, although some decline seems to be taking place. On the positive side, the abundance of tillable land presents a condition so far from population pressure that surplus food is available for export. Once favoring a self-imposed isolation similar to but not so complete as Japan's, Ethiopia's government is beginning to encourage industrialization and in other respects strive for modernization.

South Africa, the fourth largest African country, is unique in its manner of handling its racial mix. The separation of the races by the policy of apartheid permeates all aspects of the society to a greater degree than in any other country. There are four carefully-defined racial groups: Bantu constitute two-thirds of the national population, whites (Europeans, especially Dutch) make up one-fifth, Colored (mixed racially) amount to one-tenth, and Asiatics (Indians) are about one-fortieth. The European minority is far more powerful than all three nonwhite groups combined, a dominance which they may have to struggle to maintain, as the nonwhites, especially the Bantu, are increasing much faster than the Europeans. All groups have low or medium mortality, but the European birth rate is only about 15, in contrast to the rates of about 45 among the Bantu and around 35 among Coloreds. As the nation becomes progressively more

83

African and less European, the Bantu may soon threaten and eventually overturn the European stranglehold on money and power.

The continent's demographic future depends largely upon the policies of the new African nations. These fledgling countries came into existence under disheartening conditions: low income levels, little industry and capital, few cities, scarcity of trained technicians and experienced leaders, heavy youth dependency, omniprevalent malnutrition, widespread illiteracy, tribal fragmentation, and in some areas excessive aridity. Densities are not great, but huge expanses of land are practically uninhabitable. Nonetheless, the bulk of the continent is not overpopulated, and resources are plentiful and could support many more agricultural and industrial enterprises than exist.

Realization of this potential, however, would require larger investments of capital than these new nations possess, and some countries are experiencing difficulty in keeping the per capita food supply from declining, let alone increasing industrial productivity. Nonetheless, most countries are improving levels of living, albeit considerably slower than they would if population growth did not absorb most of the increased productivity. An A.I.D. report estimated that the "growth of the gross national product in the less developed countries of Africa from 1960 through 1969 was 4.2 percent. Population growth reduced this favorable rate to 1.8 percent per capita."[5]

"Living on a continent that has a quarter of the earth's surface and less than one-tenth of its people, many Africans find it hard to believe that population growth poses a significant problem to them."[6] The problems that exist at present were not caused by population growth, but in the near future, population increase may well pose a major threat to their well-being. Fortunately, "African awareness of the implications of rapid population growth is increasing. So is the readiness to go from awareness to action."[7]

The Arab Countries

Stretching across North Africa and into Asia are twelve Arab countries. From the Atlantic coast of Africa to Southwest Asia, they are: Morocco, Algeria, Tunisia, Libya, Egypt (the United Arab Republic), Sudan, Saudi Arabia, Jordan, Lebanon, Iraq, Syria, and Kuwait.

Most Arabs are Moslems, but many Moslems are not Arabs. (Turkey, Iran, Pakistan, and Bangladesh are non-Arabic Moslem countries.) Instead of being religiously defined, an Arabic person is one who is descended from the original inhabitants of the Arabian peninsula; with the Jews, they make up the Semitic classification or sub-race of the Caucasian race. (There are, however, quite a number of black citizens of Arabic countries.) Other Semitic peoples were the ancient Phoenicians, Babylonians, and Assyrians.

Arabs constitute a majority of the Near East — an intercontinental region they share with Israel, Turkey, and Iran. Although Arabs had their origin in Asia, today most Arabs inhabit Africa.

The total population of the Arabic countries is about 130 million. Their size varies from Kuwait's 0.9 million to Egypt's 37 million, and their income ranges from Kuwait's status as one of the richest nations in the world (per capita) to the impoverished condition of most people in these nations. Growth rates generally are quite high because of the exceptionally high fertility and moderate mortality. Indeed, the average crude birth rate of about 50 makes the Arab states the highest-fertility political group in the world. Data generally are of such poor quality that a study of Arabic countries made the complaint that "in none of the countries is there suitable data to analyze the past trends of its vital rates, let alone their future trends."[8] Nonetheless, so excessive is their fertility and so weak their present inclination to lower it, that the Arab peoples seem clearly destined to increase greatly during the rest of this century — and probably well into the next one.

Levels of living generally are low in the Arab nations, as would be expected in a region of widespread illiteracy and an essentially peasant-agricultural labor force. Industrialization is taking place, however, and incomes are rising in the cities. Segregation of the sexes extends to many aspects of daily life, and families, businesses, and politics are male-dominated. It will be interesting to observe to what extent a rising standard of living may be accompanied by liberation of women from their customary confinement to menial household tasks.

Arabic countries are notable for their high proportion of nomads, who roam the desert and mountain regions in search of pasture for their sheep or other animals. Census and registration officials do not appreciate nomads, for they are difficult to count accurately, and births and deaths frequently are not reported. Attachment is to a *sheik* and a tribe, never to a place; and how can you count anyone who will not stand still? Consequently, all statistics concerning nomads are approximations. An estimated two-thirds of the Arabian peninsula's 16 million inhabitants are nomadic, but elsewhere in Southwest Asia and North Africa the proportion probably falls as low as 10 percent or thereabouts. Much of the motivation for nomadism is the meagerness of pastures in areas of scanty rainfall, forcing the herdsmen to keep moving as grasslands are cropped thin. Also characteristic of these areas are oases, which attract sedentary agriculturists. Most nomads move in small tribes having patriarchal organizations emphasizing discipline and group solidarity. Very few children attend school, and most men and practically all women are illiterate. The long-run trend is toward settlement around oases or in towns, although this tendency to decrease the number of nomads is partially counterbalanced by their generally high fertility.

Because of the difficulties of enumeration, there exist few demographic studies of nomadic peoples. One of the largest in scope was made in 1965 in Mauritania, a Moslem nation to the extreme west of Africa. The nomad birth rate was estimated at 42, but because of the high divorce rate and the late average age at marriage, the completed family size was only about 4.4 — smaller than the 5.1 in Mauritanean sedentary areas. The nomad's death rate appeared to be 25 and life expectancy at birth averaged 36 years — about what one could expect in medieval Europe.[9] Probably these findings are typical of nomads in desert and semi-arid areas of North Africa and the Near East.

Latin America

Latin America is the fastest-growing continent. From a 1973 population of about 300 million, it is heading at present growth rates toward 435 million by 1985 and 640 million by 2000; both the plummeting death rate and the sluggish natality decrease are responsible. The population increase is occurring almost exclusively in and adjacent to urban areas; indeed, the influx of migrants from rural areas has created a suburban mushrooming which is rapidly altering the Latin American settlement pattern from a few giant cities coupled with a low overall degree of urbanization to a larger number of urban areas and a more regular and gradual density gradient; in other words, the era of a giant primate city dominating a predominantly rural nation may be approaching an end. Less likely to end is the present concentration of population along the Atlantic and Pacific margins, in contrast to the nearly empty core, of which the humid Amazon Basin forms a major part.

That national growth rates vary considerably is evident from the low of 1.4 percent in Uruguay to highs of 3.4 percent in the Dominican Republic, Colombia, Ecuador, Paraguay, and Venezuela, doubling in 21 years. Fortunately this spectacular growth is taking place from a base population whose size is not now a world problem.

Mexico is a country of 56 million inhabitants growing at a rate of 3.3 percent annually from a density approximately that of the United States. Some of this Mexican increase is siphoned off into the United States; an annual average of 50,000-70,000 immigrants are admitted legally, supplemented by a larger but unknown number of illegal entrants. This exodus has not seriously affected the major demographic problem confronting Mexico: youth dependency, a consequence of the high birth rate. In 1973, 46 percent of the population was under 15 years of age, in contrast to 27 percent in the United States and about 25 percent in European nations; this high proportion of children places a heavy stress on already overburdened educational facilities. Mexico's demographic future depends on what happens to fertility; the outlook is that the birth rate will decline from its present 40-45 per 1,000 per year, but the rapidity of decline is uncertain. Unless there is a marked decrease in natality, the country will reach 85 million by 1985 and by the end of the century may become one of the dozen largest in the world.

Double the size of this second largest Latin American nation is Brazil, whose 101 million inhabitants and huge area make it the seventh most populous and fourth largest in area in the world. Growing 2.8 percent annually and likely to attain 145 million by 1985, Brazil's population is notable for its heavy concentration along the coast, its migration toward urban areas, its youth dependency (43 percent of the population is under 15 years of age), and its extremely heterogeneous racial make-up, including stone-age native Indians such as the Camaiura and Xeta, Portuguese and Italian immigrants, former black slaves, and smaller numbers from Japan and elsewhere. The low overall density is misleading — a lesson in the mistaken optimism that may be derived from neglecting the great variations in habitability often found within a single nation.

Ironically, the basic cause of Latin America's population problems is the success in lowering mortality. "Declines in mortality that took over a century to accomplish in Western Europe came in Latin America in less than 30 years.... Fertility, on the other hand, remained high, unlike in Western Europe where fertility had gradually followed the mortality decline."[10]

Until a new vital balance is achieved, economic progress and improved living conditions will be difficult to attain. With few exceptions, the Latin American nations have yet to make the transition to an industrial culture, and with a significant lowering of natality unlikely in the immediate future, continued rapid growth appears inevitable. Still, plentiful natural resources and millions of acres of virgin land ensure that the continent's future growth problems are surmountable if serious and intelligent efforts are made. One important reform, for example, would be a more equitable system of land tenure, which would reduce rural unemployment and increase food production, thus providing a major impetus to social and economic melioration.

Remarking that Latin America contains fewer people than its land area should be able to support, Trewartha nonetheless believes that population pressure poses serious problems for the continent. This paradox originates in the firmly rooted inability of Latin American culture "to effectively organize the region's extensive area and considerable natural resources for the benefit of even a modest population."[11] Some observers explain the low agricultural productivity of Latin America by pointing out the huge areas that are too wet or mountainous for ready cultivation. Others note that similarly discouraging climatic and topographic liabilities have been overcome in Southeast Asia and other world regions. More influential than tropical climate and steep slopes are such cultural factors as the regrettable land-holding system prevalent through the continent: "Vast areas of potentially cultivable land are held out of active use by a small number of absentee landlords, who not only themselves make ineffective use of the land, but at the same time refuse to permit its cultivation by small operators."[12] Because it is so difficult to acquire land, peasants remain landless and poverty-stricken, and many migrate to urban areas in search of jobs that will earn a better income than scrabbling on a too-small plot of rented soil.

Although the ratio of population to agricultural land is favorable in Latin America, this advantage is nullified by the productivity per worker, which is lower than in South and East Asia.[13] Because of this low food productivity, there is a serious pressure of population on cultivated land; and because of rapid population growth, this pressure is increasing.

Anglo America

Crossing the Rio Grande River from Mexico into the United States, and hence from Latin America to Anglo America, one approaches a far different culture having a much higher standard of living.

Many demographic properties of the United States are shared with Canada. Perhaps the most salient differences lie in the national backgrounds of the two populations. Almost half of the Canadian people are of English stock, and about a third are French, heavily concentrated in the province of Quebec, where French is widely spoken; the rest are mostly of European descent. The French-English cleavage pervades Canadian life, noticeably affecting the occupational distribution, the education system, and the results of elections. The 23 million national population is heavily and increasingly urban, birth and death rates are declining slowly but persistently, growth is moderate, and density varies markedly — traits similar to those of the United States.

The United States reached 213 million population in mid-1975, from a population of less than 4 million in 1790, about 76 million in 1900, and 150 million in 1950. The manner in which this growth has come about is shown by the imprecise quantities in Table 5. Imprecision is relative: the totals are nearly as accurate as any count of a major country can be expected to be; natural increase is affected by some undercounting of births and deaths but still is fairly accurate; but net migration is known only approximately, for the number of illegal entrants can only be guessed, it being so easy to walk over the border from Canada or — which happens much more frequently — from Mexico. So great is the number of Mexican aliens illegally residing in the United States (estimates range from 4 million to 10 million) that in October 1974 Attorney General William B. Saxbe declared that such aliens create a "severe national crisis" — an attestation considerably less believable than his complaint that they "mock our system of legal immigration."

Although the United States has received the greatest influx of immigrants of any nation over a similar period in the history of the world, in every decade for

TABLE 5

NATURAL INCREASE AND NET IMMIGRATION FOR
THE UNITED STATES, 1810-1973

Decade or year (fiscal period)	Component of change (in millions)		Total increase of population (in millions)
	Natural increase (births minus deaths)	Net migration (immigrants minus emigrants)	
1810-1820	2.3	0.1	2.4
1820-1830	3.1	0.1	3.2
1830-1840	3.7	0.5	4.2
1840-1850	4.7	1.4	6.1
1850-1860	5.6	2.6	8.2
1860-1870	6.3	2.1	8.4
1870-1880	7.7	2.6	10.3
1880-1890	7.7	5.0	12.7
1890-1900	9.4	3.6	13.0
1900-1910	9.7	6.3	16.0
1910-1920	11.5	2.4	13.9
1920-1930	14.5	3.0	17.5
1930-1940	9.5	−0.1	9.4
1940-1950	17.7	1.8	19.5
1950-1960	25.4	3.0	28.4
1960-1970	20.5	3.8	24.3
1970-1971	1.8	0.4	2.2
1971-1972	1.5	0.3	1.8
1972-1973	1.2	0.3	1.5

Sources: Compiled from data in United States Bureau of the Census, National Center for Health Statistics, and Immigration and Naturalization Service; Warren S. Thompson and P.K. Whelpton, *Population Trends in the United States* (New York: McGraw-Hill Book Co., 1933), p. 303; Conrad Taeuber and Irene B. Taeuber, *The Changing Population of the United States* (New York: John Wiley and Sons, 1958), p. 294; Dorothy Swaine Thomas, "International Migration," in Philip M. Hauser (ed.), *Population and World Politics* (Glencoe: Free Press, 1958), p. 150; and U.S. Bureau of the Census, "Estimates of the Population of the United States and Components of Change: 1973 (with annual data from 1930)," *Current Population Reports,* Series P-25, No. 521, May 1974, p. 11.

which figures are available, natural increase has greatly exceeded growth by migration. This is true even in the decades of greatest immigration (1900-1910) and smallest rate of natural increase (1930-1940). In the depression decade the nation lost more emigrants than it received immigrants, whereas the nation has never experienced a negative natural increase. During the 1960-1970 decade, natural increase contributed more than five times as much to national growth as did migration. Thus despite the impression given in many history books that the United States was built mainly by immigration, the fact of the matter is that here, as in nearly all other countries, the excess of births over deaths was, is, and undoubtedly will remain for some time the major factor causing population growth.

During the first half of the 1970s the annual average growth was 0.8 percent, of which 0.6 was natural increase and 0.2 was net civilian immigration. This represents a decrease both in overall growth and in fertility from the 1950s, when annual net growth was 1.7 percent, comprised of 1.5 from natural increase and 0.2 from net immigration. The difference is solely attributable to a declining natality, whereas deaths and net immigration have been nearly constant since 1950.

Most states in the union are growing (only West Virginia and North and South Dakota lost population during the 1960-1970 decade), the fastest rates being in Nevada, Arizona, and Florida, with the greatest growth in numbers occurring in California, whose additional 4.2 million persons dwarfed the second largest growth of 1.8 million in Florida. All 50 states experienced a positive natural increase. Interstate variations in net migration are far greater than those in natural increase, presumably because a desire to move is motivated largely by one's surroundings, while having children and dying are less subject to influence by locational factors.

"California has led the nation in total growth for the past five decades, and between 1940 and 1970 its intercensal growth was at least twice that of any other state. In fact, in every decade of this century California's rate of growth was at least double the United States average, and over the entire seventy-year period its average annual growth has been 3.7 percent. The remainder of the country has had an average annual increase of 1.3 percent per year over the same time period."[14] Since 1970, however, California's growth has slowed sharply, largely because of the population drop in Los Angeles County. This most populous county in the United States is estimated to have lost about 70,000 persons from 1970 to 1973, a marked turnabout from the county's gains of 1.0 million in the 1960s, 1.9 million in the 1950s, and 1.4 million in the 1940s.

California's leadership in growth is being taken over by Florida. As Table 6 shows, Florida grew by nearly 900,000 people during 1970-1973. Its net in-migration during this first third of the decade exceeded three-quarters of a million persons — a rate which, if continued, would add by 1980 more than 2 million persons above its base population of about 7 million.

TABLE 6

NATURAL INCREASE AND NET MIGRATION FOR FLORIDA
AND CALIFORNIA, 1940-1973

Date	Population (in thousands)	Change from preceding date (in thousands)		
		Total	Natural increase	Net migration
Florida				
April 1, 1940	1,897	—	—	—
April 1, 1950	2,771	874	296	578
April 1, 1960	4,952	2,180	564	1,616
April 1, 1970	6,789	1,838	511	1,326
July 1, 1973	7,678	888	107	782
California				
April 1, 1940	6,907	—	—	—
April 1, 1950	10,586	3,679	1,021	2,658
April 1, 1960	15,717	5,131	1,989	3,142
April 1, 1970	19,953	4,236	2,123	2,113
July 1, 1973	20,601	648	511	137

Source: U.S. Bureau of the Census, "Estimates of the Population of States with Components of Change, 1970 to 1973," *Current Population Reports*, Series P-25, No. 520, July 1974, p. 2.

United States Future

The United States as a whole may reach a population of 250 to 350 million by the year 2000.[15] Certain segments of the population are expected to increase faster than others: the surplus of females over males should increase, as should the percentage urban and the percentage nonwhite.

Such growth is paid for in many ways, as the growing nation needs more and more subdivisions and automobiles. A serious threat is posed to continuing prosperity and human happiness as already overcrowded cities are enlarged and the countryside is bulldozed into readiness for streets, homes, and factories. National parks and other outdoor recreation facilities are becoming so overcrowded that some campers and hikers stay away through dislike of crowds.

Welfare agencies caring for children and the aged must be prepared to cope with more clients. Water shortages will be accentuated. Forest and ferrous products will rise in cost, as will meat and certain other foods, especially those requiring considerable space to produce. Such irreplaceable fossil fuels as coal, oil, and gas may come into short supply.

Despite magnificent technological accomplishments and the beneficial effects of an increasing population for certain areas of national life, demographic and industrial patterns in which Americans have more of everything except space and certain natural resources are unquestionably deleterious in the long run and probably harmful even in the short run. Although not facing a crisis of imminent starvation like many Asians, Americans face other more subtle dangers that threaten their admirably high standard of living and even their traditional political freedoms. With fixed known natural resources and increasing use of those resources, the nation is faced with possible shortages and skyrocketing prices. And with greater density of habitation comes almost inevitably a need for greater governmental organization to keep people in line, lest they trample on the persons or rights of their fellows. Aldous Huxley called "this blind biological enemy of freedom" the shortest road to a nightmare world of overcentralization of power and Big Brother.[16] Even the richest nation on earth is not immune to problems stemming from population growth.

The World At Large

If the United States has just cause for fear of population increase, then what of the world as a whole and especially its less fortunately endowed residents? The answer is clear: others have even more to fear. The demographic crisis is so great that there is almost no disagreement on the subject among population experts. The persistent emphasis on the distresses induced by population growth is indeed one-sided, but it is difficult to find an expert on population who is willing to take the other side. There is no real controversy within demography; the controversy exists almost entirely among non-demographers — that is, among people who have devoted relatively little time and attention to questions of population size and growth and their consequences for human welfare and happiness.

The demographic mechanisms responsible for the changes causing so much concern to scholars and national leaders are, to repeat, mortality, natality, and migration. Since the end of World War II, world mortality has decreased remarkably, particularly in the developing countries. Natality has changed less, remaining about twice as high in underdeveloped regions as in industrial areas and keeping well above mortality levels in nearly all areas. International migration has had surprisingly little effect on recent national growth, with the exceptions of Israel and Ireland; however, migration within countries redistributes population from farms to cities and from areas of unemployment to more prosperous zones. In sum, though, not only in the world as a whole but also in individual nations, the major force for population change is not so much migration as natural increase.

Implications of These Trends

In general, the nations expected to experience the most rapid population growth are the least equipped to deal with it economically, socially, and politically. Incomes are distressingly low in the countries with the highest rates of natural increase, and in some regions hunger and poverty are endemic. Large proportions of the people in such areas are children, yet educational facilities are poor; consequently, illiteracy may remain high. Most high-fertility countries have about 40 percent of their population under 15 years of age, whereas low-fertility nations have only 25 percent under age 15. High youth dependency is not conducive to social amelioration, for it requires heavy expenditures for housing, food, and schooling — expenditures that could otherwise be used to finance the producer goods that are so sorely needed. Also, large proportions of children imply a not-to-distant increase in the number of people moving into the reproductive ages, betokening a formidable fertility potential.

These differences between developed and underdeveloped nations will increase rather than decrease if demographic trends continue without alteration. Af if existing differences in the living level are not enough, it is ironic that the countries with the lowest standard of living at the present time are precisely those with the highest growth rates. And when per capita income is low, rapid population increase aggravates attempts to improve the conditions of life by demanding that a major portion of the productive capacity of the nation be devoted to providing for immediate needs, thereby making investment in the future agonizingly difficult.

If ameliorative planning is restricted, national leaders may consider the possibility of improving living conditions among their followers (who may soon cease to be their followers if more shoes and television sets are not quickly forthcoming) by the fastest of all methods: war. Practically everyone wants to improve his store of material pleasures, and if a country cannot produce enough by its own efforts, its citizens may come to believe that the fastest way to obtain more such pleasure-giving objects is to take them from others by force — and whether this belief is right or wrong is irrelevant to the motivation of their actions. In this manner, excessive population growth may provide impetus for military aggression among the "have not" nations. Fortunately, this impetus generally does not result in actual armed conflict.

Never before in history has the human species multiplied as rapidly as it is doing at present — or as it is expected to do in the rest of this century. But this unique era is bound to end in the twenty-first century, if only because the earth can feed and house only so many people. Of course, interplanetary and intergalactic colonization may eventually solve this impending density problem, but such a solution seems unlikely in the foreseeable future.

In this century, timing is the *bête noir*. But that is only the short-term story. In the long run, there is no question but that each nation, no matter how favored by natural resources, inspired leadership, and a responsible citizenry, must face the question of how many people it can support at a desirable standard of living — and hence, the corollary question of what action must be taken to achieve this "terminal" population size and living level.

NOTES

[1] Norma McArthur, *Island Populations of the Pacific* (Canberra: Australia National University Press, 1968), p. 345.

[2] D. I. Pool, "Estimates of New Zealand Maori Vital Rates from the Mid-Nineteenth Century to World War I," *Population Studies*, Vol. XXVII, No. 1, March 1973, pp. 1117-125.

[3] Glenn T. Trewartha, *The Less Developed Realm: A Geography of Its Population* (New York: Wiley, 1972), p. 152.

[4] *Ibid.*, p. 183.

[5] U.S. Agency for International Development, *Population Program Assistance* (Washington: Government Printing Office, 1971), p. 69.

[6] *Idem.*

[7] *Idem.*

[8] K. C. Zachariah, "The Demographic Measures of Arab Countries: A Comparative Analysis," in Cairo Demographic Centre, *Demographic Measures and Population Growth in Arab Countries* (Cairo: 1970), p. 317.

[9] Jacques Brenez, "L'observation démographique des milieux nomades: l'enquête de Mauritanie," *Population*, Vol. XXVI, No. 4, July-August, 1971, pp. 721-736.

[10] U. S. Agency for International Development, *Population Program Assistance, op. cit.*, p. 14.

[11] Trewartha, *The Less Developed Realm, op. cit.*, p. 37.

[12] *Ibid.*, p. 45.

[13] *Ibid.*, p. 47.

[14] U. S. Bureau of the Census, "Estimates of the Population of States with Components of Change, 1970 to 1973," *Current Population Reports*, Series P-25, No. 520, July 1974, p. 3.

[15]U. S. Bureau of the Census, "Projections of the Population of the United States, by Age and Sex: 1972 to 2000," *Current Population Reports*, Series P-25, No. 493, December 1972, p. 1.

[16] Aldous Huxley, *Brave New World Revisited* (New York: Harper & Brothers, 1958), pp. 3-17, 22-36.

This family planning message adorns an ancient highway
mileage marker between Delhi and Agra, India.

PART III. FAMILY PLANNING CONTROVERSY

If your parents didn't have any children, you probably won't either.

(Goldie Hawn)

Coito ergo sum.

(Paraphrase of René Descartes, Discours de la méthode (Paris: 1637), by Patrick Seale and Irene Beeson, "Babies Along the Nile," The New Republic, Vol. CLIV, No. 19, Issue 2685, May 7, 1966, p. 11.)

Chapter 6.   Birth Control: Background

THE most timely and controversial topic in the field of demography today is birth control, or family planning. Deliberate manipulation of fertility has raised vociferous and sometimes violent opposition, although there seem to be no objections to exercising like control over the other demographic variable affecting man's total numbers. No one argues that death control or mortality planning is against nature, immoral, or in any way undesirable.

The explanation, put in simplest terms, is that death control is acceptable because it is so obviously on our side in the struggle to increase our numbers and comforts. Traditional values, adopted at a time when men needed to do all in their power to increase their ability to fight both natural and human enemies, favored and continue to favor mortality declines. But this same value system encourages the production of many children. Birth control is opposed because it runs counter to existing mores. And although the normative system of any culture is constantly changing, such changes are generally very gradual. There are signs, however, that the social norms encouraging reproduction may be weakening.

Demographic Determinants of Fertility

Fertility levels are affected by four main factors: the age-sex structure of the population, individual biological capacity to reproduce, sexual relations, and the use of birth control. Conditions promoting high fertility are a high proportion of women of childbearing age, a large proportion of healthy and nonsterile people, heterosexual intercourse by a large proportion of the population, and absence of deliberate limitation of births. Low fertility may be induced by a low proportion of women in the childbearing ages (15 to 50 years of age), poor health of a type that reduces the ability to conceive or bear children, a high proportion of persons never engaging in coitus, and extensive and efficient use of birth control methods. Concerning all four of these variables, the capabilities and behavior of women are far more basic to and causative of national fertility than are men's attributes and performance.

Changes in fertility are brought about directly by changes in one or more of these four factors — although many other factors play antecedent parts, causing increases or decreases in these four variables and thereby indirectly affecting fertility. A number of these prior-operating variables are cited in the following four chapters, and a few are discussed in detail.

Once we discover which of these four causative elements is determinative in a particular instance, we then need to discover why that particular element behaved as it did. If there are more young adult women than before, what caused this increase? If sterility rose, why did it? If lifetime virginity increased, what social forces brought this about? If birth control is on the rise, what is causing its popularity? Because of this need to seek the indirect causes to explain the direct ones, demographers are to some degree involved with such varied subjects as medical practices and research, customs regarding marital and sexual behavior, and many other aspects of both biological and social sciences.

Social Norms Influencing Fertility

Personal though convictions concerning fertility may be, they do not arise spontaneously within each individual; rather they are a product of the culture in which the person was reared and lives. All cultures contain rules, habits, and taboos governing fertility directly or, through control over sexual behavior, indirectly. Among such normative factors are age at marriage, systems of descent and inheritance, rules concerning legitimacy and promiscuity, divorce regulations, taboos on association of males with females, taboos on intercourse, rites of passage into adulthood, financial or other prerequisites to marriage, status changes consequent upon having children, citizenship or tax privileges to parents, patriotic attitudes, obligations to one's ancestors, and acceptability of abortion and infanticide.

Societies practice innumerable variations upon these themes, sometimes for the deliberate purpose of affecting fertility but more often for religious, ethical, magical, economic, or political reasons. Thus the birth rate may be affected by social customs not consciously associated with natality. The demographic outcomes of social practices are sometimes manifest or "intended and recognized" by the members of the group and, in other instances, latent or unanticipated.[1] For example, all sisters of a king of the Uganda were forbidden to marry or beget children. The manifest function of this taboo was to prevent them from producing a possible heir to the throne, which could prove politically disruptive. The latent natality function (there were other latent functions not affecting fertility) was obviously the reduction of the fertility of all the king's sisters to zero.

Early Chinese emperors governed vast, sparsely populated territories, and some wanted more people for greater taxes, grander armies, and unassailable power. Common persons also desired high fertility, for "a male child represented the only available form of old-age insurance," and given the extremely high mortality, "a couple needed three sons to ensure the survival of one to adulthood; and to have three boys, that family would have to have had, on the average, six children"[2] But other practices had an opposite effect: coitus interruptus was used, female infanticide reduced the number of girls who reached the childbearing age, prostitution and concubinage augmented the shortage of women, inheritance patterns limited marriage choices so as to retain family holdings intact, marriages were delayed for lack of money for necessary dowries or bride purchases, and remarriage of widows was disapproved of.

In Western culture the quotation from Genesis I:28, "Be fruitful and multiply," has been taken as a directive to have as many offspring as possible. But two qualifications have been offered by Biblical scholars: first, the context suggests that the intent was that of dominating other species rather than increasing the number of people; second, when read in the original Hebrew, this imperative is in the masculine gender only, thus implying that only men and not women have a religious duty to multiply. This contextual and linguistic exegesis illustrates the insubstantiality of origin of mores in religious dogma.

Some societies place a high value on sons but care little for daughters. Son preferences is firmly imbedded in the cultures of China, India, and many other countries. A study of family planning in Korea found that among all the attitudes related to birth control, the one least affected by modernization was a preference for boys.[3] This preference is just as strong in Moslem countries, as is reflected in such popular sayings as "A boy is a joy even if he is stillborn" and "A boy who dies is better than seven girls."[4] The Koran says "children are the adornment of life" but it seems that Moslem boys adorn like diamonds, girls like zircons.

Value systems forming parts of all cultures exert potent impacts on the degree to which human beings approach their biological limits of procreative potential, which demographers call "fecundity" in distinction to "fertility," which is the actual performance. If a culture had no social norms restricting births, each healthy woman who lived to complete the childbearing period might have as many as 25 children, a number not achieved in any society.

The modern Protestant advocacy of birth control represents a shift from the traditional views of practically all Christian sects that population is not a fundamental matter or that a large and growing population makes for a thriving community or state. The agreement of political leaders with traditional views is illustrated by Napoleon's statement that every family should have six children: three die, two replace their parents, and one is "in case of an accident."[5] But these beliefs and related sexual taboos have been altered so much that of 2,713 American women interviewed in a 1955 sample survey, only 10 refused to answer questions about their personal efforts to control conception — fewer than the number of refusals for questions on income.[6] There was an almost universal approval and widespread and effective use of birth control, along with a surprising uniformity in stated preferences regarding family size, notably an almost total rejection of childlessness and a vigorous disavowal of both the one-child family and the five-or-more child family.[7] This and other evidence foretells an increasing proportion of couples practicing birth control in the future.

Fecundity and Sexual Behavior

Although birth control is coming to be defined as irregular by fewer and fewer segments of Western society, other sexual practices remain on the ban. Deviant sexual activity, defined by the normative structure to include nearly all sexual relations except marital coitus, has been credited historically with reducing the birth rate, from the pederasts of ancient Athens to modern homosexuals. The presumption is that sexual desire directed into nonreproductive outlets is subtracted from the potential amount of heterosexual coitus, thus inducing a lower birth rate. Similarly, a commonly postulated latent demographic function of prostitution is that of reducing the frequency of legitimate bisexual intercourse which may lead to procreation. The fact that neither of these assumptions has been proven correct has not deterred their use.

Many cultures define sexual frigidity as deviant behavior. Certainly unresponsiveness may lead to marital tension, interfering with close feeling between husband and wife. Such intimacy is expressed by the attitude toward sex of a wife interviewed in a recent study: "Because of it everything else runs smoothly."[8] However regarded, when aversion to sexual intercourse takes the form of complete abstinence, fertility is nil. Absence of sexual ardor is sometimes attributed to biological causes, sometimes to social ones. Results are likely to include marital frustration, unhappiness, or divorce in addition to a possibly lower birth rate. One psychology professor is fond of remarking that the greatest single cause of marital strife is the demand for a sudden change in the bride's attitude: "In the course of a few hours, the worst thing in life is supposed to become the best thing in life." A frequent scapegoat is the mother who rears her daughter according to the prevailing norms.

> Her mother taught her all the things good little girls were supposed to know. . . . She was made to feel that a good wife was synonymous with being a good housekeeper, that if she kept her husband's home well, he would love and cherish her forever. But she was never told that he might want her as a lover. . . . My wife today is all her parents ever hoped she would be — one of the neatest housekeepers in our neighborhood and a doting mother of the two sons we managed to have. I think the old folks would believe me mad if I told them I required something more of her and had to go to prostitutes because she hasn't got it to give.[9]

101

From this centuries-long Western norm that sex is what a man does to a woman, there arose in the 1950s a new attitude: sex is what a man does *for* a woman — that is, it became the man's responsibility to please his mate. Now, in the 1970s, a third norm has arisen: sex is something that a man and woman do together for mutual pleasure. In the first era the married woman received little satisfaction because she was only supposed to be a passive, even reluctant, participant. In the second period men suffered a unilateral burden of being answerable for their wives' orgasms. In the present phase both spouses are supposed to transmit an exchange of pleasure and vulnerability.

These swings of sexual obligation have loose counterparts regarding procreative decisions. Sometimes the wife is charged with bearing all of the children that the husband can beget — and the husband may not be interested in limiting his offspring. Sometimes the wife is held responsible for controlling the couple's fertility. But increasingly it is felt that both partners to a marriage should participate in the decision as well as its mode of implementation. Even though most birth control methods are designed for use by the woman, both spouses can talk over their preferences (if any) concerning the number of children and the most acceptable way to achieve the mutually-acceptable or compromise goal.

Economic Influences on Natality

The intermittent persistence of sexual incitements is inescapable, and the waxing and waning of social inducements was acknowledged in the preceding pages. Yet there remains the perpetually-powerful impetus, whether toward or against fertility, of money — the effect of each couple's financial resources on their desire to have or to not have their next child, or any number of children later on. Questions sometimes asked are "How many children can we afford?" and "How many can we send to college?" — and, conversely, "How many are needed to assure us a comfortable old age, secure from financial worries?"

Children can be regarded as liabilities when they have to be fed and clothed in the early years, as assets as soon as they are old enough to work and bring home their salaries, as liabilities if parents must put them through high school and provide a dowry or set them up in business, as neither assets nor liabilities during their self-sustaining adulthood, and finally, as ultima-terma assets who keep the old folks alive by supplying food and shelter when the parents are too enfeebled to fend for themselves.

All these possibilities considered (and some parents do, indeed, think of them), the optimal solution seems to be to have some children, but not too many. At least one child, and preferably two or several children, can help peasant parents; on the other hand, many children (especially if they are girls) may damage family economics through presenting too great a strain on the family's ability to rear the next generation. What generally is needed, optimally, is one or two sons (and, in traditional cultures, preferably no daughters). A Chinese peasant was reported to say in 1968: "You need two sons because you have to make sure that at least one has ability."[10] Whether a daughter has ability or not remains, in many regions, incidental.

A Summary of Fertility Motives

As has been pointed out earlier in this chapter, a number of factors influence a family's fertility: social and cultural norms, biological fecundability, sexual behavior, economic forces, psychological values, and a miscellany of other determinants. This is a gigantic subject on which definitive conclusions have yet to be reached; indeed, it appears that there always have been and always will be wide differences in motivation among different sorts of people. Inspecting the summary of these motivating factors given in Table 7, it should be easy for anyone to recall similar statements, on both sides, that he or she has heard expressed in recent years.

Today, in the United States generally, the low-fertility motives seem to be increasing in popularity. More and more couples are coming to favor what will be described later in this chapter as "the small family system."

Preferences for high fertility still exist, especially among traditionally oriented religious groups. In contrast to a United States national birth rate that dropped in 1974 below 15 per 1,000 persons per year, the Amish sect — centered in Ohio and Pennsylvania but now dispersed into nearly half of the fifty states — is maintaining its birth rate at about 30, and the Hutterites of South Dakota, Montana, and Canada are keeping their birth rate at about 45. Any religious order that can persevere at a fertility level that doubles or triples the national average is worth discussing.

Two High-Fertility American Sects

The Amish are family-centered to an extent unparalleled elsewhere in America.[11] They think and behave as if the conjugal family were their whole life. Derived from the sixteenth-century European Anabaptists by way of the Mennonites (named for Menno Simmons, a former Dutch Catholic priest), the Amish were named for Jakob Ammann of Switzerland, who found the Mennonites insufficiently fundamentalist. Moving to the United States in small groups, the Amish have grown by 2 to 3 percent a year to a total of somewhat more than 50,000 persons.

TABLE 7
MOTIVES FAVORING LARGE OR SMALL FAMILIES

High-Fertility Motives	Criterion	Low-Fertility Motives

Economic Level

Children are useful or needed to help the family earn a living. At worst, they can pay for themselves as they grow. And the more children you have, the more financial support you will have in old age.

The fewer the children, the smaller the everyday expenses. If one is poor, children may worsen this condition. With few children, one can gain a higher level of living, more vacation fun, a better house, and a bigger car. One can even save toward retirement. Finally, one's inheritance remains intact, rather than being divided among many children.

Family Organization

Children can help with work around the house, including the supervision of babies. "Large families are happy families." The family name is continued, especially by sons. Sons also can help fight your battles and uphold family rights.

Small families have less conflict and tension, more compansionship. The house is less crowded; there is more peace and quiet. It is easier to find a suitable house or apartment.

Health and Survival

Because children often die, it is necessary to have a large family to ensure that your children will survive to adulthood.

The life of the mother must be preserved. Fewer children means healthier children. Less work is needed to support a small family.

Attitude Toward Contraception

Contraceptive devices are unhealthy, unnatural, unpleasant, and interfere with sexual gratification.

Reducing the fear of an unwanted pregnancy improves sexual gratification and decreases marital worries.

Husband-Wife Relationship

The best way to keep a man and wife from separating is to have a baby, and the best way to keep them happy is to have a large family.

A small number of children means that husbands and wives have more time for each other, to enjoy each other's companionship.

TABLE 7 (Continued)

MOTIVES FAVORING LARGE OR SMALL FAMILIES

High-Fertility Motives	Criterion	Low-Fertility Motives

Emotional Benefits

Children support the ego by demonstrating virility, manliness, or feminity. It is pleasant to have a child around the house, so that one has an additional person to love.

Lack of children permits husbands and wives to pursue occupational ambitions and vocational aims. An intelligent or talented wife can fulfill herself outside the home if she does not have too many children. Friendships outside the home are facilitated, as are community activities.

The Children Themselves

Children with many brothers and sisters have better personalities — better adjusted, better able to get along with others, and not so spoiled or egotistical.

In small families, it is easier to give each child a good education and a start on a career. Parents can devote more time to each child's education and socialization.

Religious and Cultural Values

Large families are God's will. Large families promote morality by helping to prevent divorce and infidelity. If you have a big family, you are looked up to in the community.

Everyone is entitled to have the number of children that he or she wants, and no one is required to have any to satisfy his God, his relatives, or his community.

Nation and Community

Large families are desirable because they promote national growth and make the nation strong. The community benefits from the added marketing and tax base.

Small families avoid overcrowding and overpopulation. They make it easier for the community to meet demands for schools and other services, plus reducing the welfare burden. National technical progress is not eaten up by having more bodies to feed, clothe, and house.

Source: Information adapted from Donald J. Bogue, *Principles of Demography* (New York: Wiley, 1969), pp. 840-841.

The Amish religion is characterized by high fertility (contraception is declared a sin), mistrust and avoidance of the outside world, affinity toward nature, anti-intellectualism, and refusal to use any product of modern technology, including electricity, telephones, motor vehicles, or even air-filled rubber tires. Amish families may be seen on highways near their farms, driving their horse-drawn black buggies while completely enveloped in black clothing. Their unwillingness to benefit from modern agricultural techniques, combined with a fertility averaging six or seven children per woman, ensures that most Amish families have a hard time providing for their members, and especially offering their young men enough land to fulfill their sacred duty to farm. One result is a defection rate of about 10 percent; another is a very slow adoption by "New Order" Amish of a limited number of modern farm practices; a third result is the reluctant acceptance of nonagricultural jobs by some young Amishmen. They still oppose compulsory public school attendance, knowing that an Amish teenager who reaches high school and associates with non-Amish peers may be lost to the church.

The Amish are thus trapped: beginning as a revolt against the religious orthodoxy of their time, they proceeded to establish an even more rigid theocracy which insists that its adherents have many children, yet does not permit them to use the modern farming procedures that might enable them to compete on equal terms with non-Amish neighbors. How the Amish will resolve the increasing problem of population pressure within the family is, and will remain for some time, a fascinating conundrum. Here we see a classic example of a group that wants to make its own world stand still, but which is surrounded by accelerating change.

Even higher fertility is shown near the Canadian border by the Hutterites (founded by Jakob Huter of what is now Austria), who are among the fastest-growing groups on earth.[12] Averaging about ten children per woman, the Hutterites are doubling their numbers every 15 to 20 years. From ages 25 to 40, married Hutterite women normally have a child nearly every two years; by contrast, most women in the United States cease childbearing by age 30. Even the Amish women reduce their childbearing — albeit slowly — after age 30. It is interesting to speculate how high Hutterite fertility might go if it were not for the rigid taboo against premarital sexual relations and the prohibition of teenage marriage. As it is, their average age at marriage in 1965 was 23 — slightly older than the United States average.

Like the Amish, the Hutterites originated from the Anabaptists and maintain persistent fundamentalist and anti-intellectual views, but they differ by living in communes rather than family units. Each Hutterite community of one hundred or so persons is a self-sufficient agrarian and economic colony which keeps itself almost completely isolated from its neighbors.

Not only is the Hutterite birth rate among the highest in the world, but because they have so many persons in the younger and less death-prone ages, their death rate is exceptionally low (indeed, lower than that in any sovereign country). Such a low mortality is also possible because the Hutterites, unlike the Amish, accept the impedimenta of modern medicine. Although there exist a few cases of sterilization for unquestionably valid threats to the mother's life, Hutterites generally believe as strongly as the Amish that all forms of birth control are sinful, including the rhythm method. It should not be surprising, then, that middle-aged Hutterite women have a high death rate.

The Hutterites' carefully remembered persecution in sixteenth-century Europe, supplemented by modern-day hostility from neighbors who resent their continual search for additional land on which to establish new colonies needed to support their numerous progeny, has bred into the Hutterians a justified paranoia. As a bulwark against the world, they seek large families — and given their prohibition of birth control, almost universal marriage, nearly nonexistent divorce, and a high level of health, large families are easy to achieve. Given additionally the communistic nature of Hutterite life, which provides equally for all families without regard for the number of children, there is no economic motivation to avoid having another child. The carpenter just makes another bed.

Less austere in religious doctrine than the Amish, Hutterites use farm machinery and chemical fertilizers. And because their land is owned by communes rather than families, their plots are large and therefore can bestead bulk purchases and sales. Household maintenance also benefits from the Hutterian ability to purchase food and other necessities in price-reducing bulk quantities. For this reason, non-Hutterite farmers often object to Hutterites as having an unfair competitive advantage, claiming the ordinary farmers cannot obtain such large-quantity discounts for farm and household machinery and supplies.

Yet the Hutterites are not free from economic strains. Every generation must establish a new colony, in addition to the parent commune, to house and feed the doubled population. Thus another 4,000 or 5,000 acres must be found and paid for, plus a new batch of farm equipment and the raw materials to build a 100-person dormitory. Given the concentrated and efficient effort of the Hutterians on working the soil, they tend to become rich; given their fertility, they tend to become poor; the net result is that they survive and even may be said to prosper in a subdued fashion. But in the long run, the race against this generational doubling, with its demand for doubling the land and equipment, offers the Hutterites little surplus money. Their future, like that of the Amish, will be interesting to observe.

Sterility and Subfecundity

Other factors of demographic interest are sterility (inability to have children) and subfecundity (partial sterility). Subfecund couples are capable of having children, but do so less frequently than the fully fecund and also require more time to conceive. Some couples making every effort to have as many children as possible still manage to bring forth only one or two in a lifetime. Most couples conceive within six months, but subfecund ones may take two or three years. Of couples discontinuing contraception with the intent to have a child, about 30 percent conceive during the first month, some 60 percent within three months, and 90 percent within a year.

Without paying much attention to facts, moralists from the ancient world to the twentieth century have voiced the belief that luxury breeds inability to reproduce. A recent study of American families found about one-third to be subfecund and one-tenth permanently sterile, usually as the result of an operation to make conception impossible; but no evidence has been found supporting consistent differences in ability to beget children among different socioeconomic strata.[13]

Among both sterile and subfecund people — that is, all those suffering from some physical impairment reducing reproductive capacity — as well as those affected by frigidity, numerous substances have been ingested or applied externally in an effort to combat these ills. So many methods have been advanced to cure impotence and sterility that one's imagination is humbled upon considering their seemingly infinite variety. Indiscriminate use is frequently dangerous to health and sometimes may prove fatal; hence such "high-potency capsules" are proscribed by law in most Western countries. Effectiveness of these potions seems to lie primarily in psychological rather than chemico-biological properties, as is illustrated by distilled and fermented drinks, whose biological properties tend to lower fecundity rather than increase it; the same is true of narcotics. The best conception-inducing drugs seem to be beauty and imagination — a fact pointed out as long ago as the fourth century A.D. by physician Theodorus Priscianus, whose cure was to "let the patient be surrounded by beautiful girls or boys; also give him books to read."[14]

While pharmacological agents designed to promote fertility are of doubtful efficacy, it is certain that dietary deficiency which interferes with general health and vigor adversely affects sexual, and hence procreative, ability. Experimental rats reared on deficient diets have delayed sexual maturation. In humans, semistarvation interferes drastically with sexual processes, and extreme inanition produces impotence. Conversely, adequate caloric and other nutritional intake aids sexual functions.

Surely health must have been adequate in the case of Mrs. Fedor Vassilet, who before her death in 1872 purportedly produced 69 little Vassilets: 16 pairs of twins, 7 sets of triplets, and 4 sets of quadruplets (very few of the children survived infancy).[15] But plural births are not generally so common, the number of cases per million confinements being about 10,000 twins, 100 triplets, and 1 quadruplet; these proportions, incidentally, all reach their highest point among mothers aged 35-39.

Ways to Measure Fertility

When demographers study the fertility of a nation, tables and rates become necessary tools. Most familiar is the crude birth rate (CBR), which is simply the number of babies born in one year, divided by the population, and multiplied by 1,000 in order to avoid a decimal. For example, if a country of 8 million inhabitants had 240,000 births during 1975, then the CBR would be:

$$\frac{240,000}{8,000,000} \times 1,000 = 30 \text{ (per 1,000 persons per year)}$$

This rate deserves the label "crude," for it does nothing more than report the number of births relative to the size of the total population. It explains nothing about the demographic forces that operate: for example, what is the proportion of persons too young to have children? What is the proportion of women too old for childbearing? Is the ratio of men to women equal?

To answer these three questions, demographers use age-sex-specific birth rates. That is, they calculate the birth rate separately for each age group of women. (There is little point in calculating the age-specific fertility of fathers — although this is occasionally done.) For instance, we determine the birth rate for women aged 15-19, for those 20-24, for those 25-29, and so on throughout the childbearing ages. A close reading of these specific rates can tell a statistician far more than could be learned from the crude rate. One might learn, for example, that women in Thailand continue bearing children at fairly high (although decreasing) rates through their 30s and 40s, whereas American women demonstrate a much more rapid decrease in age-specific rates after age 30.[16] Such information can be highly important to manufacturers of garments for pregnant women (to what age-group should the styles appeal?) as well as to family-planning directors (which age groups are having the most children?).

Age-specific birth rates, although very useful for examining a single country, become tedious for the comparison of two or more nations. Hence demographers have developed standardized birth rates. To compare the fertility of Thai and American women, a statistician might multiply each age-specific birth rate of the Thai women times the proportion of American women in each age group; this would tell the overall fertility that the Thai women would experience if they had the same age distribution as the American women. Conversely, one could apply the age-specific birth rates of the American women to the age distribution of the Thai women; this would estimate what would be the overall fertility of the American women if their proportions in each age group were the same as those of the Thai women. In this way, age is held constant or equalized between the two populations. A compromise procedure avoids adopting the age structure of either nation, but instead applies the age-specific birth rates of both the Thai and the American women to the age distribution of a third nation, which might be chosen because its age structure is intermediate between those of Thailand and the United States.

The reasoning underlying the use of standardized rates is as follows: It is possible — and occasionally happens — that Country A and Country B both have the same tendency toward fertility, as observed according to the ages of the women, but that the crude birth rates are not the same in the two nations. That is, the 15-19-year-old A's have exactly the same fertility as the 15-to-19-year-old B's, the 20-24-year-old B's have precisely the same fertility rate as the 20-24-year-old A's, and so forth throughout the entire childbearing period. But if Country A has a larger proportion of older women (and older women nearly always have lower fertility than young women), then the crude birth rate of Country A would be lower than that of B. This does not mean that the CBRs are incorrect, for they report correctly what is going on, in total, in the two nations. But they do not show details, and it is the detailed birth rates by age that provide the most realistic future estimates to political and business leaders who want to plan school building construction or estimate beer consumption X years from now.

But age-specific rates cannot be calculated without knowing the ages of women who are having babies — and in some countries, these ages are not accurately known. In such cases, demographers calculate a child-woman ratio — the number of children under five years of age, divided by the number of women in the childbearing ages (normally 15-49, although the childbearing ages are not the same in all countries because of the variations in social practices mentioned at the beginning of this chapter).

Another technique is cohort analysis, whereby a group of women is studied throughout their lives or for stated time periods. For instance, the cohort of women who were married in 1950 could be studied year by year, noting their fertility in 1951, 1952, 1953, and so forth. They could be compared with the cohort that married in 1970 by observing the latter group's production of children for 1971, 1972, 1973, and so on. In this way, women married, say, for seven or eight years (1958 and 1978, respectively, for the two cohorts) could be compared. Additionally, each cohort can be examined by age group to permit age-specific fertility comparisons. Cohorts need not be defined by date of marriage: often cohorts are defined as all women born in 1900, 1910, 1920, and so on. In principle, any event will do: women catechized in 1937 versus 1946, or females reaching puberty in 1919 or 1932.

Some measures of fertility make allowance for deaths to children. The simplest example is the size of completed family, which is the number of children in a family whose mother has completed her childbearing years. This figure equals the number of children ever born minus those who died.

More complicated are the gross reproduction rate (GRR) and net reproduction rate (NRR). To put it incompletely (a full explanation is very cumbersome), the NRR measures the extent to which one generation of women replaces their mothers. The GRR does the same thing, but without allowance for deaths to females in the second, or replacing, generation. Reproduction rates of 100 represent exact replacement of the present generation by the oncoming one; rates above and below 100 signify changes. Reproduction rates are distinctive because they measure intergenerational change rather than the annual changes that are the focus of the measures previously described and ordinarily reported.

A particularly important set of measures are the natural increase (NI) rates: crude (CRNI), standarized (SRNI), and intrinsic or life table (this third rate requires construction of a life table, which is discussed briefly in Chapter 9). Natural increase equals the birth rate minus the death rate. For example, if Slobbovia has a CBR of 44 and a CDR of 20, then the CRNI is 24 — which tells us that there are 24 more Slobbovians this year than last year, not allowing for migration.

Small Family Systems

The term *small family system* refers to the preference exhibited in many places in modern times for four children or fewer. The first nation to espouse the small family was France, a Roman Catholic country.

The French birth rate began to decline around 1770, long before similar trends were set elsewhere, in response to widespread adoption of coitus interruptus and contraception;[17] by 1850 most French families were probably practicing some form of birth control.[18] Urban dwellers were the first to know about and use birth control, but Jacques Houdaille notes the appearance of birth control in rural villages in eastern France as early as 1780.[19] Natality continued to decline until during 1936-1944 deaths exceeded births, and France appeared to be facing depopulation. However, since the World War II demobilization, the birth rate has risen to a level slightly above that required for replacement of each generation by the next.

This lowering of fertility has also occurred in other Roman Catholic nations; in fact, the birth rates of all Catholic countries in Europe are now approximately equal to, and in most cases smaller than, that of the United States. The other large Catholic area, Latin America, still maintains high natality rates.

Residents of most industrial nations have accepted the small family, but those in underdeveloped areas frequently have not, although there are signs of attitudes favoring contraception, abortion, and sterilization, even where these methods have not traditionally been favorably regarded.[20] Haiti exemplifies what now seems to be a minority position which rests upon the fatalistic belief that human beings cannot control the number of their offspring, coupled with the further conviction that people should not attempt to form preferences: "People can't do anything to not make children because it is God who gives them children." "If God gives me ten I would be happy. If He gave me two I would be happy too."[21] In a survey of 2,314 couples in India, 34 percent acknowledged knowing some technique by which fertility could be curtailed, but only 5 percent reported having occasionally used such a technique; furthermore, couples having no knowledge of birth control methods rarely expressed any interest in learning about them. However, this apparent lack of knowledge and interest does not necessarily mean that Indian couples are not interested in limiting their family size: 70 percent said they wanted a small number of children for economic or health reasons, but there is a powerful feeling that fulfillment of this wish should or must stem from divine intervention rather than human initiative.[22]

In most parts of the world, family planning interest and knowledge are usually greatest in upper social classes, urban areas, educated and high income persons, and certain religious groups. All of these tendencies are exhibited in the United States, where the most significant differentials are the higher birth rates and lesser use of birth control among Catholics, nonwhites, southerners, farm residents, and nonworking wives. Of all of these high natality groups, the most striking is the American Indian, whose fertility level is nearly double that of the white population.

The fact that new family planning practices ordinarily have been adopted first among upper-class persons has led many demographers to explain changes in reproductive habits and birth control as a filtering-down process of successive acceptance first among people of high education, income, and social status, next by persons of moderate standing, and finally among those of low rank.[23] However, in recent years this process has been weakening and may ultimately vanish. Under certain conditions — extreme poverty, high density, and little opportunity — the poorest and least educated classes may be as likely to adopt fertility planning as more educated and prosperous persons, especially when exposed to an educational or promotional program on birth control techniques.[24]

Around the world, the number of live births per 1,000 population per year has declined from the traditional level of 40 or 50 to half that amount in many nations. Recent birth rates are supplied in Table 8, which includes countries primarily on the basis of the accuracy and completeness of their statistics. The strongest intercontinental difference is between Europe and Africa — but note the "white-colored" contrast in the Union of South Africa.

United States Trends

The long-term decline of fertility and the adoption of the small family system characterize many nations, including the United States, where natality dropped year after year with hardly a break for a century and a half after the nation was founded. This gradual but virtually uninterrupted reduction in fertility is documented by changes in the total fertility rate (the average number of births that would occur to women living through the childbearing ages exposed to the existing birth rates at each age): 7.0 in 1800, 6.7 in 1820, 6.1 in 1840, 5.2 in 1860, 4.2 in 1880, 3.6 in 1900, 3.2 in 1920, 2.2 in 1940, and, reversing the previously consistent trend, 3.5 in 1960.[25]

During 1946-1957, Americans could speak with some accuracy of a trend toward larger families, but the increase was slight. Furthermore, these so-called large families of four or five children were large only by twentieth-century standards. In colonial times, a family of four or five children was regarded as small; the average was, in fact, eight.[26] Viewed in this light, the resurgence of fertility through the "baby boom" following World War II constituted "a trendlet rather than a trend."[27]

The number of live births per 1,000 women aged 15-44 dipped to an all-time low of 76 in 1936, thereafter rising to a high of 123 in 1957. This "trendlet" then began to play itself out, for since 1957 there has been a steady downward movement. Similarly, the annual number of births slowly but steadily declined from a ceiling in 1957 of 4.3 million to 3.1 million in 1973.

Reasons for both the rise during the 1940s and 1950s and the subsequent decline are to be found in changes in marriage folkways, age composition, and economic events. For some decades early marriage has been becoming increasingly fashionable, encouraged by such other changes in American culture as reduced financial burdens (because both spouses work), relief from mistakes through divorce, and elimination (through contraception) of the necessity of having children. Once wed, young couples tend to have babies sooner than did previous generations. They also complete their childbearing at an earlier age, most women now bearing their last child before reaching the age of 30. This advance in timing or concentration of childbearing between the ages of 18 to 29 resulted in a temporary "bunching up" of births and helped to cause the baby boom; but once this new age-fertility folkway was established, the birth rate resumed its long-run decline as other forces came into play.

TABLE 8
BIRTHS PER 1,000 POPULATION PER YEAR IN
SELECTED COUNTRIES, 1955-1972

Continent and country	1955-59	1970	1972
Anglo America			
Canada	27.8	17.4	
United States	24.9	18.2	15.6
White	23.7	15.5	
Nonwhite	34.8	25.2	
Latin America			
Argentina	24.0		
Chile	35.9	29.6	
Costa Rica	48.1	33.2	
El Salvador	49.3	40.0	
Guatemala	48.7	40.9	
Jamaica	39.2	34.4	
Panama	39.8	37.1	35.6
Uruguay	20.8	22.4	
Europe			
Austria	16.8	15.2	13.8
Belgium	17.0	14.7	13.8
Bulgaria	18.7	16.3	15.3
Czechoslovakia	18.5	15.9	
Denmark	16.8	14.4	16.2
Finland	19.9	13.8	12.7
France	18.4	16.7	16.9
Germany, East	16.3	13.9	11.7
Germany, West	16.9	13.4	11.4
Greece	19.3	16.5	
Hungary	17.8	14.7	14.7
Ireland	21.1	21.9	
Italy	18.0	16.8	16.3
Netherlands	21.3	18.3	16.1
Norway	18.1	16.6	16.6
Poland	27.1	16.8	17.4

TABLE 8 (Continued)
BIRTHS PER 1,000 POPULATION PER YEAR IN
SELECTED COUNTRIES, 1955-1972

Continent and country	1955-59	1970	1972
Portugal	24.2	19.3	
Spain	21.3	19.6	19.4
Sweden	14.5	13.7	13.8
Switzerland	17.5	15.8	14.4
United Kingdom	16.4	16.2	14.9
England and Wales	15.9	16.0	14.8
Northern Ireland	21.4	21.1	
Scotland	18.9	16.8	15.1
Yugoslavia	24.8	17.8	18.2
Asia			
Hong Kong	36.3	20.0	19.4
Indonesia	52.0		
Israel	27.9	26.7	26.9
Japan	18.2	18.8	
Malaysia (West)	44.4	33.8	
Singapore	42.8	23.0	23.3
Sri Lanka	36.6	29.4	
Africa			
Egypt	40.6		
Liberia		51.0	
Nigeria	49.2		
South Africa			
Colored	45.6	36.8	
White	24.9	23.6	
Tunisia	42.8	36.2	
Oceania			
Australia	22.6	20.6	20.5
New Zealand	26.3	22.1	
U.S.S.R.	25.3	17.4	18.0

Source: Adapted from *Population Index,* Vol. XXXIX, No. 3, July 1973, pp. 475 -478 and 485-487.

NOTES

[1] Robert K. Merton, *Social Theory and Social Structure* (Glencoe: Free Press, 1949), p. 51.

[2] Leo A. Orleans, *Every Fifth Child: The Population of China,* Eyre Methuen, London, 1972, p. 36.

[3] Bom Mo Chung, James A. Palmore, Sang Joo Lee, and Sung Jin Lee, *Psychological Perspectives: Family Planning in Korea* (Seoul: Korean Institute for Research in the Behavorial Sciences, 1972), p. 51.

[4] Laila Shukry El-Hamamsy, "Belief Systems and Family Planning in Peasant Societies," in Harrison Brown and Edward Hutchings Jr. (eds.), *Are Our Descendants Doomed?* (New York: Viking, 1972), p. 353.

[5] J. Christopher Herold (ed.), *The Mind of Napoleon* (New York: Columbia University Press, 1955), p. 24; from Gaspard Gourgaud, *Sainte Hélène: Journal Inédit de 1815 à 1818,* Vol. I, p. 461.

[6] Ronald Freedman, Pascal K. Whelpton, and Arthur A. Campbell, *Family Planning, Sterility and Population Growth* (New York: McGraw-Hill, 1959), p. 14.

[7] *Ibid.,* pp. 401-402.

[8] Lee Rainwater, *Family Design* (Chicago: Aldine Publishing Co., 1965), p. 74.

[9] John M. Murtagh and Sara Harris, *Cast the First Stone* (New York: McGraw-Hill, 1957), pp. 200-201.

[10] Janet W. Salaff, "Institutionalized Motivation for Fertility Limitation in China," *Population Studies,* Vol. XXVI, No. 2, July 1972, p. 240.

[11] John A. Hostetler, *Amish Society* (Baltimore: Johns Hopkins Press, 1968).

[12] Joseph W. Eaton and Albert J. Mayer, "The Social Biology of Very High Fertility among the Hutterites: The Demography of a Unique Population," *Human Biology,* Vol. XXV, No. 3, September 1953, pp. 206-264.

[13] Freedman, Whelpton, and Campbell, *op. cit.,* pp. 18-19.

[14] Quoted in Hans Licht (Brandt), *Sexual Life in Ancient Greece* (New York: Barnes and Noble, 1952), pp. 514-515.

[15] Norris and Ross McWhirter, *Guinness Book of World Records* (New York: Sterling Publishing Co., 1973), p. 25.

[16] Ralph Thomlinson, *Thailand's Population: Facts, Trends, Problems, and Policies* (Bangkok: Thai Watana Panich Press Co., 1971; republished in Winston-Salem, North Carolina: Wake Forest University, 1972), pp. 69-70.

[17] Alfred Sauvy, *Fertility and Survival* (New York: Criterion Books, 1961), p. 157.

[18] Peter R. Cox, *Demography* (London: Cambridge University Press, 1959), p. 248.

[19] Jacques Houdaille, "La population de sept villages des environs de Boulay (Moselle) aux xviiie siécles," *Population*, Vol. XXVI, No. 6, November-December 1971, p. 1069.

[20] Ronald Freedman, John Y. Takeshita, and T. H. Sun, "Fertility and Family Planning in Taiwan: A Case Study of the Demographic Transition," *American Journal of Sociology*, Vol. LXX, No. 1, July 1964, pp. 16-27.

[21] Men and women interviewed in Haiti in 1959, quoted in J. Mayone Stycos, "Haitian Attitudes Toward Family Size," *Human Organization*, Vol. XXIII, No. 1, Spring 1964, pp. 42-47.

[22] Edwin D. Driver, *Differential Fertility in Central India* (Princeton: Princeton University Press, 1963), pp. 113-130.

[23] E. Lewis-Fanning, *Report on an Enquiry into Family Limitation and Its Influence on Human Fertility During the Past Fifty Years* (London: His Majesty's Stationery Office, 1949), pp. 7-10.

[24] A Majeed Khan and Harvey M. Choldin, "New 'Family Planners' in Rural East Pakistan," *Demography*, Vol. II, 1965, p. 7.

[25] Ansley J. Coale and Melvin Zelnik, *New Estimates of Fertility and Population in the United States* (Princeton: Princeton University Press, 1963), p. 36.

[26] Wilson H. Grabill, Clyde V. Kiser, and P. K. Whelpton, *The Fertility of American Women* (New York: John Wiley and Sons, 1958), p. 5.

[27] George J. Stolnitz, "The Demographic Transition: From High to Low Birth Rates and Death Rates," in Ronald Freedman (ed.), *Population: The Vital Revolution* (New York: Doubleday and Co., 1964), p. 32.

Chapter 7. Birth Control: Arguments

DIFFERENT degrees of enthusiasm for small-family ideology and motivation accurately but incompletely imply differences in the degree of acceptability of birth control implementation. "Men and women have always longed for both fertility and sterility, each at its appointed time and in its chosen circumstances."[1] Thus abiding value systems are supplemented by economic and other motives which fluctuate from year to year.

Traditional Family Planning Methods

Given sufficient motivation and a permissive ideology, each individual is faced with the question of birth control techniques – of which there are many. Contemporary American folk practices include eating crushed egg shells, drinking water containing a rusty nail, sitting in a basin of turpentine, and taking a laxative immediately following intercourse. A physician related the disgust of a middle-aged farm woman, successful in twenty-eight self-induced abortions using a goose quill and a mirror, who failed in the twenty-ninth. Less practical is one woman's belief that "short women don't become pregnant easily."[2]

The most effective method is the one requiring the greatest self-control: abstention from coitus. Rejected by some as psychologically injurious or even masochistic, abstinence is supported by moral conservatives such as Edouard Charret, who in a 1965 French election campaign opposed all birth control measures except abstinence with the high-minded warning: "If you don't want to reap, don't sow."

The vaginal douche of plain water or a mild spermicidal solution is a well-known method and can be slightly efficacious if performed immediately after intercourse. European hotels provide bidets for this purpose. In lovers' lanes, women irrigate the vagina with carbonated, acidulated soft drinks.

Three kinds of male-controlled coitus are used to prevent semen from entering the vagina during intercourse. Coitus interruptus or onanism consists of withdrawing the penis immediately before emission of semen; while this is the most widely used birth control technique in the world, its effectiveness is limited. The rarely practiced coitus obstructus calls for a firm pressure with a finger at the base of the penis at the moment of emission, thus channeling the semen into the bladder instead of the vagina. Coitus reservatus consists of prolonged intercourse without ejaculation; some people consider it to be the most sublime form of sexual relations because it provides practically unlimited gratification for the woman, demonstrates admirable self-discipline by the man, permits lengthy enjoyment, and offers vaguely Calvinist renunciation of the power of sex over man's will.

The rhythm method adapts intercourse to the woman's monthly cycle in such a manner as to try to avoid impregnation. Ambiguously approved by the Roman Catholic Church on the basis that it is a version of abstinence, this method is widely used. However, its efficiency is low.[3] Ironically, the rhythm method is especially unsuitable in underdeveloped regions of high illiteracy and low income, where people are not equipped to perform the necessary calculations and where more efficient but also more expensive techniques are not financially feasible. Nonetheless, the receptiveness of Catholic authorities makes rhythm a good choice for research; if some method can be devised whereby women can easily and accurately identify their safe and unsafe periods, this procedure would become one of the best, for it is already morally acceptable and always has been inexpensive.

A permanent technique is sterilization, an operation having a long history and which is occasionally still suggested as a punitive measure for sex criminals and congenitally defective persons. Today the operation usually is applied by personal preference to avoid having unwanted offspring. Women are most frequently sterilized by tubal ligation, an operation resembling appendectomy in risk and complexity and requiring a few days of hospitalization. The male operation, vasectomy, is much simpler, normally being performed in a physician's office in about fifteen minutes. Tubal ligation is permanent, but reversal of vasectomy is possible in about 50 percent of the cases. No disturbing after-effects occur for either sex, and sexual activity is unimpaired. In the United States, the Roman Catholic Church remains the only major group opposed to the operation.[4] Ironically, the intransigent position of the Church is responsible for sterilization of many Catholics who wish to avoid the embarrassment of confessing to using contraception week after week; sterilization solves both the ethical and practical problem once and for all.[5]

Contraceptive devices for both men and woman antedate written records. For males the condom, an inexpensive rubber sheath whose sales reach three-quarters of a billion annually in the United States, is highly efficient when properly used.[6] Since rubber condoms tend to dull sensation, while animal membrane poses less interference with sexual enjoyment, the skin condom made of lamb caecum is growing in use in the United States, catering to the luxury market.[7]

Women have a choice of the occlusive diaphragm (a dome-shaped cup of thin rubber fused to a base containing an oval metal spring), the cervical cap (a small

119

cup fitted by a physician over the cervix), spermicidal jellies (creams inserted with a tube applicator), and foam tablets (melted by body heat and not requiring an applicator). Since the major reason for contraceptive failure is faulty use by the individual, efficiency is largely a function of acceptance and motivation,[8] which are greatly influenced by education and social class.

Lately the intrauterine rings, first suggested by Aristotle and later developed by Ernst Grafenberg in the 1920s and others in the 1960s, have come into increasing use, the most recent application being insertion into Indian sacred cattle to lower their fertility. Intrauterine devices, abbreviated as IUDs, are small metallic or plastic spirals, loops, rings, or bows which prevent maturation of fertilized ova in a manner not yet known. Insertion of this inert mechanical device into the uterus of a woman is quick and painless, and side effects are confined to transient uterine cramping and bleeding; the greatest hazard is occasional spontaneous expulsion, with a resultant restoration of fecundity. But reliability is sufficiently high that the most significant development in birth control in the mid-1960s is the extensive world use of IUDs, especially in underdeveloped areas having large numbers of inhabitants of little education and small income. Commonly regarded as contraceptive, IUDs are literally abortive, for they inhibit growth of the fetus rather than prevent conception. However, this feticide occurs at such an early stage of development (immediately following fertilization) as to be tantamount in its practical consequences (although not in its manner of biological operation) to contraception.

Abortion also has a long history and may well be the second most widely used method in the world today. Women in primitive cultures try to terminate pregnancy by jostling themselves against a stone while squatting, applying hot coals or black beetles to the abdomen, having themselves buried to the waist, eating herbs or goat dung, wearing magical garments, inserting foreign bodies into the uterus, bathing, and lying in the sun.[9] Abortion always was, and still is, very frequently resorted to (in 1963 more than 30 percent of all pregnancies were intentionally aborted in Seoul, South Korea[10]), and there is evidence that very few abortions fit the sentimental but fallacious image of the abortionist's client as a recently-innocent girl who tearfully climbs out of a teen-age boy's convertible to slip into the side entrance of a dilapidated frame house. Actually, most abortions are performed on married women who already have children and want to quit. Although the risk to life from an abortion performed by a qualified physician in a hospital is considerably smaller than the risk ordinarily accompanying childbirth, many American women have died as a result of illegally and improperly performed abortions. Partly because of this statistic and partly on the premise that each woman should be able to govern her life, including the decision to have children, there has arisen heated controversy over therapeutic voluntary abortions.

In the nineteenth century, most American states enacted laws prohibiting abortion, but in 1967, the tide began to turn with the passage of Colorado's permissive law. Colorado was soon followed by a dozen other states, and in 1973, the Supreme Court nullified restrictive laws by ruling that "the right of privacy" gives to a woman the power of decision whether or not to end her pregnancy.[11] Women still cannot get abortions on demand everywhere, but abortion certainly has become far easier to obtain. And the "dangerous, discriminatory, undignified, and costly illegal abortions" are replaced by legal abortions performed under the same safe medical conditions as childbirth.[12] Other major nations that recently liberalized their abortion laws include China in 1957, India in 1971, the Soviet Union in 1955, and Japan in 1952. By 1973, "the majority of the world's population" had access to legal abortion.[13]

If abortion often results from a failure of contraception, so infanticide sometimes follows a failure to abort. In spite of the revulsion with which many persons regard it, infanticide is widespread throughout the world and a standard topic in anthropological literature.[14] Its use in medieval and modern Europe has been much greater than is commonly realized. It is easy for a midwife or obstetrician to "inadvertently" fail to perform a certain action necessary to the life of a deformed neonate. Infanticide is sometimes defended by the argument that a quick death shortly after birth is less painful than a lifetime of too much work, too little food, and too few comforts — but nonetheless youthanasia remains a sin according to Christian mores.

A new and less disturbing approach lies in contragestion — preventing the ovum from growing once fertilized. Being both more efficient and cheaper, as the woman need only take a pill when she suspects pregnancy, contragestive pills are a subject of contemporary medical research. Although opponents of contragestion cry "murder," proponents make a distinction between the vegetative state of embryonic development and the stage when sensory and rational (and therefore human) attributes begin to appear. If we accept this distinction, destruction of the embryo before it attains the human stage does not constitute feticide[15] — and to be fair, opponents should acknowledge that Thomas Aquinas believed that the soul did not appear until the fortieth day of pregnancy for a male fetus and the eightieth day for a female.[16] Still other persons argue that since fetuses have not yet been born, they can nowise be regarded as human beings, and hence their destruction is discretionary; as a Japanese remembering Hiroshima remarked: "A people who have had the sublime opportunity of experiencing firsthand the full expression of modern war do not appear too compunctious over the removal of a few grams of fetal protoplasm from the uterus."[17]

The Pill and the Future

"The pill' ushered in a new era of birth control. Recently synthesized progestational steroid compounds have yielded several orally administered, clinically effective, commercially available products. Producing a marked effect on the uterus, ovaries, and pituitary, these drugs inhibit ovulation and are accompanied by several minor side effects similar to those experienced in pregnancy. Although oral contraception provides a higher degree of protection than most other methods, it has the defect of requiring sustained motivation and attention to the calendar — in contrast, for instance, to intrauterine contraception, which demands only a single decision to have a device inserted and may therefore have a greater demographic impact among people of little education. Religious views about these pills vary: some clergymen accept them, some prohibit them. Justifying use on the basis of regulating ovulation and thereby increasing efficiency of the rhythm method, some Catholic clergymen are highly enthusiastic.

Development of the pill and the newer, smaller-dosage mini-pill began in the 1940s with the discovery of a practical method for synthesizing the hormone progesterone from plants; chemists developed a workable steroid pill by 1956. Since that time, use has skyrocketed, so that today, oral contraceptives are taken by about 30 million women. Taken properly, the pill is 99-plus percent effective against pregnancy. Although the pill has been attacked for inducing cancer and heart ailments, it is safer than many other types of medication. In fact, research by medical statisticians shows that it is safer than the absence of contraception. That is, if 100,000 women of reproductive age take the pill, there will probably be 3 to 6 deaths as a result; but if 100,000 women refrain from birth control, many will become pregnant and 10 to 300 will die during childbirth (from about 10 in modern countries to 200 to 300 in underdeveloped countries).[18] Psychologically, many people feel better about the childbirth deaths because they seem "natural" and the women did not "bring it on themselves," whereas a pill-taker who dies can be said to have died unnaturally because of something she herself did. This tradition-oriented interpretation neglects to note that a dead young woman is a tragedy, regardless of the cause.

Of course there are demurrers, from the amateur psychiatrist who opposes all forms of birth control because they frustrate a natural need and hence generate psychic discord and frustration, to the moralist who worries that efficient means of birth control may encourage free love, to the taxpayer who fears enlargement of welfare expenditures for babies born to irresponsible women, and to the demographer who points out that decreasing fertility may result in a more rapidly aging population. So it seems once more that we do not face a single isolated problem, but rather a problem in a nexus of related problems.

No birth control technique is truly modern. The pill is about the best, but for how many other conditions must one take medication 20 or 30 times a month? What is really needed is a pill or injection that will make a woman or a man infertile for at least a year and preferably indefinitely — plus another pill or injection that will restore fertility on demand. But when, if ever, we will get such a substance is uncertain. Our present cumbersome methods result essentially from two circumstances. First, because of attitudes toward procreation and sexual relations, research on birth control became serious only in the present century (by contrast, research on death control has a long history). Second, the male reproductive system is complicated, and the female system is unbelievably convoluted.

The main reason for the greater number of female birth control methods is that the female system has many more stages at which interruption prevents impregnation. Men possess merely three stages: sperm production, maturation, and transport — and research is being done on all three stages. So, to those who complain that there is no pill for men, we can only say: wait and hope, for researchers are trying.

Beyond Family Planning

Proposals going beyond the usual reach of family planning were gathered by Bernard Berelson:

Extensions of voluntary fertility control
    Institutionalization of maternal care in rural areas of developing countries
    Liberalization of induced abortion
Establishment of involuntary fertility control
    Mass use of fertility control agent, to be included in water supply
    Licenses to have children
    Temporary sterilization of all girls, with reversibility allowed only upon governmental approval
    Compulsory sterilization of men with three or more living children
    Requirement of induced abortion for all illegitimate pregnancies
Intensified educational campaigns
    Inclusion of population materials in primary and secondary schools
    National satellite television systems for direct informational effect
Incentive programs
    Payment for the initiation or the effective practice of contraception
    Payment for periods of nonpregnancy or nonbirth
Tax and welfare benefits and penalties
    Withdrawal of maternity benefits, perhaps after N children
    Withdrawal of children or family allowances, perhaps after N children
    Tax on births after the Nth
    Limitation of governmentally provided medical treatment, housing, scholarships, loans, and subsidies to families with fewer than N children
    Reversal of tax benefits to favor the unmarried and the parents of fewer rather than more children

Provision by the state of N years of free schooling to each nuclear family, to be allocated by the family among the children as desired

Pensions for poor parents with fewer than N children

Shifts in social and economic institutions

Increase in minimum age of marriage

Promotion or requirement of female participation in labor force

Manipulation of family structure, reducing the noneconomic utilities of offspring

Two types of marriage, one childless and readily dissolved, and the other licensed for children and designed to be stable

Encouragement of long-range social trends leading toward lower fertility, innovation that may break the "cake of custom"

Improved status of women

Lower infant and child death rates, on the inference that birth rates will follow them down

Approaches via political channels and organizations

Insistence on population control as the price of food aid

Reorganization of national and international agencies to deal with the population problem

Promotion of zero growth as the ultimate goal in order to place intermediate goals of lowered fertility in proper context

Augmented research efforts

More research on social means for achieving necessary fertility goals

Focused research on practical methods of sex determination

Increased research toward an improved contraceptive technology [19]

Freedom and Civil Liberties

Most individuals and organizations want their own beliefs to determine the laws governing dissemination of information and availability of equipment for the control of fertility. Ordinarily one group succeeds in this power struggle, bringing about legislation restricting family planning to within whatever limits that group deems appropriate; persons of other faiths are unwillingly constrained to practice or at least to simulate adherence to these rules.

Civil liberties advocates resent such birth control legislation as a curb on the freedom of each individual to govern his own life as long as it does not interfere with the liberty or happiness of other persons. They contend that what a couple practice in their bedroom is their own business and no one else's, on the principle that each person should be allowed to decide according to his own conscience — not held to the conscience of someone else.

Opponents of this view argue that an evil act — and certain family planning actions are sometimes so labeled — remains evil regardless of whether or not the person committing it believes that it is evil. Therefore, preventing anyone from performing such an action is inherently desirable, even if the culprit is convinced that the action is morally acceptable. Better yet is the solution of convincing the ignorant but good-intentioned evil-doer of the right path; sometimes this persuasion goes far enough to be called religious conversion.

Most states have restrictions governing birth control techniques, often enacted by officials who sincerely believed that dispersal of knowledge or instruments for family planning would send the country straight down the road to purgatory. Sometimes legislators were pressured by religious lobbies to vote for an anti-birth control bill or be branded as favoring sin — and run out of office in the next election. Moral and social problems arise when one group succeeds in forcing its code upon all citizens, compelling minorities (or sometimes the majority) to conform or be punished. Implications of this situation are eloquently traced in J. S. Mill's classic plea for the social and civil rights of the individual. [20]

History of Birth Limitation

In prehistoric times, birth limitation was accomplished through reduced frequency of intercourse, coitus interruptus, castration, vaginal obstructions, abortion, and infanticide. In primitive cultures, crude tampons or vaginal plugs were made from cloth, leaves, and whatever other substances came to hand: Djuka women inserted a large seed pod in the vagina as a sort of intravaginal condom.

Early religious and medical writings contain more references to family planning than one might expect. The oldest Chinese medical book, dating from earlier than 2500 B.C., contains a prescription for abortion. Both the Petri papyrus of 1850 B.C. and the Ebers papyrus of 1550 B.C. include contraceptive advice. In the fourth century B.C., Plato and Aristotle advocated keeping down population growth by abortion and infanticide. Roman writers Lucretius (95-55 B.C.) and Pliny (23-79 A.C.) recommended birth control techniques. The Bible refers to the safe period and withdrawal. The second-century Greek physician Soranus of Ephesus described the rhythm method and declared the advantage of contraception over abortion. The third-century Hebrew Tosephta Niddah discussed contraceptive methods. Vatsya Yana's *Kama Sutra,* an Indian work of the fourth century, describes occlusive and chemical contraception. And so on through the literature of many cultures in many times.

But there have also been countercurrents. Early Christian fathers lifted out of context the Biblical phase "Be fruitful and multiply" for the purpose of combating the first- and second-century Gnostic heresy, which regarded procreation as the imprisoning of divine souls in evil bodies. St. Augustine extended the argument in writings that enshrined him as "the chief architect of the position

125

imbedded in the Western tradition. Not only was procreation the end of marriage but the end of each conjugal act." [21] If any other purpose is intended, said the great fifth-century bishop, a sin is committed (though only venial if the partners are married and provided "there is no attempt to prevent such propagation either by wrong desire or evil appliance" [22]). The Roman Catholic Church has maintained approximately this stand up to the present time.

Twentieth-century Protestant churches of many nations and denominations have issued formal proclamations and informal advice over the last three decades; the usual position is advocacy of all means of contraception and rejection of abortion. [23]

The present furor over the distribution of birth control information can be traced directly back to nineteenth-century England and America. James Mill, father of the famous philosopher John Stuart Mill, wrote in the 1821 *Encyclopedia Brittanica* that "the grand practical problem, therefore, is to find the means of limiting the number of births." Francis Place published a pamphlet in 1822 in England advocating interruptus and the sponge. In 1832 a Massachusetts physician, Charles L. Knowlton, promoted birth control by astringent douche in a book ambiguously entitled *Fruits of Philosophy.* In 1877 Annie Besant and Charles Bradlaugh were tried in England for publishing Knowlton's treatise, on the charge of "corrupting the morals" by selling an "indecent, lewd, filthy, bawdy, and obscene book;" at the trial Mrs. Besant seized the opportunity to testify at inordinate length about the benefits of birth control, with the result that, although both defendants were found guilty (but exonerated of corrupt motives), the circulation of *Fruits of Philosophy* skyrocketed.

During this same period Anthony Comstock and his colleagues in the Society for the Suppression of Vice were pushing through the legislatures of several states and the United States Congress a set of laws prohibiting manufacture or sale of contraceptives and banning dissemination of birth control information. These laws were enforced, and some physicians were Federal imprisoned. The Comstock Act was repealed in 1971. Until the Connecticut law was struck down by the United States Supreme Court in 1965, even use of contraceptives was against the law — a stipulation next to impossible to implement. For several decades the Connecticut was law challenged almost annually by court cases involving married women claiming interference with their health and personal liberties, clergymen alleging infringement upon their religious freedom under the First Amendment, physicians complaining of restriction of their right to practice medicine according to scientific standards accepted by the American Medical Association, members of the Planned Parenthood League arguing for the constitutional right of each individual to decide whether or not to have children, and lawyers stating that such laws cannot be justified as a valid extension of police power. Still, these laws stood for ninety-one years.

Four methods of natality control escaped proscriptive legislation: the time-honored technique of absolute abstinence; periodic continence, popularly called the rhythm method; the widely practiced coitus interruptus; and the exacting coitus reservatus.[24] In addition to these legally permissible methods are contraception, sterilization, and abortion, each of which is still entangled in a web of regulations and prohibitive laws of ethical rather than demographic intent. Most such restrictions were put on the books by Protestants, but by a curious reversal, it appears to be the Roman Catholic Church which is keeping them there.

Values and Preferences

The value systems forming parts of all cultures have tremendous effects on how closely human beings approach their limits of biological fecundity. The mores of Western countries have in recent centuries encouraged a lowering of natality toward the small family system now common in Western Europe and the United States — although it has not been uniformly accepted by all subgroups and individuals within these areas.

Some subcultures favor high birth rates. A few sociologists favor the generalization that high fertility is created by minority status. In the modern world, argues Lincoln Day, it is not the doctrines of Roman Catholics that cause their relatively high fertility, but rather their minority status and consequent feelings of being threatened. Day supports this contention by citing statistics that show that a Catholic subculture encouraging high fertility only develops in those nations where Catholics are a minority. Where Catholics are a majority, their birth rates are sometimes high and sometimes about as low as anywhere in the world — France, for example.[25]

A more extreme variant of this hypothesis claims that the American birth control movement is a white conspiracy intended at black genocide. Literature issued by the Black Muslims, the Black Panthers, and several other black activist organizations argue this interpretation, but suspicion concerning family planning programs extends well beyond black nationalist and black revolutionary groups. A survey of black attitudes in a New England city indicates that some blacks, particularly men under age 30, agree with this black-genocide thesis.[26] This viewpoint has a long history, extending back to the first state-supported birth control programs of the 1930s and 1940s, which were believed by some persons to be disguised attempts to reduce the black population. The birth control debate among blacks began in the 1920s with "a dispute between those blacks who believed that in sheer numbers there was strength and those blacks, such as W. E. B. DuBois, who argued that among human races, as among vegetables, quality and not quantity counted."[27] In the 1960s and 1970s the genocide-conspiracy theory gained strength, abetted by such strident protagonists as H. Rap Brown in his book *Die Nigger Die*[28] and entertainer Dick Gregory in his article "My Answer to Genocide."[29]

127

Yet in the United States nearly all groups have some sympathy with family limitation, for it is "almost universally approved and is practiced widely and effectively," and "all classes of the American population are coming to share a common set of values about family size."[30] The consensus on the two-to-four child family and the almost total rejection of childlessness and vigorous disavowal of the one-child family may indicate increasing importance of the family in American life — a change from its decline over the past century. The proportion of couples practicing birth control should increase in the future, bringing about a decline in the number of really large families, a greater responsiveness of fertility to social and economic changes and hence increased volatileness of the birth rate, and perhaps less variation in the marriage rate as couples do not postpone marriage until they can afford children (they would marry but postpone pregnancy instead). If Americans do concentrate on the three-child family, the national population will almost surely exceed 300 million by the year 2000 and reach 600 million by 2050. Thus "Americans may soon have to choose between the consequences of a very large population or a revision of their present values about marriage and childbearing."[31]

Receptivity to Birth Control

Residents of modern nations are not alone in being ready to adopt birth control. In a rural area of Thailand having a mean income of about $100 per person, an average schooling of four years, high illiteracy, and wives who were "almost totally ignorant of the elementary workings of their reproductive systems," two-thirds of 1,207 women interviewed in 1964 stated a desire to learn how to control their fertility, and three-fourths said they wanted no more children than they had.[32] "Many women lamented their inability to adapt the number of their children to the financial resources of their households, and nearly all of those who had five or more children expressed a wish to cease reproduction."[33] After a subsequent two-year educational program, these proportions increased further, and the percentage who reported ever using contraception increased from 2 in 1964 to 28 in 1967. This survey advanced the notion that "poor, ill-educated, rural people may be as ready to accept birth control as middle-class, urban people."[34] Indeed, the desire to have no more children may even be strongest among the least modernized segments of Thailand. Rather than crediting the upper socioeconomic strata with the greatest readiness to adopt family planning, the reverse is conceivable: the Thai data suggest that "deprivation rather than higher aspiration affects desire for additional progeny."[35] If this hypothesis is true, then what the women of underdeveloped nations need is not persuasion but information and supplies.

Interviews in 1965 of 5,617 American women disclosed that they seemed, on the average, to want slightly more than three children. When asked the number of children they considered ideal for the average American family, the women gave answers that averaged 3.3; when asked the number of children they personally desired, their answer again averaged 3.3; and when they were asked how many children they intend to have, the answer averaged 3.2.[36] At the time they were interviewed, the women already had an average of 2.8 children, so it appears that they did not want many more. Indeed, it is probable that the true number wanted is smaller than 3.2. The number intended cannot be fewer than the number the women already have, and the number desired often is rationalized to be at least as large as the present number even if the last child was not wanted before conception. There appeared also a preference for an even number of children: 2 and 4 were preferred more frequently than 1 or 3 or 5. Perhaps the women thought in terms of an equal number of each sex, perhaps they believed that children are best reared in pairs, or perhaps there is another explanation. Whatever their reasons, the blacks and the white non-Catholics tended to show a strong mode of 2, and the white Catholics a strong mode of 4.[37] "If there is developing in the United States a single reproductive norm for the total population, the evidence presented here would suggest that it is more likely to become established at 2 rather than at 3." Because this difference "represents the crucial distinction between a stationary and a rapidly growing population," it deserves our fullest attention.[38]

The Number of Children Wanted

The reported number of children wanted, as conventionally measured in the above-cited and other studies, probably overestimates the true number. Many are the children who were not wanted at the time of conception, even to the point of the mother's considering an abortion, but whose loving presence was subsequently accepted, thereby raising by one the number of children reported as desired. Therefore we need a measure of the number of children that truly were wanted before conception, no matter how fervently they are adored thereafter. In 1970 two demographers developed a new way to ascertain the number of children wanted: for women who intend to have more children than they now have, the total number intended is used; but for women who intend to have no more, the number wanted is the current number of children minus the number reported as having been unwanted at the time of conception.[39] There remains the problem of how to get interviewees to admit that a pregnancy was unwanted, but at least this definition is a step in the right direction. Applying it to the 1965 data just described yielded an estimate of the wanted number of children as 2.7 — a sufficiently large reduction from the 3.3 previously cited to have a serious effect on estimates of future fertility in the United States.[40]

When the number of children wanted is smaller (and the true number probably is below 2.7) than the number that one actually has (2.8 in this survey), there is a clear implication that improved use of birth control methods would result in a smaller national population.

This study disclosed powerful racial and religious differences. In all but the lowest income groups, black women expressed a desire for fewer children than did white women, but they expected to have more than the white women — because they already had more. Obviously, there is a race-related difference in the ability to control fertility. Apparently this is a matter of education: for both races, the less the education, the larger is the discrepancy between the number of children desired and the number expected. And as black women generally have had less schooling than whites, the over-all discrepancy might be expected to be larger among blacks.[41]

Consistent with these findings are the results of 1969-1970 interviews of 1,500 black and 1,600 white women living in low-income neighborhoods in seventeen American cities. The researchers, Bauman and Udry, found three reasons why black women had more unwanted births than whites: the blacks desired fewer children in the first place; they were more likely not to use birth control or to use methods not administered by a physician; and they had higher failure rates when they did use physician-administered methods.[42]

These same data, plus hospital interviews with new mothers, showed that poor people have higher rates of unwanted births than do the nonpoor, but that this difference is not attributable to greater use of "drugstore methods" or less frequent use of physician-administered techniques, for both high- and low-income persons use both types of method in about the same proportion. Since such differences "do not account for the large differences in unwanted fertility between the poor and nonpoor, between blacks and whites, and between educational levels, then it is unlikely that increasing the use of physician-administered contraception among the poor, the black, and the less educated . . . will by itself substantially reduce the gap in unwanted fertility between the more favored and the less favored segments of the population."[43]

It is clear that Catholic women both desire and expect more children than do either Protestant or Jewish women, regardless of how many they already have. Protestant denominations differ little among themselves, but among Catholics, the greater the involvement with their religion, the greater their commitment to large families. Among Protestant women, the more the education, the fewer the expected children; among Catholics, college graduates are a "distinctive high-fertility group," as a result of which, the greatest Protestant-Catholic differential occurs at the college-graduate level. The higher the income and occupational status, the more the Catholic expected fertility exceeds that of the Protestants. Other variables produce no religious differences: the region of the country, the size of the community, and the proportion of women working all have the same influence on Catholic as on Protestant women. The lowest fertility for both groups is expected by career women.[44]

Another indicator of potential receptivity to birth control is the frequency of failures in family planning. Among those women who have been pregnant, the failures to achieve the number of children intended amounted to 32 percent; the failures of timing reached 62 percent. These startling failure rates were higher for blacks than for whites, for white Catholics than for white non-Catholics, and for wives who did not finish high school than for those with more education.[45] Neglecting the relatively inconsequential failures of timing, this statistically-conjectured lack of success in planning the number of one's children is substantial for all races, religions, and educational levels in the United States. If these figures are to be believed — and they have yet to be substantiated by other research — then there is considerable room for improvement in the efficiency of birth control methods in America.

Expectations and Ideals

Ideals and expectations vary tremendously. At one extreme, a few cults in the United States and other nations do not believe in sexual activity. An opposite view is illustrated in a Teheran court in 1969: Abdollah Ranjbar was granted a divorce because his wife refused to bear him any more children. Said the 42-year-old wife: "After the eighteenth delivery, I decided I'd had enough of it" and began to use birth control. Her 86-year-old husband left the courtroom saying, "Now I can look for a decent and proper wife who will give me children."

That Iranian man would have been especially ill-advised to marry an American woman, for interviews conducted in the Current Population Survey over 1967-1973 indicate a continuing desire for and expectation of fewer children. The most critical group — because it is the group most exposed to having children — is the married women aged 18 to 24. The expectations of these women concerning the number of children they will bear in their lifetimes were reported in the 1967 interviews as an average of 2.9; by 1973, the new set of 18- to 24-year-old wives reported an expectation of only 2.3 children.[46] Although this decrease of 0.6 children may not seem large at first glance, it represents a reduction (allowing for women who never marry plus those whose marriages are interrupted by death or divorce) to almost exactly the replacement level — that is, the level that would result in zero population growth.

"To the extent that expectations of young American women regarding the number of children they will eventually have can be accepted as an indication of future levels of fertility, it appears that the two-child family will be the wave of the future."[47] The word "appears" is well taken, for three factors may intervene between these expectations and actual performance: first, changes in the timing of births may affect temporarily annual birth rates and rates of national increase; second, some of these women will not be able to restrict their production of children to the levels they expect; and third, fads and other expectations have a way of changing, and these 18- to 24-year-old women might change their preferences in the future if the "spirit of the times" should come to favor larger families. Although a shift of public opinion toward bigger families seems unlikely, Judith Blake reminds us of the demographic instability inherent in the fact that many people do not possess consistent attitudes regarding family size.[48] The babies born in the 1980s and 1990s will have mothers who are, in the 1970s, teenagers or young children; obviously their natality preferences are ill-formed or not formed at all and therefore are subject to influence by any number of unforeseeable happenings and opinion alterations.

Lifetime childbearing expectations are affected by many variables, including especially age, ethnicity, and education. The younger the women interviewed, the greater is the buildup of expectation of having precisely two children: under age 30, most women decisively prefer two children, whereas 30- to 39-year-olds favor two, three, or four-or-more children almost equally. Age by age, black women expect more children than do whites, and women of Spanish origin expect even more.[49] College women (meaning those completing one or more years of college) expect 2.3 children, high school graduates expect 2.6, and those with less education expect 3.1 offspring. Childlessness is expected by 4 percent of whites, 5 percent of blacks, and 3 percent of Spanish-origin women; among wives having one year or more of college, this percentage rises to 6.[50]

The long-term trend is toward homogenization, with few women favoring not having children and increasing numbers opposed to large families. A consensus is developing for two children, especially if the second child is of opposite sex from the first. This nationwide American preference is shared increasingly by residents of developing countries, although many parents still insist on having a son. When females achieve worldwide equality of occupational, educational, familial, and inheritance treatment, then this international preference for sons may weaken; if so, the change will affect childbearing practices as well as non-natal behavior.

NOTES

[1] Norman E. Himes, *Medical History of Contraception* (Baltimore: Williams and Wilkins, 1936), Introduction.

[2] Ronald Freedman, Pascal K. Whelpton, and Arthur A. Campbell, *Family Planning, Sterility, and Population Growth* (New York: McGraw-Hill, 1959), p. 175.

[3] Christopher Tietze and Robert G. Potter Jr., "Statistical Evaluation of the Rhythm Method," *American Journal of Obstetrics and Gynecology,* Vol. LXXXIV, No. 5, September 1, 1962, pp. 692-698.

[4] Ralph J. Campbell, "Legal Status of Therapeutic Abortion and Sterilization in the United States," *Clinical Obstetrics and Gynecology,* Vol. VII, No. 1, March 1964, pp. 22-36.

[5] Kurt W. Back, Reuben Hill, and J. Mayone Stycos, "Population Control in Puerto Rico: The Formal and Informal Framework," *Law and Contemporary Problems,* Vol. XXV, No. 3, Summer 1960, p. 572.

[6] Christopher Tietze, "The Condom as a Contraceptive," in Society for the Scientific Study of Sex, *Advances in Sex Research* (New York: Harper and Row, 1963), pp. 88-102.

[7] Christopher Tietze, "The Current Status of Fertility Control," *Law and Contemporary Problems,* Vol. XXV, No. 3, Summer 1960, p. 428.

[8] Christopher Tietze, "The Use-Effectiveness of Contraceptive Methods," in Clyde V. Kiser (ed.), *Research in Family Planning* (Princeton: Princeton University Press, 1962), pp. 357-369.

[9] George Devereux, *A Study of Abortion in Primitive Societies* (New York: Julian Press, 1955).

[10] Ronald Freedman, "The Transition from High to Low Fertility: Challenge to Demographers," *Population Index,* Vol. XXXI, No. 4, October 1965, p. 417.

[11] U.S. Supreme Court, *Roe et al. v. Wade,* 70-18, January 22, 1973; and U.S. Supreme Court, *Doe et al. v. Bolton,* 70-40, January 22, 1973.

[12] Christopher Tietze, "Two Years' Experience with a Liberal Abortion Law: Its Impact on Fertility Trends in New York City," *Family Planning Perspectives,* Vol. V, No. 1, Winter 1973, p. 41.

[13] Luke T. Lee, "Five Largest Countries Allow Legal Abortion on Broad Grounds," in George Washington University Medical Center, *Pregnancy Termination,* Series F., No. 1, April 1973, pp. 1-8.

[14] See for example Baldwin Spencer and F. J. Gillen, *The Arunta* (London: Macmillan, 1927); and E. Adamson Hoebel, "Law-ways of the Primitive Eskimos," *Journal of the American Institute of Criminal Law and Criminology,* Vol. XXXi, 1941, pp. 670-682.

[15] Paul S. Henshaw, *Adaptive Human Fertility* (New York: McGraw-Hill, 1955), pp. 220-223.

[16] John T. Noonan Jr., *Contraception: A History of Its Treatment by the Catholic Theologians and Canonists* (Cambridge: Harvard University Press, 1965), pp. 89-90.

[17] W. T. Pommerenke, "Abortion in Japan," *Obstetrical and Gynecological Survey,* Vol. X, April 1955, pp. 145-175.

[18] R. T. Ravenholt, P. T. Piotrow, and J. J. Speidel, "Use of Oral Contraceptives: A Decade of Controversy," *International Journal of Gynaecology and*

Obstetrics, Vol. VIII, No. 6, November 1970, pp. 941-956; and Christopher Tietze, "Mortality with Contraception and Induced Abortion," *Studies in Family Planning,* Vol. I, No. 45, September 1969, pp. 6-8.

[19] Reprinted with the permission of the Population Council from Bernard Berelson, "Beyond Family Planning," *Studies in Family Planning,* Vol. I, No. 38, February 1969, pp. 1-3.

[20] John Stuart Mill, *On Liberty* (London: 1859).

[21] Richard M. Fagley, "The Population Problem and Family Planning," *The Ecumenical Review,* Vol. XI, No. 1, October 1958, p. 10.

[22] St. Augustine, quoted in P. Schaff, *Nicene and Post-Nicene Fathers,* First Series V (1888), pp. 270-271.

[23] Richard M. Fagley, *Statements on Parenthood and the Population Problem* (Geneva: World Council of Churches, 1960), mimeographed. Many of these statements are reproduced in Fagley, "A Protestant View on Population Control," *Law and Contemporary Problems,* Vol. XXV, No. 3, Summer 1960, pp. 470-489.

[24] Alvah W. Sulloway, "The Legal and Political Aspects of Population Control in the United States," *Law and Contemporary Problems,* Vol. XXV, No. 3, Summer 1960, pp. 593-613.

[25] Lincoln H. Day, "Natality and Ethnocentrism: Some Relationships Suggested by an Analysis of Catholic-Protestant Differentials," *Population Studies,* Vol. XXII, No. 1, March 1968, pp. 27-50.

[26] William A. Darity, Castellano B. Turner, and H. Jean Thiebaux, "Race Consciousness and Fears of Black Genocide as Barriers to Family Planning," Population Reference Bureau, Washington, Selection No. 37, June 1971, pp. 5-12.

[27] Robert G. Weisbord, "Birth Control and the Black American: A Matter of Genocide?", *Demography,* Vol. X, No. 4, November 1973, p. 571.

[28] H. Rap Brown, *Die Nigger Die* (New York: Dial Press, 1969).

[29] Dick Gregory, "My Answer to Genocide," *Ebony,* Vol. XVI, No. 12, 1971, pp. 66-72, cited in Weisbord, *op. cit.,* p. 579.

[30] Freedman, Whelpton, and Campbell, *op. cit.,* pp. 401-402.

[31] *Ibid.,* p. 405.

[32] Ralph Thomlinson, "Overview and Assessment of the Potharam Study: 1964-1969," in Visid Prachuabmoh and Ralph Thomlinson (eds.), *The Potharam Study,* Institute of Population Studies, Chulalongkorn University (Bangkok: 1971), pp. 5 and 13.

[33] *Ibid.,* pp. 5-6.

[34] *Ibid.,* p. 10.

[35] Visid Prachuabmoh, "Factors Affecting Desire or Lack of Desire for Additional Progeny in Thailand," in Donald J. Bogue (ed.), *Sociological Contributions to Family Planning Research* (Chicago: Community and Family Study Center, University of Chicago, 1967), p. 408.

[36] Norman B. Ryder and Charles F. Westoff, *Reproduction in the United States: 1965* (Princeton: Princeton University Press, 1971), pp. 19-31.

[37] *Ibid.*, pp. 31-34.

[38] *Ibid.*, pp. 34-35.

[39] Larry Bumpass and Charles F. Westoff, "The 'Perfect Contraceptive' Population," *Science,* Vol. CLXIX, September 18, 1970, pp. 1177-1182.

[40] Ryder and Westoff, *op. cit.,* pp. 92-95.

[41] *Ibid.*, pp. 53-67 and 90-91.

[42] Karl E. Bauman and J. Richard Udry, "The Difference in Unwanted Births Between Blacks and Whites," *Demography,* Vol. X, No. 3, August 1973, pp. 315-328.

[43] J. Richard Udry and Karl E. Bauman, "Unwanted Fertility and the Use of Contraception," *Health Services Reports,* Vol. LXXXVIII, No. 8, October 1973, p. 732.

[44] Ryder and Westoff, *op. cit.,* pp. 66-86 and 91-92.

[45] *Ibid.*, pp. 223-235.

[46] U.S. Bureau of the Census, "Birth Expectations of American Wives: June 1973," *Current Population Reports,* Series P-20, No. 254, October 1973, p. 1.

[47] U.S. Bureau of the Census, "Fertility Expectations of American Women: June 1973," *Current Population Reports,* Series P-20, No. 265, June 1974, p. 1.

[48] Judith Blake, "Can We Believe Recent Data on Birth Expectations in the United States," *Demography,* Vol. XI, No. 1, February 1974, pp. 25-56.

[49] U.S. Bureau of the Census, "Fertility Expectations of American Women: June 1973," *op. cit.,* p. 2.

[50] *Ibid.*, p. 3.

Chapter 8.   Birth Control: Religion

RELIGIOUS bodies take varying stands on birth control, but most of the major world religions now offer to their members the privilege of using most of the techniques described in the preceding chapter. The major exception to this liberality is the Roman Catholic Church, which was described by a leading demographer as one of the "two widespread international value systems which actively oppose birth control measures," the other being the Marxist.[1] The two differ, however: Marxists view overpopulation as a capitalist plot impossible in a socialist state, while the Catholic Church recognizes some means of population limitation, and Popes John XIII, Pius XII, Paul VI, and other leaders have spoken of the need to control population growth.

Still, the Catholic Church presents one of the most forthrightly negative stances taken by any organization, whether religious or secular. To put it bluntly, the Church regards most birth control methods as morally wrong.

The Concept of a Prevented Birth[2]

Intermingled in the quarreling over birth control are the concepts of prevented births and of natural law. The twentieth-century concept of a prevented birth, wrote Lyle Saunders, "has all the purity of a mathematical symbol" while yet reminding one of a bit of doggerel popular a few years ago:

> The other day upon a stair
> I passed a man who wasn't there.
> He wasn't there again today;
> Oh, gee, I wish he'd go away.[3]

The family planning paraphrase, suggested Saunders, might go like this:

> Yesterday from dark to morn
> Ten thousand babies were not born.
> Like autumn leaves the non-born fall;
> I wonder where we'll put them all?[4]

But prevented births are not merely subjects for whimsical humor; they are worth money, as is attested by an article on the value of nonbirths to under-developed countries[5] and also by policy-oriented papers analyzing the results of active birth control programs.[6] A medical statistician even went so far as to publish an article on the curious exercise of analyzing the timing of averted births![7]

Averted births have a positive economic value for many families and most countries today. Moreover the nonaverted births present a real economic threat to both families and nations.

Papal Actions from 1958 to 1967

In recent years, many Catholics and non-Catholics had been hoping for a liberalization of the Roman Catholic Church's prohibition of most means of controlling fertility. These optimists were disappointed by the release of Pope Paul's encyclical letter "Humanae Vitae" ("Of Human Life") on July 25, 1968. The hopes of these liberals were not without basis, for both Paul VI and his immediate predecessor expressed views implying a possible loosening of the restrictive policies of the Church, as stated definitively in the Encyclical "Casta Connubii" ("On Christian Marriage") by Pius XI in 1930 and the address "Moral Questions Affecting Married Life" by Pius XII in 1951.

Soon after John XXIII became Pope in 1958, he instituted a program of "aggiornamento" intended to "let some fresh air into the Church" and "bring it up to today." Supported by an upsurge of tradition-shattering opinion among many leaders of the priestly hierarchy, Pope John's progressive attitude seemed to be setting the stage for a long-awaited modernization of dogma affecting birth control.

When Paul VI ascended to the Papacy in 1963, some observers believed that he might continue John's policy of attending first to the contemporary needs of living people, and only second to the desire to preserve dogma and, thereby, to ensure our spiritual survival. This expectation was buttressed by his appointment in March 1964 of a fifty-member commission to study contraception vis-à-vis divine and natural law.

In April 1967, it was revealed that a majority of the Papal birth-control study commission had recommended that all forms of contraception should be allowed, including a qualified endorsement of the contraceptive pill. On the other hand, the fact that the report had been kept secret since its presentation to the Pope in June 1966 was not encouraging. Still, the printing of this explosive document, albeit ten months late, offered evidence of a doctrinal revolution taking form within the Church; indeed, the leak of the report to the press apparently was motivated by the desire of some theologians to push the Pope into more rapid action toward modernization. One member of the Papal commission predicted that the Pope might approve the pill, vaginal diaphragms, and even sterilization, although continuing to forbid use of the condom and coitus interruptus on the basis that the latter two methods prevent insemination, which most Catholic theologians regard as the legal test of the consummation of a marriage.[8]

Such predictions had counterparts in pleas to the Pope from many sides. In 1965, 78 Nobel prize laureates signed statements asking Pope Paul to reconsider the Church's ban on artificial birth control. In 1967 the executive assembly of the third world congress of Roman Catholic laymen, meeting in Rome, voted 67 to 21 to urge the Church to permit Catholics to choose whichever birth control methods each couple deems best.

The 1968 Encyclical "Humanae Vitae"

But whatever practices are in actual use by Roman Catholic parents, and whether the decree is regarded as a tragic backward move or a reaffirmation of unchanging principles, the 1968 encyclical undoubtedly constitutes an officially binding dictum directing Roman Catholics how to proceed — or more properly, how *not* to proceed — in the begetting of children.

The encyclical is quite clear: "direct interruption of the generative process" is strictly forbidden; contraception, abortion, and sterilization are "absolutely excluded as licit means of regulating birth."[9] Branding all forms of mechanical and chemical contraceptives as morally degrading, Pope Paul thus upheld without qualification the Church's traditional position, urging national governments to outlaw contraceptives and "calling men back to the norms of the natural law," which "teaches that each and every matrimonial act must remain open to the transmission of life."[10] This definitive conclusion was not arrived at so quickly as might be supposed, for the Prelate required several years of "mature reflection and assiduous prayers" to arrive at his absolutistic and logically exhaustive conclusion: "Excluded is every action which, either in anticipation of the conjugal act, or in its accomplishment, or in the development of its natural consequences, proposes, whether as an end or as a means, to render procreation impossible."[11] Because all anti-procreation efforts — whether before, during, or after the act of intercourse, including both purposes and techniques — are ruled out, and because each "matrimonial act" must permit "the transmission of life," all forms of fertility limitation, including even the rhythm method, are thereby clearly declared to be morally illicit. (A later passage, however, indicates that Pope Paul regards the rhythm method as legitimate.[12]) Thus was upheld the natural law in opposition to the requests of many clergymen, both Catholic and other, for acceptance of the use of pills and other contraceptives.

Pope Paul did not choose to make this encyclical infallible or irreversible, although it could have been so labeled if the Pope had wished to make it so. Thus contraception is not ruled out forever, although presumably Paul's successor would have to marshall new and powerful theological arguments to justify a later shift to acceptance of such now firmly denied actions.

Two ways are left to limit fertility acceptably: remaining celibate and abstaining from intercourse during the wife's fertile period. Both have their defects: celibacy keeps men and women from participating in one of the most sublime of all the experiences open to humanity, and the rhythm method is a ludicrously ineffective way to limit the number of one's offspring. Nor is sexual love as regulated by the rhythm system much more romantically appealing than total abstinence; in the opinion of Catholic layman Clare Booth Luce, the rhythm method's calendar-watching is derided and dismissed as "checked-off love and clocked-out continence." In addition, both permanent and periodic abstinence have powerfully irritating qualities, including both affectional and sexual frustration which may upset the harmony of life and which, when continued for a long period, can even be dangerous for mental health.

Serendipitously supplementing these two avenues of escape from parenthood is a recently added indirect possibility that seems to be acceptable under the 1968 mandate: birth control pills may be used if − but only if − their purpose is to treat sickness; they may not be used directly to prevent pregnancy. Some Catholic obstetricians and gynecologists prescibe birth control pills to women whose menstrual cycles are so irregular and unpredictable as to make the rhythm method unreliable, a practice condoned by Father John J. Lynch and other priests, who believe that while the pills are theologically unacceptable when used directly to avoid pregnancy, they are licit if used to improve the efficiency of the rhythm method. "Blessed are the women that are irregular, for their daughters shall inherit the earth." [13]

Support for the Encyclical

Controversy blossomed immediately following issuance of the encyclical, and the multiverse argument has continued to the present date. Many clergymen sprang to the Pope's support. Archbishop Philip Pocock of Toronto offered his "complete assent" to the Pope's decision. The 77 archbishops and bishops of Mexico warned their constituents that the encyclical was not "a simple opinion" with which one could disagree, but rather "a solemn confirmation of a constant teaching of the authority." The Scottish Catholic hierarchy announced that "Humanae Vitae" must be obeyed. In Poland, primate Stefan Cardinal Wyszynski declared ceremoniously that the "wonderful" encyclical must be "received with great relief" by this nation "ready for sacrifices," and that acceptance of contraception would reduce man to "a pack of dwarfs, a pack of all sorts of imbeciles and disfigured humans." James Francis Cardinal McIntyre, Archbishop of Los Angeles, called the encyclical a "positive expression of fundamental principles of morality." The Archbishop of New York, Terence J. Cooke, greeted the proclamation as an "authoritative teaching" that requires assent by all Catholics. The Bishop of Des Moines, Maurice Dingman, described himself as a "firm believer in the position of the Pope."

Many priests lauded the encyclical as a restraint that could save the world from the moral ruin of increasing sensualism and hedonism: Monsignor Valencia Cano of Colombia applauded it as a "violent but necessary brake to sexual corruption in the western world." Others, such as the Archbishop of Tegucigalpa, Hector Enrique Santos, welcomed the Pope's pronouncement as a defense against the foreign influence that "seeks to reduce us to permanent impotence."

More explicit was an editorial in the Buenos Aires newspaper *Primera Blana,* complaining of "the United States attack on the birth rate in countries receiving aid" and concluding with the lament that "the poor people have to resign themselves to vacant land so that a foreign power with enough capital may someday colonize their underpopulated areas." Equally intemperate was a Turkish editorial acclaiming Pope Paul for "condemning those who made us swallow pills" in the war against progeny; "after this resounding Roman slap in the face, if the enemies of birth keep trying to propagandize the pill, it will be the duty of every Turk to strike them in the name of the fatherland." Competing in naiveté with this diatribe is another from an Islamic paper: "Birth control pills are being brought to Turkey as a microbe which will stop the population increase. Not for our prosperity, but as a microbe which will make us economically more miserable." One more example: the American Black Power paper, *Muhammed Speaks,* has repeatedly carried inflammatory articles likening family planning workers to "pushers" of dope who seek to destroy Black Power by diminishing the number of Black babies being born and thereby to "exterminate Black people"; it also proudly displays its exposés of "the genocide mission of the Peace Corps."

Catholic leaders themselves often took ambiguous stands. In some cases, the support seemed to be a reluctant acceptance of the mandate of a superior authority: the Bishop of London, G. Emmett Carter, simultaneously expressed his disappointment with the Papal decision and his unequivocal acceptance of it.

A second set of clergymen accepted it with qualifications: the Archbishop of Toulouse, Jean Guyot, warmly saluted the new encyclical while cautiously advising that some Catholics might use contraceptives without incurring the damnation that the encyclical implies.

A third group accepted the encyclical unqualifiedly, yet managing to combine obeisance with sympathetic understanding of the difficulties thus imposed on married couples: examples are the meetings of the Italian and West German bishops.

140

A fourth stance consisted of the weakly-expressed, tritely-formal plea to recognize the importance of humanity's eternal procreative destiny: for instance, the Rhodesian Bishops issued a statement accepting "Humanae Vitae" and commending to the Faithful "earnest prayer and confident recourse to the Sacraments."

A fifth exemplar was the carefully ambituous summation to Milanese Monsignor Gusetti's verbose article in the *Los Angeles Times*: "We can therefore conclude that the theme, the morality of the use of contraceptives, was revived because it is impossible easily, or indeed without real heroism in the proper sense of the word, to reconcile the so-called responsible parenthood with a demographic policy of deceleration of population growth on the one hand, and a normal and harmonious marriage-life on the other."

Opposition to the Encyclical

But others disagreed — and sometimes vigorously so. Verging on iconoclasm was the statement of the Belgian bishops that the decision whether or not to have children belonged to the parents and not to the celibate clergymen.

Before the encyclical was issued, Leon Joseph Cardinal Suenens of Belgium warned that the Church could not afford another Galileo decision. (In 1632 Galileo stated that the planets, including the earth, revolve around the sun; for that he was branded a heretic, and it was not until the 1960s that the Church expressed its willingness to re-examine the case and to consider restoring Galileo to the good graces of the Church.)

Julius Cardinal Doepfner of Munich and the Most Reverend Sergio Mendez Arceo of Cuernavaca, Mexico, instructed their priests not to withhold the sacraments from couples who decide to use contraceptives. Describing the encyclical as ambiguous and confusing, the Roman Catholic bishops of Austria ruled that Austrian Catholics could practice birth control if their consciences permitted, adding that "new life must have the opportunity to realize itself under favorable social conditions." In America, the weekly *National Catholic Reporter* editorialized pungently that "the birth control issue poses a serious question and the encyclical does not give a serious answer."

Priestly opinion seems to be divided according to age. A large majority of priests over age 50 agreed with "Humanae Vitae," whereas those under age 30 tended to disagree.

A 1969-1970 interview study of 5,155 priests, 165 bishops, and 155 superiors concluded that "over half of the priests of the United States no longer agree with their Church's official teaching on contraception."[14] So significant is this disclosure that a professor at the Jesuit Center for Social Studies at Georgetown University was motivated to write that "the existence of such extensive disagreement among the clergy has serious implications for the future solidarity of the Church," implying a need for a "critical reappraisal" of the "essential components" of Catholic faith.[15]

Protestations against recidivism characterized many objections. A 1969 article in *Commonweal* opened by castigating "Humanae Vitae" as Pope Paul's "brave leap into the middle ages." Dr. Spencer P. Austin, chairman of the world relief branch of the United States National Council of Churches, described the encyclical as a "backward move," adding pejoratively: "In the light of modern knowledge regarding population pressures and massive malnutrition, the failure of the church to share in family planning would constitute gross immorality." Dr. Hudson Hoagland, one of the developers of the contraceptive pill, called the recent encyclical "a tragic mistake" which "reaffirms a medieval theological concept which it is a moral crime against humanity to maintain." The Reverend Robert E. Hunt of Catholic University of Washington, D.C., labeled the decision as "theologically myopic," and the governing board of the Los Angeles Association of Roman Catholic Laymen went farther, bitterly declaring the bachelor Pope to have an "antisexual bias."

In deciding not to label his encyclical infallible, Pope Paul left the door ajar for dissenting opinions and even dissenting behavior; and dissenters of all religious persuasions were not tardy in arriving. The noted Swiss Catholic theologian, Reverend Hans Kung, declared that not only was the Pope's statement not infallible, but it was also wrong. Even the ghostwriters of the encyclical did not all view it as a behavioral command; within a week after issuance of "Humanae Vitae," one of its writers, Father Gustave Martelet, stated that "following the encyclical is a matter of individual conscience."

In 1970 a Dutch Catholic priest, Dr. Leo Alting von Geusau, published a summary of 4,000 worldwide reactions, classified by the nationality and specialty of each writer. Opinions varied widely, from (a) "general approval" in "black Africa" and the claim by a Chilean professor that there was "no population problem on his continent," to (b) the moderate positions of some Catholic and non-Catholic theologians that "the personal conscience of the married couple was the final authority on the subject," to (c) the antagonistic statement of the 2,600 American scientists who signed a document averring that "Paul VI has sanctioned the death of endless numbers of human beings with his wrongly inspired and immoral encyclical." Some non-Catholics affirmed strong agreement with the encyclical (mainly for its stand against hedonism), but enough adverse criticism flowed from within the Church to indicate a major schism: many theologians objected to "the fact that never in recent history had a pope issued a statement with so little support from the Church" Nor did the dissenters agree among themselves: some scholars attacked the encyclical for its lack of supporting Biblical evidence, while others complained that it was not up to date, being based on an "impersonal concept of nature which had been abandoned since the Middle Ages.[16]

Who Knows the Unchanging Truth?

One prominent lawyer remarked that "The lengths to which the Roman Catholic Church, as the principal opponent of contraception, will go to enforce its views pose a continuing threat to personal freedom in this area of human life. The Roman Catholic Church believes that it has a duty to intervene in the secular affairs of the state or of its non-Roman Catholic citizens wherever the spiritual welfare of its own members is concerned."[17] Monsignor Kelly agrees: "Many persons think that contraception is a sin only for Catholics. Contraception is a sin for everyone."[18]

And so we have the most prominent (and yet not really clearly defined) demographic controversy confronting the world today: the disagreement between the Roman Catholic Church and others regarding fertility control. This dispute is aggravated partly because Catholic religious leaders are exceptionally articulate and rational in argument, and partly because the Church claims uncompromisingly to be the sole possessor of the absolute, unchangeable, and final truth. Contraception is rejected as "contrary to the law of God. The Roman Catholic Church bases its condemnation on the natural law, binding on all men, and not merely on Roman Catholics."[19]

This insistence on applying the 1968 encyclical to non-Catholics tends to infuriate the non-Catholics. Yet Cardinal McIntyre of Los Angeles and Vatical columnist Monsignor Ferdinando Lambruschini, to name only two, are credited with declaring that this edict of His Holiness is binding on all Christians, and perhaps all people of whatever faith. But if that were true, the Catholic Church surely would not be so isolated among religious groups in rejecting artificial birth control as inherently evil. And even Catholics experience difficulty in accepting this edict. An editorial in *The National Catholic Reporter* declared mournfully that "the men of our day find the teaching incomprehensible — and rather sad."

The conviction of a necessity to be the only church to know the truth leads to a persistent fear of losing followers: "If the Church could err in such a way, the authority of the ordinary magisterium in moral matters would be thrown into question." Thus the Minority Report of the Papal Commission fearfully presented the various undesirable practices that might result from any change in the dictates of the Church, specifically deploring (as likely consequences of changes in Catholic teaching following papal acceptance of family planning) the sins of extra-marital relationships, oral and anal copulation within marriage, masturbation among youths, and sterilization. And as if this were not enough, the Minority Report added the prediction that "more serious evils can yet be expected." The worst of these evils is unquestionably the dread prospect of diminishing "the value and dignity of the Church's teaching authority." To wit: "If the Church should not admit that the teaching passed on is no longer of value, teaching which has been preached and stated with ever more insistent solemnity until very recent years, it must be feared greatly that its authority in almost all moral and dogmatic matters will be seriously harmed." Perhaps it is not primarily ethical principles which are involved, but rather the unchanging and supposedly undeviatingly-complied-with consistency of Church mandates. The Minority Report concludes with this despairing sentence: "For the Church to have erred so gravely in its grave responsibility of leading souls would be tantamount to seriously suggesting that the assistance of the Holy Spirit was lacking to her."

Natural Law and Sexual Relations

In the controversy over birth control, the concept of natural law is prominently argued.[20] The principles of natural law are discerned by reason and logic; they are inherent in things and behavior. Being that part of the divine law which is not revealed directly by God, but which instead must be discovered by human powers of observation and rational thought, natural law still is universal and immutable, in contrast to the arbitrary and changeable laws established by societies to regulate conduct in accordance with   local conditions. Ordinary laws written by society to maintain order are presumably directed toward practical and humanistic ends; natural laws are fixed and God-given.

According to natural law, the purpose and hence the proper use of an object or a part of the body can be disclosed by application of reason to knowledge of its form and function. In this way, theologians have concluded that the purpose of the sexual organs is procreation and not pleasure. And if the reproductive organs were intended for reproduction, then any interference with the reproductive process is in violation of the natural law. It is in the nature of certain parts of the body to produce children, and any frustration of this nature is contrary to one's duty to God. The advocates of natural law deduce logically the natural purpose of marriage from the teleology of the genitalia, the act of coitus, and the chemistry of the sexual fluids, all of which so clearly are structured for generative purpose.

The patron saint of the natural law prohibition of family planning, St. Augustine, was willing to permit "only those sexual relations which are necessary to procreation." To conceive a child usually would require from one to twenty acts of coitus. Thus Kinsey's estimate of the average lifetime cumulative frequency of intercourse of American males and females as 3,000 to 4,000 must be regarded, with great misgiving, as at least fifty and perhaps a thousand times higher than that allowed under this compelling religious norm.

Relevance of Natural Law to Fertility

To some people it is natural to take an antibiotic pill but not a birth control pill. But both pills are man-made and artificial. And in what sense is the use of such technological equipment as a thermometer or a rhythm-aiding calendrical slide-rule more natural than the use of a vaginal diaphragm or pills to achieve the identical objective — avoiding conception? Elaborate theological argumentation aside, the only purpose of the rhythm method is obviously to avoid procreation; since rhythm's intent and use are clearly the same as any other means to achieving fertility control, results-oriented persons tend to decry the Church's distinction between it and other anti-conception procedures as intellectual and moral hair-splitting. People who take scientific gadgets for granted as aids to happiness and comfort are beginning to see the rhythm method more as an artificial disruption of conjugal love than as a natural process for avoiding procreation.

Many people believe that unlimited procreation is humanity's only natural reproductive condition; yet no society — no matter how primitive — has ever been known to practice unrestricted fertility. Others contend that birth limitation is natural as long as it is conducted in certain ways, sometimes including chastity and always accepting specified forms of marital organization and customs; the fact that these social norms differ vastly from group to group and from era to era (even to the extent of being opposite to each other) raises a serious question as to the legitimacy of the appellation "natural." Still other people argue that sexual continence — even temporarily — is unnatural, and that sexual intercourse is a necessity for sane and healthy human life. Careful observation discloses systematic disagreements in these opinions according to the cultural nexus in which the speaker was reared and now lives. Insofar as people are a product of their times, so generally are their beliefs concerning reproduction. Where then is naturalness? In the eloquent words of Cambridge University essayist Frank L. Lucas: "All civilization is 'unnatural.' To be purely 'natural' we must perch nude in trees." As for deaths and births: "Our forefathers denounced sanitation and vaccination as thwarting Providence. Even within living memory there were men who opposed the use of anaesthetics for women in childbirth, as if some Heavenly Shylock were being defrauded of his due of pain."[21]

Demographic Implications of "Humanae Vitae"

Assessment of the probable demographic consequences of the 1968 encyclical is best illustrated by Latin America, the continent with the most rapid rate of population increase. Given the Catholic majority, the official dicta of the Holy Father cannot be contradicted openly by governments with assurance of impunity. Demographically, the most visible governmental reaction to "Humanae Vitae" is a reluctance to enlarge the existing feeble — although viable — birth control programs. Birth control will continue to be practiced by individuals and family units, but nationwide programs may be difficult to proclaim publicly by elected officials.

"Opposition to family planning among decision makers in Latin America stems primarily from three overlapping sources: the Church, the Marxists, and the Nationalists. Of these, only the Church presents institutionalized opposition and, in the light of the recent encyclical, its influence on public policy may prove to be of considerable significance."[22] Prominent among the reasons for this significance is the encyclical's enhancement of the "nationalist psyche" and its fanning of the "fertility mystique" beloved by traditionalists who view the United States as mounting an antinatal plot to diminish the power of Latin American nations. There had been hints that this chauvinistic paranoia was decreasing, but after the encyclical, "what might have been dying embers may now be rekindled."[23]

In the mid-1960s, exiguous pro-birth control programs were established in a few Latin American nations, but since the encyclical, augmentation of these programs is as hard to arrange as is the institution of new programs in other Latin countries. This difficulty is not insurmountable, however, as illustrated by the Mexican government's decision to offer birth control services in government health clinics for the first time beginning in 1974. Many Latin American citizens still want to limit their family size; and consequently, the birth control controversy continues to flourish. Some conservative Catholics are torn between rigidly restrictive instructions to refrain from sexual intercourse or face its reproductive consequences, and the anti-Papal direction to do as their individual consciences direct but to contribute as few mouths to feed in A.D. 2000 as can be arranged.

One of the strongest short-term effects of the encyclical on Latin American fertility is to highlight the birth control issue in the newspapers and, unintentionally, to give considerable free publicity to the arguments of pro-family planning and anti-encyclical spokesmen. Thus the effect of the Pope's pronouncement may be, to some extent, the opposite of what was intended — an outcome that might have been foreseen in view of such prior lessons as the inadvertent spreading of knowledge about sterilization in Puerto Rico by priests who felt impelled to protest against the practice, regardless of whether or not their hearers knew about sterilization.

Behavior of Catholic Couples

Despite all the high-flown theological arguments, it is within the ordinary family that the most consequential demographic decisions are made. Whatever Pope Paul says, each couple will probably continue to make its own decisions regarding reproductive behavior. Leon Joseph Cardinal Suenens of Belgium went so far as to afirm that the Church is losing members because of its birth control policy, and those who remain in the Church may avoid going to confession.

Dogma does not always accord with the practices of church members. Thirty percent of married Catholic women interviewed in a fertility survey in the United States in 1955 reported they had used a method not approved by the Church[24] — a fraction that grew to 38 percent in 1960, became a majority (53 percent) in 1965, and rose to 76 percent by 1969, the year following issuance of the encyclical.[25] In Latin America, sample surveys conducted during 1964-1965 in ten cities in nine countries showed that most married women had used a forbidden antinatal technique at one time or another.[26]

Public opinion also is nonsupportive. Several surveys have revealed that a majority of rank and file American Catholics would like to see their church remove the ban on the use of contraceptive devices, and a Gallup Poll following the issuance of "Humanae Vitae" disclosed that only 28 percent of the sampled Americans favored the encyclical, whereas 54 percent opposed it (the other 18 percent expressed neutrality or no opinion).[27]

Many poor Catholic couples — and especially illiterate ones — know too little of the 1968 encyclical to be directly affected by it. J. Mayone Stycos reported that two weeks after the encyclical was issued, 90 percent of the women attending out-patient clinics in Tegucigalpa, Honduras, said they had not heard of the Pope's new proclamation. A month after issuance of the encyclical, only 20 percent of a sample of 330 women in low-income Tegucigalpa homes (most of which contained radio sets) had heard about it. Of those who had heard of it, nine out of ten stated that the encyclical had not changed their thinking about family planning, and none said that it would change what they were actually doing. When asked why, they offered such explanations as: "The Pope does not know the true life of the poor" and "I am a Catholic but I am also poor and it hurts to see my children without shoes and naked."[28]

In 1969 Charles Westoff and Norman Ryder conducted telephone interviews with 473 married Catholic women in the United States (whom they had previously interviewed in 1965), inquiring whether their behavior was affected by the encyclical. The proportion currently using some method of birth control other than rhythm increased from 58 to 64 percent over the four-year interval. "There is very little indication of return to the Church-approved method after the encyclical," and among those who had formerly used the rhythm method, "30 percent had switched to the pill." These findings imply that the encyclical has not reversed the trend toward nonconformity and "has probably not even slowed it down."[29]

As to the attitudes of the Westoff-Ryder respondents, 16 percent spoke "for" the encyclical, 60 percent declared themselves "against" it, and 24 percent proffered divided or unclassifiable responses. Cross-tabulation by age, attendance at mass, and education indicated proportions "against" the encyclical varying from 80 percent of women under age 24 down to 54 percent of those aged 39 to 43; from 39 percent among those who attend mass several times a week to 92 percent of those who attend only once a year or less; and from 47 percent among college graduates to 64 percent among women having less than a high school education.

This apparent reversal of the usual expectation of educational influence is explained by several studies indicating that increasing amounts of education in Catholic schools and colleges promote traditionalism and conservatism, whereas increased education in Protestant and secular institutions promotes liberation from traditional thoughtways. Clearly, individualistic thinking is not necessarily advanced by higher education; the orientation of the education is crucial.

Regarding consistency between attitudes and behavior, 65 percent of all women in the 1969 study who spoke "against" the encyclical were using nonapproved methods, whereas only 8 percent of women "for" the encyclical were using nonapproved techniques. Some interviewees expressed themselves quite firmly: "I reacted like a lot of other women. . . . I stopped going to Church. . . . It seemed like a farce." Eloquence was supplied by the plaintive "It's my religion. I was born into it, and I believe it. I wish they'd change it though; they're changing everything else."

The common presumption that the dominant religious body in a country determines the reproductive practices of the populace is a fond fallacy — and has been for centuries. Historically, the first nation to shift from large families to what demographers like to call "the small family system" — signifying a norm of two to four children rather than the traditional eight or twelve — was France, which was then, and remains, a predominantly Roman Catholic country. Late in the eighteenth century, birth control knowledge and practice spread throughout France, without official Church approval but possibly with some clerical connivance. No other nation can claim that probably most married couples were using some type of birth control more than a hundred years ago. It is apparent that other factors in an individual's value system may counteract the religious component; in some cases, they may overcome stern priestly pronatalist directives.

Prospects for Papal Change

The position of the Roman Catholic Church retains, nevertheless, tremendous world prominence. If the Catholic Church one day comes to accept birth control, who then will oppose it? Certainly no other major religion now takes a stance so strenuously negative. Numerous individuals will continue to fight against family planning programs in many countries, including such influential personages as cabinet ministers of various persuasions, generals wanting larger armies to defend their territories, and the like. But no large and powerful international organization would remain to object to family planning through the application of speeches and writings by excellently trained personnel, ample money for lobbying and propaganda, a centuries-long history with its extensive cumulated literature, and a large quantity of faithful followers.

The question immediately confronting us all is whether the prospect for liberalizing the official Vatican stand has vanished: what is the likelihood of rescinding "Humane Vitae"? Surely Paul VI will not abrogate his own painfully achieved pronouncement, so no significant change can be expected as long as he remains Pope. The future thus may be determined by three circumstances: how soon there will be a successor, what his views on birth control will be, and how much respect he will feel he owes to the statements of his predecessor. It would appear rather insulting to the memory of Pope Paul if, shortly after his burial, the succeeding Pope publicly proclaimed the 1968 encyclical to be invalid. However, the history of the Papacy does offer extensive evidence that new Popes do not always give full honor to the spiritual wisdom of the men they succeed. Further, it is possible that the intensity and extent of the furore aroused by this latest encyclical may combine with the pleas of scientists, citizens, ministers, and priests to impel the next Pope toward a renewed confrontation. And because Paul VI did not elect to declare his July 1968 words to be infallible, the possibility of a partial modification or even a complete reversal remains alive.

NOTES

[1] Philip M. Hauser, *Population Perspectives* (New Brunswick: Rutgers University Press, 1960), p. 163.

[2] This chapter is primarily an abridged and rewritten adaptation of Ralph Thomlinson, "Prevented Births, Naturalness, and Roman Catholic Doctrine," *Population Review,* Vol. XIV, No. 1, Jan. 1970, pp. 17-35; issue destroyed by fire, therefore article revised and republished in *Journal of Sex Research,* Vol. VIII, No. 2, May 1972, pp. 73-100.

[3] Hughes Mearns, untitled poem, 1910.

[4] Lyle Saunders, "Research and Evaluation: Needs for the Future," in Bernard Berelson (ed.), *Family Planning and Population Programs* (Chicago: University of Chicago Press, 1966), p. 786. © 1966 by The University of Chicago. Reprinted by permission.

[5] J. L. Simon, "The Value of Avoided Births to Underdeveloped Countries," *Population Studies,* Vol. XXIII, No. 1, March 1969, pp. 61-68.

[6] Robert G. Potter Jr., "Estimating Births Averted in a Family Planning Program," in S. J. Behrman, Leslie Corsa Jr., and Ronald Freedman (eds.), *Fertility and Family Planning* (Ann Arbor: University of Michigan Press, 1969), pp. 413-434.

[7] J. C. Barrett, "The Time Response in Averted Births," *Population Studies,* Vol. XXVI, No. 3, November 1972, pp. 507-514.

[8] Peyrefitte, Roger, *The Prince's Person* (New York: Farrar Straus, 1965) (translated by P. Fryer).

[9] Pope Paul VI, Encyclical Letter *Humanae Vitae* (Of Human Life), July 25, 1968, U.S. Catholic Conference, Washington, D.C., p. 8.

[10] *Ibid.,* p. 7.

[11] *Ibid.,* p. 9.

[12] *Ibid.,* p. 10.

[13] Garrett Hardin, "A Second Sermon on the Mount," *Perspectives in Biology and Medicine,* Vol. VI, No. 3, Spring 1963, p. 370.

[14] Maurice J. Moore, *Death of a Dogma?: The American Catholic Clergy's Views of Contraception* (Chicago: University of Chicago Community and Family Study Center, 1973), p. 111.

[15] John L. Thomas, S.J., "Foreword" to Moore, *ibid.,* pp. vii and xi.

[16] von Geusau, Leo Alting, "International Reaction to the Encyclical *Humanae Vitae,*" *Studies in Family Planning,* The Population Council, Vol. I, No. 50, February 1970, pp. 8-12.

[17] Alvah W. Sulloway, "The Legal and Political Aspects of Population Control in the United States," *Law and Contemporary Problems,* Vol. XXV, No. 3, Summer 1960, p. 608.

[18] George A. Kelly, *Birth Control and Catholics* (New York: Doubleday and Co., 1963), p. 81.

[19] Norman St. John-Stevas, "A Roman Catholic View of Population Control," *Law and Contemporary Problems,* Vol. XXV, No. 3, Summer 1960, pp. 445-469.

[20] For historical perspective, see John T. Noonan, Jr., *Contraception* (Cambridge: Harvard University Press, 1965).

[21] Frank Laurence Lucas, "The Greatest Problem of To-Day," in Lucas, *The Greatest Problem and Other Essays* (London: Cassell and Co., 1960), p. 327.

[22] J. Mayone Stycos, "Opposition to Family Planning in Latin America: Conservative Nationalism," *Demography,* Vol. V, No. 2, 1968, p. 846.

[23] *Ibid.,* p. 853.

[24] Ronald Freedman, Pascal K. Whelpton, and Arthur A. Campbell, *Family Planning, Sterility, and Population Growth* (New York: McGraw-Hill, 1959), pp. 181-182.

[25] Norman B. Ryder and Charles F. Westoff, *Reproduction in the United States: 1965* (Princeton: Princeton University Press, 1971), pp. 186 and 206.

[26] Centro Latinoamericano de Demografia and Community and Family Study Center, *Fertility and Family Planning in Metropolitan Latin America* (Chicago: University of Chicago, 1972), p. 175.

[27] *Ibid.,* p. 201.

[28] J. Mayone Stycos, "Ideology, Faith and Population Growth in Latin America," Washington, D.C., Population Reference Bureau, January 1969, pp. 4-5.

[29] Charles F. Westoff and Norman B. Ryder, "The Papal Encyclical and Catholic Practice and Attitudes, 1969," *Studies in Family Planning,* Vol. I, No. 50, February 1970, pp. 1-7.

A Moroccan peasant family on the move.

Klong (canal) residents spread litter and disease
in Bangkok, Thailand.

PART IV. DISPUTES OVER DEATHS AND MOVES

Undesirable forms of control effected by man could include homosexuality — which is never accompanied by a high birth rate — and cannibalism [which] would have the beautiful symmetry of population decreasing as food supply increased.

> (Philip M. Hauser, "Population: More than Family Planning," Journal of Medical Education, Vol. XLIV, No. 11, Part 2, November 1969, p. 20.)

Mississippi water tastes like turpentine, but Michigan water tastes like sherry wine.

> (Jelly Roll Morton)

Chapter 9.   Death Control

THE population explosion was caused primarily by declining mortality — or, more specifically, by the lag between a slowly decreasing birth rate and a rapidly decreasing death rate. The divinely appointed scourges symbolized by the four horsemen of the Apocalypse — famine, pestilence, war, and death — once kept population growth down by seeing to it that deaths were plentiful. Today the death rate has been reduced to a level where problems are changing from "how to live to a ripe old age" to "what do we do after retirement?"

Confronted with increasing numbers of old people, geriatricians and social workers are trying to make the aged feel better physically and emotionally. Employers are beginning to recognize that many persons are still employable after they reach 65 years of age. If present trends toward an increasing proportion of the aged continue, Americans may be obliged to retreat from their "youth cult" and give elders an honored place in the social structure, making better use of the experience and wisdom that accumulate with the years. But before the social consequences of lowered mortality are discussed, whether they be pleasures introduced or problems added, the amount and causes of the reduction should be made clear.

Ways to Measure Mortality

As might be surmised, many techniques to measure mortality resemble their fertility counterparts. The crude, age-specific, standardized, and intrinsic or life table death rates are constructed in exactly the same ways as the corresponding birth rates.

The supreme tool in analyzing mortality is the life table. Having its origins in the work of several Englishmen in the 1600s, the life table was brought to perfection by A. J. Lotka in the 1920s.

Essentially, the life table is the mortality history of a cohort of people all born at the same time. Take, for example, a life table for the 1880 United States cohort: starting with 100,000 persons, suppose 4,000 die during the first year of life. This represents a survival rate of 96 percent. Then, given these 96,000 persons reaching their first birthday, we note how many live to age 2 (and what is the survival rate from age one to age two). We continue thus until all of the cohort has died or to the oldest age for which we have information.

Unfortunately, given the above description, one must wait nearly a century to complete the table (that is, until most persons — but not necessarily everyone — in the cohort has died); this waiting period clearly is disastrous for application. Consequently, demographers developed the current life table, which is constructed in the same way, has the same tabular appearance, and yields the same kinds of results, but with one very important difference. A current life table is a hypothetical construction based on the assumption that the age-sex-specific death rates (or survival rates) for a given year — say, 1970 — can be applied successively to a fictional group of people who somehow manage to live every year of their lives in 1970. If mortality conditions did not alter for 80 or 100 years, the current life table would be the same as the actual life table described above. But if survival rates change drastically, then the current life table will turn out to represent mortality assumptions considerably removed from the conditions under which a cohort actually lives. Even with this defect, however, current life tables are more useful than actual life tables because of the time lag inherent in the latter.

Using a life table, demographers can calculate the expectation of life beginning at any age. The expectation of life at age 20, for example, is the number of years lived by all members of this cohort after age 20, divided by the number of people alive at age 20. Although the expectation of life at age 0 is the most widely used (because it is the most inclusive of mortality experiences), expectations of life at other ages are valuable figures to know.

Once a life table has been prepared, statisticians can calculate intrinsic or life table birth and death rates, which are based on the age-sex distribution shown in the life table. These rates, together with the expectation of life and the survival ratios, constitute widely useful applications of the life table. Insurance rates are based on life tables, as are pension programs, and they also are used in such contexts as lawsuits for accidental injury compensation, in which it is desirable to be able to estimate what, most likely, would have been the future lifetime earnings of a killed or crippled person.

Preindustrial Mortality

From early man's probable death rate of about 50 per 1,000 population per year and an expectation of life at birth that seems rarely to have exceeded 20 years, the more advanced nations have lowered their death rates to below 10 and raised the expectation of life to about 75 years. This improvement did not occur gradually; rather, mortality and longevity gains were very slow throughout history until the industrial revolution, which made possible the higher standard of living essential to death rates below 25 and life expectancies above 40. Studies of ancient Greeks and Romans indicate an expectation of life between 25 and

35 years, and research on medieval and early modern Europeans shows evidence of little improvement, the most accurate computation being astronomer Edmund Halley's estimate of 35 years for the city of Breslau during 1687-1691.[1]

Reasons for this brevity of life are easy to see: contagious diseases were very poorly controlled, partly because both public and personal sanitation were deplorable, and partly because the state of medical knowledge did not permit understanding of causes; malnutrition was widespread and chronic, and famine was a recurrent threat. The noted epidemiologist Hans Zinsser declared that the flow of history has been guided less by the actions of great leaders than by the waxing and waning of the epidemic and often pandemic diseases before which even the best informed and richest persons were helpless.[2] In 1348 the Black Death (probably bubonic plague) is estimated to have killed one-fourth of the inhabitants of Europe — about 25 million deaths in a single year, a performance that threatened to be repeated on several succeeding occasions. The diary of Samuel Pepys recorded conditions in London during 1665:

> June 29th. This end of the towne every day grows very bad of the plague. The Mortality Bill is come to 267; which is about ninety more than the last.
> August 10th. In great trouble to see the Bill this week rise so high, to above 4,000 in all, and of them above 3,000 of the plague ... The towne growing so unhealthy, that a man cannot depend upon living two days to an end.
> August 31st. Thus this month ends with great sadness upon the publick, through the greatness of the plague every where through the kingdom almost. Every day sadder and sadder news of its encrease. In the City died this week 7,496, and of them 6,102 of the plague. But it is feared that the true number of the dead this week is near 10,000; partly from the poor that cannot be taken notice of, through the greatness of their number.[3]

Daniel Defoe drew a vivid picture of the mental agonies induced by the 1665 epidemic:

> People in the rage of distemper, or in the torment of their swellings, which was indeed intolerable, running out of their own government, raving and distracted, and oftentimes laying violent hands upon themselves, throwing themselves out at their windows, shooting themselves, mothers murdering their own children in their lunacy, some dying of mere grief as a passion, some of mere fright and surprise without any infection at all, others frighted into idiotism and foolish distractions, some into despair and lunacy, others into melancholy madness.[4]

Prescientific Medicine

The list of causes under which deaths were classified in seventeenth-century London implies the ignorance of the physicians; in order of their occurrence, the leading purported causes were: consumption and cough; chrisomes (that is, neonates) and infants; ague (a severe fever) and fever; plague; aged; teeth and worms; flox and smallpox; and dropsy (swelling attributable to excess fluid) and tympany (gas in the abdomen).[5] Clearly this list of supposed causes is mainly a catalog of symptoms, but that was all the physicians of the time knew. Despite the fact that natural science was then experiencing one of its great periods of discovery, medical knowledge did not improve. Locke, Leibnitz, and Descartes regarded seventeenth-century developments in hygiene and therapeutics as highly promising, and it seemed likely that medical practice would follow. Unfortunately, a strange and tragic thing happened: "Medicine at first faltered, and then fell behind; physic failed to keep up with physics."[6]

This medical culture lag resulted in considerable part from antagonistic folkways and mores. Experimentation on the human body was unthinkable, and corpses were not to be dissected. Even the idea of illness as a natural phenomenon was repugnant; for sickness was accepted as a manifestation of divine dissatisfaction. Anatomical research was frowned upon to such an extent that Andreas Vesalius, chief physician to Charles V and Philip II of Spain, was accused of heresy and condemned to death by the Inquisition. Social norms did not exert such a powerful retardation upon physics and chemistry: "Imagine Galilei's difficulties, had the local mores prohibited the profane handling of pendulums and falling bodies!"[7]

As a result, medieval and early modern physicians were more concerned with the symptoms of the sick man than with the disease itself, clinging to the traditional depleting procedures of bleeding, purging, and blistering. The seventeenth century was "a period of excrementory therapeutics,"[8] the pharmacopoeia listing such repulsive medications as blood, bile, hair, sweat, saliva, lice, and lead bullets; patients not fond of these prescriptions could switch to other physicians who cured ailments with tobacco, barley malt, and maple sugar. Monistic systems of pathology were popular then as in the nineteenth century, based on hypertension, gastroenteritis, or psoric itching. If learned doctors could evolve such grand Newtonian syntheses, one is tempted to question their superiority to the gullible adherents of Galvanism, Mesmerism, Naturopathy, Couéism, Orgonomy, and Dianetics — several of which were founded in recent years by M.D.s.[9]

Fads and fashions come and go in medicine as in anything else that man undertakes; yet "resistance to innovations in medicine may be said to be the rule rather than the exception." B. J. Stern cites the twentieth-century adage that "it takes ten years to get a medical discovery into a medical textbook and at least ten years more to get it out after it has been superseded."[10] William Harvey's discovery of the circulation of the blood in the early seventeenth century was strongly opposed by contemporary physicians; Harvey claimed that no man over forty accepted the new fact. Asepsis was not accepted for centuries: as early as the thirteenth century, Theodoric challenged Galen's belief that suppuration in wounds was natural, arguing correctly that "laudable pus" was an undesirable complication that could be avoided; but asepsis was rejected by surgeons until the nineteenth century.[11] Similar treatment was accorded to the ideas of Ignaz Semmelweis in Vienna and Oliver Wendell Holmes in Boston when they charged that puerperal fever, the leading cause of death to women during childbirth, was carried from patient to patient by physicians (some of whom did not even realize the need to wash their hands between deliveries) and encouraged by insanitary hospital conditions (frequently bed linen was not changed between patients); Semmelweis's career was ruined by head physicians who drove him out of one hospital after another, but Holmes survived to write in a medical journal:

> It is as a lesson rather than as a reproach that I call up the memory of these irreparable errors and wrongs. No tongue can tell the heart-breaking calamity they have caused; they have closed the eyes just opened upon a new world of love and happiness; they have bowed the strength of manhood into the dust; they have cast the helplessness of infancy into the stranger's arms, or bequeathed it, with less cruelty, the death of its dying parent. There is no tone deep enough for regret, and no voice loud enough for warning.[12]

Pasteur's germ theory, on which Lister's contributions to antisepsis and asepsis were based, was vigorously disparaged by medical teachers and practitioners and only adopted after decades of struggle. Vaccination to achieve immunity against epidemic disease was fought by the medical profession.

Modern Medical Science and Drugs

Sweeping reforms initiated by the Flexner reports of the 1910s and 1920s,[13] added to the general progress of biological science, brought both preventive and curative medicine to a respectable level. But there remain laggard areas: even now the methodological and statistical competence of many general practitioners is insufficient to enable them to properly evaluate controlled experimentation on new drugs. In 1957 the head of the department of preventive medicine at Harvard Medical School wrote: "The profession of medicine . . . must apply more rigorous experimental design to the testing of new drugs, and elevate the standard of research publications."[14] The problem is further aggravated by the fact that, to quote the editor of a leading pharmacological journal, "a large proportion of claims for superiority for new drugs are patently invalid," and "drugs are being marketed and promoted and advertised by precisely the same techniques used for soaps and detergents."[15] There are now so many drugs, some of which are extremely potent in interfering with basic physiologic functions and many of which are poorly understood because of limited experimentaton before release, that physicians are hard put to be knowledgeable about more than a few; the result is an increasing reliance on drug salesmen for information that should come from less biased sources. "Physicians are led to use drugs when the indications are lacking, to use drugs that are not the best available or even those which do not apply."[16] It is no wonder that untoward reaction to drugs is becoming one of the commonest ailments encountered by physicians. New drugs have proliferated so rapidly in the last century that the renowned Canadian physician Sir William Osler admonished practitioners to "treat as many patients as possible with a new drug while it still has the power to heal," and a physician at Cornell University complained that in view of the "150,000 preparations on the market" and the fact that there is generally one best drug for each ailment, "we simply don't have enough diseases to go around."[17]

Research physicians are becoming highly scientific and are turning increasingly to computers to analyze the large numbers of cases they study. The day is not far off when computers may be used by ordinary physicians in examinations and diagnoses as routinely as blood tests and X-rays are now made. Another important use of computers will be to measure the effectiveness of treatment. Several Markovian states may be identified: patient in critical condition, patient sick but not critical, disease quiescent, patient fully recovered, or patient dead. A patient traverses a path from one state to another, although not necessarily in any specified sequence, and one objective of medical research is to ascertain, when a patient is in any given state, his probable length of time of remaining in that state and the likelihood of his entering each other state — a probability influenced by dozens of variables. Since some variables are not measureable for all patients, and others are not measureable for anyone in the present condition of medical expertise, a probability approach may be the most effective method of prognosis (in fact it has been used by physicians — although not always consciously — from time immemorial). With the aid of such a model, new treatments may be evaluated and afflicted patients may be helped.[18]

Disease Prevention

Medical and sanitary sciences have enabled men to achieve remarkable control over acute infectious ailments. Plague, cholera, smallpox, and yellow fever have been largely eliminated in Western countries, although they maintain a foothold in Asia and Africa; protection comes mainly from immunization and quarantine. Of the major epidemic diseases, smallpox is the only one that had a truly serious outbreak in recent years anywhere in the world. However, millions of people living in areas where infectious diseases are endemic are still threatened. International agreements dating back to 1903 plus national health regulations have generally confined epidemics to limited regions. Control is complicated by the fact that certain communicable diseases, notably plague and yellow fever, seem to persist more or less permanently in wildlife, thus providing a reservoir of potential infection. Typhus and typhoid, once deadly throughout the world, have been virtually eradicated in areas having safe water supplies, sewage systems, and pasteurized milk.[19]

Pneumonia, tuberculosis, and malaria are now vestigial problems in modern countries. Elsewhere, epidemics are still widely reported. Penicillin and other antibiotics have brought about a striking worldwide drop in deaths from pneumonia. Pulmonary tuberculosis has declined precipitously in the twentieth century. The insecticide D.D.T., coupled with other public health measures, has drastically lowered malaria death rates in many underdeveloped areas, and other diseases carried to humans by insects are also controllable by insecticides.

Childhood diseases are practically conquered in modern nations, some being nearly eliminated and others reduced to nuisances so harmless that some mothers now deliberately expose their children to them at an early age simply to avoid the discomfort of getting through the illness at some inconvenient later date. Incidence and death rates from diphtheria, measles, scarlet fever, and whooping cough are generally lower than in former times.

Similar progress has not yet been made with diseases of the aged, for gerontologists are not yet able to identify what aging is, let alone what causes it. They do know, however, that it is always with us. Even in the fastest stage of human growth (the embryo), deterioration occurs; conversely, even in advanced senescence the hair grows, cuts heal (although relatively slowly), and body cells replace themselves. Deterioration begins at different ages for different organs: the lenses of the eye begin to lose their elasticity before age 15; hearing starts to decline at age 20 (especially the high tones); muscular strength weakens after age 25; bones become brittle and cartilage hardens after 30; production of digestive juices declines steeply after age 35; certain vision defects appear after age 40; basal metabolism commences to fall at 45 (accompanied by an endocrine system slowdown); the sense of taste begins to weaken at age 50; the sense of smell commences to fail at age 60; saliva, sweat, and other secreted products gradually fall off in volume with age; protective antibodies and immunities gradually wear out (explaining why more grandmothers die of whooping cough than do grandchildren); and the homeostatic balance or equilibrium of the body fluids and cells deteriorates, subjecting elderly persons to lowered adaptability to extremes of, or sudden changes in, temperature, exercise, diet, or emotion. By way of compensation, certain abilities continue unimpaired to advanced ages and may even increase with age: judgment and accuracy of comprehension are frequently maintained to very great ages; endurance increases through age 45; and wisdom, achieved painfully through the application of intelligence to experience, is a product of aging. Furthermore nearly all of the elements of decline are gradual, and people rarely die of worn-out digestive systems or lack of glandular durability. However there is a lowered resistance to disease, and recovery is far slower.

How we fight physical and mental sickness and death is closely tied to our attitudes toward illness. Men once regarded sickness as a mysterious phenomenon of supernatural origin; indeed, the ancient antagonism toward a naturalistic explanation of disease still prevails in many parts of the world, especially regarding mental disorders. Fear of sickness motivates adoption of special diets, and gullible food faddists have made rich men of charlatans. Good health and slenderness are being merchandised in the same way as the automobiles that eliminate walking and the foods that have no calories.

As communicable diseases are coming increasingly under our control, while the mental and degenerative diseases and fetal and infant deaths remain serious threats, the risk of dying is greatest at two extremes of life — the months immediately following birth, and the older ages. At present the United States death rate is lowest at about age 10, whereas mortality during the first year approximately equals that in the seventieth, mortality in the first month is similar to that at age 95, and mortality during the first day resembles that of persons aged well over 100. In other words, the death rate increases slowly with increasing age among adults and decreases rapidly among infants as they pass through the first few dangerous hours and weeks of life.

World Levels of Mortality

The result of these medical and sanitation improvements has been a lowering of national death rates to the levels indicated in Table 9. In the more advanced countries, crude annual death rates are now below 10 persons per thousand, and in those nations which have an exceptionally large proportion of their populace in the ages between 10 and 25, death rates are considerably lower. The mediocre showing of the United States is partly attributable to its relatively old age distribution, partly also to the higher mortality among blacks and in the rural south, and partly to the increasingly unsatisfactory manner in which medical care is delivered to the public. Whatever the cause of our ranking below a number of other nations, Americans cannot be proud; to the contrary, there is some cause for shame that the richest country in the world cannot keep its citizens from dying at a rate higher than several less favored nations.

Death rates of 10 or below represent commendable achievements. At the beginning of the present century, even the most accomplished countries had rates of 15 or 20. One of the longest historical records is supplied by Sweden, always a forerunner in quality of statistics: from crude death rates of 25 to 30 in 1750-1800, the Swedes managed to improve their mortality slowly but steadily

TABLE 9

DEATHS PER 1,000 POPULATION PER YEAR IN
SELECTED COUNTRIES, 1955-1972

Continent and country	1955-59	1970	1972
Anglo America			
Canada	8.1	7.3	7.4
United States	9.4	9.4	9.4
Latin America			
Chile	12.5	9.4	
Costa Rica	9.6	5.9	5.7
Uruguay	8.8	9.2	
Europe			
Austria	12.5	13.4	12.6
Belgium	11.9	12.4	12.0
Bulgaria	8.9	9.1	9.8
Denmark	9.1	9.8	10.2
Finland	9.1	9.4	9.5
France	11.8	10.6	10.6
Germany, East	12.4	14.1	13.8
Germany, West	11.0	12.1	11.8
Hungary	10.3	11.7	11.4
Italy	9.6	9.7	9.6
Netherlands	7.6	8.4	8.5
Norway	8.8	10.0	10.0
Poland	9.0	8.2	8.0
Spain	9.4	8.5	8.2
Sweden	9.6	9.9	10.4
Switzerland	9.9	9.1	8.7
United Kingdom	11.6	11.7	11.9
Yugoslavia	10.5	8.9	9.1

TABLE 9 (Continued)

DEATHS PER 1,000 POPULATION PER YEAR IN
SELECTED COUNTRIES, 1955-1972

Continent and country	1955-59	1970	1972
Asia			
India	22.8		
Israel	6.2	7.0	7.2
Japan	7.8	7.0	6.5
Malaysia (West)	11.3	7.3	
Africa			
Egypt	16.9	15.0	
South Africa			
Colored	16.1	14.3	
White	8.6	9.2	
Oceania			
Australia	8.8	9.1	8.5
New Zealand	9.1	8.8	8.5
U.S.S.R.	7.7	8.2	8.5

Source: Adapted from *Population Index,* Vol. XXXIX, No. 3, July 1973, pp. 478-481, 485-487; Vol. XL, No. 3, July 1974, pp. 600-603, 606-608.

until dipping below 10 in the middle of this century. Other Western European countries probably had similar performances, although evidence is fragmentary for the eighteenth century. Certainly, with nineteenth-century industrialization and improved production and distribution of food came lower death rates, to which the twentieth century offered additional benefits from medical and level-of-living improvements.

Another indicator of mortality is the life table and especially its prime statistic, the expectation of life. Table 10 reports the life expectancy for selected countries in various regions of the world. Clearly, the Biblically famous three-score-years-and-ten quota is being achieved in some nations and exceeded in Scandinavia. Many nations in Africa and Asia, however, are little more than half-way toward that goal — especially those countries that have too poor a statistical system to provide data for inclusion in this table.

TABLE 10
EXPECTATION OF LIFE AT VARIOUS AGES
FOR SELECTED COUNTRIES, 1950-1971

Continent and country	Years	Males			Females		
		Birth	Age 20	Age 60	Birth	Age 20	Age 60
Anglo America							
Canada	1965-67	68.8	51.5	16.8	75.2	57.4	20.6
United States	1969	66.8	48.4	15.8	64.3	56.3	20.3
White	1969	67.8	50.1	16.0	75.1	56.9	20.5
Nonwhite	1969	60.5	43.9	14.9	68.4	51.2	18.5
Latin America							
Chile	1969-70	60.5	47.3	15.5	66.0	52.7	18.0
Costa Rica	1962-64	61.9	51.1	17.0	64.8	53.0	18.2
Dominican Republic	1959-61	57.2	49.4	14.6	58.6	50.2	15.2
Ecuador	1961-63	51.0	46.2	14.9	53.7	48.1	16.6
El Salvador	1960-61	56.6	47.9	17.5	60.4	51.2	18.9
Guatemala	1963-65	48.3	43.2	14.8	49.7	44.6	14.7
Jamaica	1959-61	62.6	49.3	15.9	66.6	52.6	18.2
Mexico	1959-61	57.6	47.3	17.1	60.3	49.7	17.6
Panama	1960-61	57.6	49.0	16.1	60.9	51.3	18.5
Peru	1960-65	52.6	45.3	14.8	55.5	47.3	16.1
Uruguay	1963-64	65.5	50.0	15.9	71.6	55.5	19.5
Europe							
Austria	1971	66.6	49.6	15.2	73.7	56.0	19.0
Belgium	1959-63	67.7	50.3	15.5	73.5	55.5	18.7
Bulgaria	1965-67	68.8	52.4	16.8	72.7	55.6	18.6
Czechoslovakia	1969	66.2	49.0	14.6	73.2	55.3	18.4
Denmark	1969-70	70.8	52.8	17.1	75.7	57.2	20.4
Finland	1961-65	65.4	47.8	14.3	72.6	54.4	17.5
France	1970	68.6	50.6	16.2	76.1	57.6	20.8
Germany, East	1967-68	69.2	51.7	16.4	74.4	56.4	19.6

TABLE 10 (Continued)
EXPECTATION OF LIFE AT VARIOUS AGES
FOR SELECTED COUNTRIES, 1950-1971

Continent and country	Years	Males			Females		
		Birth	Age 20	Age 60	Birth	Age 20	Age 60
Germany, West	1966-68	67.6	50.3	15.3	73.6	55.7	18.9
Greece	1960-62	67.5	52.9	17.0	70.7	55.8	18.8
Hungary	1968	66.6	50.2	15.3	71.9	54.9	18.0
Iceland	1961-65	70.8	53.2	18.6	76.2	57.9	20.9
Ireland	1965-67	68.6	51.2	15.6	72.8	54.9	18.4
Italy	1964-67	67.9	51.6	16.4	73.4	56.4	19.5
Netherlands	1971	71.0	52.8	16.9	76.7	58.1	20.6
Norway	1961-65	71.0	53.3	17.6	76.0	57.7	20.1
Poland	1965-66	66.8	50.9	16.1	72.8	56.1	19.3
Portugal	1970	65.3	51.3	16.2	71.0	56.4	19.2
Romania	1968	65.5	51.4	16.3	69.8	54.8	18.2
Spain	1960	67.3	51.4	16.3	71.9	55.3	18.8
Sweden	1969	71.7	53.4	17.4	76.5	38.3	20.3
Switzerland	1960-70	69.2	51.6	16.3	75.0	56.9	19.6
United Kingdom							
England and Wales	1969-71	68.8	50.9	15.2	75.1	56.7	19.8
Northern Ireland	1969-71	67.8	50.3	15.1	73.7	55.7	19.0
Scotland	1969-71	67.1	49.4	14.6	73.4	55.2	18.8
Yugoslavia	1967-68	64.3	49.9	14.8	68.8	54.4	17.8
Asia							
Burma	1964	45.0	39.8	11.9	47.8	42.6	13.7
Hong Kong	1968	66.7	50.5	15.6	73.3	56.9	20.5
India	1951-60	41.9	37.0	11.8	40.6	35.6	13.0
Israel	1971	70.1	52.8	17.2	73.4	55.4	18.6
Japan	1968	69.0	51.2	15.9	74.3	55.9	19.2
Korea, South	1966	59.7	46.5	14.1	64.1	51.2	17.0

TABLE 10 (Continued)
EXPECTATION OF LIFE AT VARIOUS AGES
FOR SELECTED COUNTRIES, 1950-1971

Continent and country	Years	Males			Females		
		Birth	Age 20	Age 60	Birth	Age 20	Age 60
Malaysia (West)	1969	63.8	49.4	16.0	66.7	51.7	17.4
Pakistan	1962	53.7	47.8	15.6	48.8	42.8	15.5
Sri Lanka	1962-64	63.3	50.8	16.6	63.7	50.9	17.0
Taiwan	1970	66.1	49.4	15.0	71.2	54.0	18.0
Turkey	1966-67	52.5	48.0	15.3	56.3	50.7	17.5
Africa							
Egypt	1960	51.6	47.7	15.1	53.8	52.9	18.0
Kenya	1969	46.9	53.0	14.5	51.2	45.7	15.7
Nigeria	1965-66	37.2	39.2	12.5	36.7	38.1	12.4
South Africa							
Asiatic	1959-61	57.7	44.5	12.5	59.6	46.0	12.4
Colored	1959-61	49.6	43.0	13.8	54.3	47.4	15.9
White	1959-61	64.7	48.0	15.0	71.7	54.4	18.6
Southern Rhodesia							
European	1961-63	66.9	49.4	14.9	74.0	56.2	19.9
Upper Volta	1960-61	32.1	34.5	10.3	31.1	33.9	7.8
Zaire							
African	1950-52	37.6	34.4	10.6	40.0	36.3	12.3
Oceania							
Australia	1960-62	67.9	50.4	15.6	74.2	56.2	19.5
Fiji							
Fijian	1966	67.0	50.0	16.2	72.0	55.2	20.8
Indian	1966	65.0	48.4	15.6	67.0	50.4	16.3
New Zealand	1965-67	68.7	50.9	15.8	74.8	56.5	19.7
Western Samoa	1961-66	60.8	47.3	15.2	65.2	50.6	17.0

Source: Adapted from *Population Index,* Vol. XXXIX, No. 4, October 1973, pp. 549-557.

But where do we go from here? Clearly, the underdeveloped nations can sharply improve their death rates and drastically extend their expectation of life by copying — insofar as they are able — the ways of life of the industrial nations. But the latter have almost nowhere to go in mortality reduction unless they can diminish mortality at the oldest ages. In modern countries today, mortality already is quite low at all ages between one and 60, after which the mortality curve rises steeply. If the advanced nations are to push their expectation of life at birth to age 80 or 90, they must subdue the afflictions of age — the degenerative diseases that strike everyone who survives the communicable diseases of the young and adult ages. To date, there has been less progress than anticipation. Whether or when a large proportion of people will come to live 100 or more years is, of course, a question for the future.

Health Laws and Services

Pure food and drug laws have been enacted in many countries to protect the public from spoiled food, food preserved with poisonous substances, food diluted with cheap nonnutritious substances, drugs containing nothing more therapeutic than sugar or alcohol, drugs improperly or insufficiently tested, deceptive packaging, and false and misleading labeling and advertising. Such legislation in the United States is far weaker than that in European countries. The Federal Food and Drug Administration has a grossly inadequate budget, and related agencies such as the Federal Communications Commission are ineffective. Courts are not able to issue cease and desist orders until after the mischief has been done. But as Good King Wenceslaus said in 867 A.D.: "No law, no remedy."

Several million persons are engaged in occupations geared to improving the health of the people of the United States. Employed persons most directly involved consisted in 1971 of about 345,000 M.D.s, 15,000 osteopathic physicians, 97,000 dentists, 524,000 full-time nurses, and 224,000 part-time nurses. Their numbers per 100,000 population was 170 physicians (of both types), 48 dentists, and 361 nurses (both full- and part-time).[20] Wide regional variations exist, and cities generally are much better supplied than are rural areas.

Hospitals totaled 7,733 in 1971, of which 6,630 were general, and 1,103 specialized. Beds numbered 1,512,000, or 7.4 beds per 1,000 population — a decrease from 8.3 in 1967, 7.9 in 1968, 7.8 in 1969, and 7.6 in 1970. On an average day in 1971, these hospitals contained 773,000 patients, which means that of every 100,000 Americans, 3.8 were hospital in-patients. As with health personnel, the number of beds per 1,000 persons varied regionally, the highest numbers being 8.7 in the Middle Atlantic and 8.6 in New England, the lowest 5.9 in the Pacific states. State ratios varied from 9.9 in Massachusetts and South

Dakota to 4.9 in Idaho and 4.5 in Utah.[21] Of course, hospitals and beds are more numerous per capita in urban than in rural areas.

If all of this American medical expertise were marshalled fully effectively against disease, mortality and morbidity would be reduced. Actuaries have estimated the increase in life expectancy that would result from a 50 percent reduction in mortality from each of the major causes of death. The largest accomplishment from such a halving of mortality would stem from the heart and circulatory diseases, the half-elimination of which would add 6.5 years to the United States expectation of life. By comparison, the advantages of halving mortality induced by all other causes of death seem insignificant: reduction of cancer deaths by 50 percent would increase longevity by 1.2 years, followed by tuberculosis, 0.5 years; influenza and pneumonia, 0.3 years; motor vehicle accidents, 0.3 years; other accidents, 0.3 years; and other causes, 0.1 or less per disease.[22] Clearly, the two greatest killers are heart disease and cancer.

The Cost of Medical Care

Despite preventive efforts, people still get sick — and when they do, payment must be made to physicians and hospitals. Most industrial countries have adopted some form or other of socialized medicine; compulsory health insurance is in force in all European nations except Spain, all Latin American states, and several other countries, and complete socialized health care has been applied in Great Britain and elsewhere. The United States approach differs, based on group and individual medical insurance, prepayment plans operated by local medical societies, fees graduated according to ability to pay, free municipal clinics, medical examinations in public schools, and hospitals supported by government subsidy, private charity or patients' fees — a widely-assorted collection of procedures. The American Medical Association, the strongest labor union in the country, has consistently and energetically fought socialization of medical care, usually winning and, when loss cannot be avoided (as in the case of the Kaiser and Ross-Loos plans in Southern California), removing the tainted label "socialization" by clasping such group practices to their bosom. In 1950 the president of the American Medical Association opened his inaugural address by asserting:

> American medicine has become the blazing focal point in a fundamental struggle which may determine whether America remains free, or whether we are to become a Socialist State. .·. . But it is not just "socialized medicine" which they seek; that is only their first goal. Their real objective is to gain control over all fields of human endeavor. . . . I call upon every doctor in the United States, no matter how heavy the burdens of his practice may be, to dedicate himself, not only to the protection of the people's physical health, but also to the protection of our American way of life.[23]

Other opponents include some large business and industrial firms which campaign against socialized medicine but which, ironically, sometimes compel all their employees to have annual medical and semiannual dental examinations by the company's physicians and dentists at dates set by the company on company time in company offices, thus espousing "welfare business" while fighting the good fight against the "welfare state."

Between 1939 and 1946 Senator Wagner of New York introduced several bills seeking to add compulsory health insurance to the national social security system. These Wagner-Murray-Dingell bills called for medical care and disability payments for almost the entire labor force. They provided for free choice of physicians by the patient, physicians could work either on a fee or salary basis at their preference, and 1 to 2 percent of the insurance premiums were to be earmarked for medical education and research. None of these bills passed, and later efforts were unsuccessful until the Medicare Act of 1965.

Dissatisfaction with the rising costs of medical care is spreading through the United States. Public complaints allege soaring hospital and laboratory fees, increased tendencies for physicians to regard medicine as a way to get rich quick, refusal of physicians to make home calls in emergencies, preposterous mark-ups on drugs, and inflated charges when the patient has insurance coverage (thus driving up insurance rates).

But many families do not carry health insurance, and the ones who do are often disappointed to learn that the insurance covers only a portion of the expenses incurred. Home and office calls are frequently excluded from coverage, medications are usually excluded, dental care is omitted, and policies place maximum limits on the amount payable for specific conditions, operations, room charges, and so forth.

Many employers pay for half or all of this insurance as a fringe benefit; some even force employees to carry health insurance. A few communities are so thoroughly covered by voluntary but incomplete prepayment plans that there remains, except in cases of unusually large expenses, remarkably little practical difference between present programs and federal health insurance. The family doctor is becoming extinct, physicians work in groups and as employees, and their desks are littered with insurance reports. Patients, physicians, and hospital administrators often adopt one or another of the so-called welfare attitudes: if the insurance company is paying the bill, cost is no object, waste is meaningless, "they have plenty of money," and "I've got it coming to me."

In this wealthiest of all countries, with excellent medical facilities, hospitals are on the verge of bankruptcy, there is a critical shortage of physicians, crises arise over unethical practices of "ethical" drug companies, the physician-patient relationship is rapidly deteriorating into a business rather than a personal association, medical societies "run scared" before the gliding specter of socialism, and quacks remain uncontrolled in many states. In short, although we never had it so good, it can stand getting better, and we have to figure out how to pay for it. As Johnny Mercer and Frank Sinatra say, "Something's gotta give."

Mortality in Different Groups

These health care problems are not shared equally by all Americans. Nor is mortality the same for all groups. Differences in social status, occupational level, educational achievement, and income play important parts: as would be expected, the higher the social rank, occupational status, amount of education, and income, the lower is mortality; conversely, persons at the lowest ends of the status, work, education, and income scales have the highest mortality. Although readily understood to be undesirable, these socially induced mortality differentials at least are susceptible to change, for an individual can, in principle, get more schooling and thereby qualify for the better job that will raise his income and status.

Other group differentials are not so readily avoided. Mortality in the United States is higher among males than females, among the old than the young (exception: mortality is very high shortly after birth and decreases thereafter until reaching its lowest point at age 10, after which it rises with every additional year of age), and among blacks than whites. Although there is little we can do about the male-female and young-old differences, they do not bother us unduly because the former is not very large and the latter is accepted as an inescapable part of the aging process. But the black-white differential is widely deplored, and legitimately so, for the higher mortality of blacks smirches the national reputation by keeping the United States from joining the world's leaders in curbing mortality and, more importantly, by demonstrating that equality does not exist in what may be the most significant indicator of egalitarianism — the duration of life, or the ability to survive another year or twenty.

The magnitude of this differential and its impact on national mortality can be assessed by using the concept of "excess mortality" — the deaths that could be saved if the mortality of all persons were the same as that of white persons of high social class, occupation, education, and income. Kitagawa and Hauser calculated excess mortality for 1960 by adopting as a standard the age-specific death rates of white men and women of age 25 years and over who completed at least one year of college. In this manner they estimated an excess of 292,000 deaths — 92,000 males and 200,000 females. This represented 19 percent of all deaths of persons 25 or older — 17 percent among whites and 36 percent among nonwhites. [24] Blacks and Indians are especially hard hit by mortality differentials — "stark evidence of their underprivileged status in this nation. Moreover, the emergence of large mortality differentials by socioeconomic level within the nonwhite population suggests that much, if not all, of the excess mortality of blacks and Indians can be reduced with increases in levels of living and life styles."[25] Medical knowledge is not fully available to the lower socioeconomic classes and deprived ethnic groups. "Perhaps the most important next gain in mortality reduction is to be achieved through improved social-economic conditions rather than through increments to and application of biomedical knowledge."[26] Whether the United States ever will achieve sufficient equality of treatment among its various racial and social groups is questionable, only to be known by watching what happens in the future.

Infant and Maternal Deaths

In any country, one of the best measures of sanitation, health care, and level of living is infant mortality, which is particularly sensitive to the conditions under which life is lived by the general population. Infant and maternal mortality were quite high throughout the world during most of history, but many countries have reduced these rates dramatically in the twentieth century. Today there is little excuse — but always an explanation — for high perinatal (around birth) mortality or reproductive wastage. Such deaths truly are a waste, for most of them are preventable, and the emotional and economic costs are considerable. As the Vietnam military forces have produced extensive publicity for the term "waste" as an attempted euphemism for "kill," it is worth noting that the demographic use of "waste" has a long history and is restricted to deaths associated with the reproductive process.

In the United States, infant and maternal mortality was reduced sharply in the first half of the twentieth century: in fifty years the infant mortality rate was brought down to one-fourth of its 1900 level, and maternal mortality was reduced to merely one-tenth of its former level. Contributing to this improvement were "advances in medicine, the expansion and improvement of health facilities, the greater availability of medical and other health personnel, and aggressive action by public and private health and welfare agencies." At midcentury, public health officials were pleased with recent progress and optimistic about the future. Unfortunately their expectations were not fulfilled: during the 1950s there were even years in which infant mortality increased, "by 1965 it was possible to look back over a 15-year period in which there had been no sizable decrease in the infant mortality rate," and lack of significant change in maternal mortality also attracted concern, especially as certain segments of the population do not share in the generally low reproductive risks.[27] Fortunately these rates have begun to fall again in the 1970s, a trend which may or may not be continued throughout the decade.

In developing nations, perinatal mortality remains far higher than it should be — a condition that could be improved by introducing to all countries modern medical expertise, adequate diets for mothers and babies, improved community sanitation and personal hygiene, and greater knowledge by mothers of how to care for themselves while pregnant and for their babies following delivery. Under such conditions, any nation can make its maternal mortality rate very small, reduce the numbers of stillbirths and spontaneous abortions, and greatly reduce deaths during the first — and hardest — year of life.

NOTES

[1] Edmund Halley, "An Estimate of the Degrees of Mortality of Mankind," *Philosophical Transactions of the Royal Society of London*, Vol. XVII, 1693, pp. 596-610.

[2] Hans Zinsser, *Rats, Lice and History* (Boston: Little, Brown and Co., 1935).

[3] Samuel Pepys, *Diary* (London: G. Bell and Sons, 1924).

[4] Daniel Defoe, *A Journal of the Plague Year* (London: J. M. Dent and Sons, 1908), p. 93.

[5] John Graunt, *Natural and Political Observations Made Upon the Bills of Mortality*, London, 1662 (Baltimore: Johns Hopkins Press, 1939), table facing p. 80.

[6] Richard H. Shryock, *The Development of Modern Medicine* (New York: Alfred A. Knopf, 1947), p. 17.

[7] *Ibid.*, p. 40.

[8] *Ibid.*, p. 20.

[9] Martin Gardner, *Fads and Fallacies in the Name of Science* (New York: Dover Publications, 1957).

[10] Bernhard J. Stern, *Historical Sociology* (New York: The Citadel Press, 1959), pp. 345 and 347.

[11] *Ibid.*, pp. 362-363.

[12] Oliver Wendell Holmes, "The Contagiousness of Puerperal Fever," *New England Quarterly Journal for Medicine and Surgery*, Boston, 1843.

[13] Abraham Flexner, *Medical Education in the United States and Canada* (New York: Carnegie Fund for the Advancement of Teaching, 1910).

[14] David D. Rutstein, "The Cold-Cure Merry-Go-Round," *The Atlantic Monthly*, April 1957, p. 66.

[15] Walter Modell, "The Drug Explosion: On the Need for Self-control in the Introduction and Exploitation of New Drugs," *Clinical Pharmacology and Therapeutics*, Vol. II, No. 1, January-February, 1961, pp. 1-7.

[16] *Ibid.*, p. 3.

[17] *Ibid.*, p. 2.

[18] Samuel Zahl, "A Markov Process Model for Follow-Up Studies," *Human Biology*, Vol. XXVII, 1955, pp. 90-120; and Evelyn Fix and Jerzy Neyman, "A Simple Stochastic Model of Recovery, Relapse, Death, and Loss of Patients," *Human Biology*, Vol. XXIII, 1951, pp. 205-241.

[19] United Nations, *Report on the World Social Situation* (New York: 1957), pp. 29-30.

[20] U.S. National Center for Health Statistics, *Health Resources Statistics: Health Manpower and Health Facilities, 1972-73* (Washington: Government Printing Office, 1973), pp. 95, 185, and 216.

[21] *Ibid.*, pp. 356, 367-9, and 371.

[22] Metropolitan Life Insurance Company, "Gains from Reductions in Principal Causes of Death," *Statistical Bulletin*, Vol. XLIX, No. 7, July 1968, pp. 2-3.

[23] Elmer L. Henderson, "Medical Progress versus Political Medicine," *The Journal of the American Medical Association*, Vol. CXLIII, July 1, 1950, pp. 783-785.

[24] Evelyn M. Kitagawa and Philip M. Hauser, *Differential Mortality in the United States: A Study in Socioeconomic Epidemiology* (Cambridge: Harvard University Press, 1973), pp. 166-168.

[25] *Ibid.*, p. 179.

[26] *Ibid.*, p. 180.

[27] Sam Shapiro, Edward R. Schlesinger, Robert E. L. Nesbitt Jr., *Infant, Perinatal, Maternal, and Childhood Mortality in the United States* (Cambridge: Harvard University Press, 1968), p. v.

Chapter 10.   Migration Control

As natural increase is comprised of mortality and fertility, so net migration is the residuum after out-migration has been subtracted from in-migration. Volition plays a large part in migration, with reasons for moving as well as effects varying according to many factors: attributes of the person migrating, whether the move involves crossing a national boundary or altering the rural-urban distribution, cultural patterns and conflicts, and other mutable elements both of the individual and of his old and new environments.

Frederick Jackson Turner became famous for postulating that the character of the American people was formed by the presence of the frontier throughout so much of the nation's history. Others, including Everett Lee and George Pierson, argue that it was not the frontier, but rather the act of migrating, that was crucial. The geographic frontier, of course, was a temporary phenomenon, whereas mobility continues to characterize the American scene. Pierson claims that the American population was formed by immigration and is continually re-formed by internal migration, which supplies "a never-failing ozone of hope."[1]

The Measurement of Migration

Migration is troublesome to study, partly as a result of difficulties in defining what constitutes a migrant and the act of migration. A migrant is someone who moves, but not all persons who move are migrants. To be classified as a migrant, one must move across a boundary line to a different political unit. Also, one must make this move on a somewhat permanent basis; commuters are not migrants, nor are tourists.

The study of migration involves four subvariables: in, out, gross, and net migration. An in-migrant is a newly arriving person, whereas an out-migrant is someone who is leaving. If the move crosses an international boundary, the mover is called an emigrant as he leaves his country of origin and an immigrant as he enters his country of destination. If a man goes from Italy to Brazil, the Italian authorities regard him as an out-migrant or emigrant, while the Brazilians call him an in-migrant or immigrant. Gross migration is found by summing the total number of persons moving, whether outward or inward. Net migration is

174

the difference between in-migration and out-migration; if more people move in than out, the net number is positive, whereas if more people move out than in, net migration becomes negative. People moving in the same direction between the same two places constitute a stream.

For illustration, let us assume that 50 people move from Paris to Marseilles and 70 people move from Marseilles to Paris (and let us disregard all other movement in order to keep the illustration simple). From the standpoint of Paris, there are 70 in-migrants, 50 out-migrants, 120 gross migrants, and +20 net migrants. To the Mayor of Marseilles, there are 50 in-migrants, 70 out-migrants, 120 gross migrants, and −20 net migrants. There are two streams, one heading north and a smaller one going south. The inclusion of migrants to and from Versailles, Bordeaux, Chartres, Rome, and the Canary Isles adds more numbers and streams, but the principle remains the same. Gross migration may become quite large (say, 151,000 persons) while net migration remains quite small (say, 75,000 in-migrants minus 76,000 out-migrants, or a net of −1,000).

Sources of Data

Because migration involves these four subvariables, because it does not occur in a single place, because it is repeatable and reversible, and because demographers began serious study of migration only recently, both the collection and the analysis of migration data are weaker than that for mortality or fertility.[2] Consequently, we know less about migration than about the other two fundamental variables.

There are five ways to acquire migration statistics: by keeping a continuing record of the movement of every inhabitant; by recording moves when they occur; by interviewing people concerning their past moves or earlier residences; by a statistical procedure called the residual method; and by secondary use of other data. A continuing register is almost ideal, but it is very expensive, and only a few small countries maintain such detailed records. Observation of each move is ideal but has two inherent obstacles: it takes considerable alertness to locate a person crossing a border in a brief moment, and migrants sometimes conceal their move by claiming to be tourists or simply by evading all official notice. Asking people where they lived thirty or even three years ago opens up prospects of inaccurate and incomplete recall. Use of the demographic balancing equation (described in Chapter 1) to estimate the unknown residual, migration, is logically sound but nonetheless indirect and cumbersome. Occasionally demographers are able to secure migration data from sources that have no manifest connection with migration; examples of this secondary use of data that originally were collected for another purpose are the systematic culling of Federal Social Security records for changes of address, the customer service records of utility companies, and the smoking and residential histories of cancer sufferers. In sum, all methods have their weaknesses.

However they get their basic statistical material, demographers calculate rates. A migration rate shows the frequency with which migration occurs among a given group of persons. Unfortunately, setting up a simple fraction for a migration rate has two trouble spots: the numerator and the denominator. Problems in learning the number of migrants (the numerator) have just been summarized, but ascertaining the correct denominator (the base population) is not as easy as it seems.[3] Two places (and therefore two populations) are involved — the origin and the destination — and the time period (one year? five years? ten?) and distance traveled present complications. Migration rates for one year are bound to be smaller than those for ten years — but how do we allow for the difference? A ten-mile move is less consequential than a ten-thousand-mile transfer, and should be treated so in drawing conclusions.

In principle, the numerator should include all moves, but does a move across the street really mean anything? Should we, then, include only moves of a certain distance or across certain political boundaries? And to which year do we allocate an ocean voyage that starts in December and ends in January? One solution commonly used is to record lifetime migration by comparing present residence with place of birth. But some people move many times in their lives, so we prefer to have lifelong migration histories reporting every permanent change of address. And so it goes.

It might appear, from all that has been said, that practical analysis of migration is impossible, but such is not the case. There are partial or multiple answers to all of the above (and other, unmentioned) questions, and definitive answers to a few. But these answers are too lengthy for discussion here, and sometimes the mathematics becomes recondite. However, it is consoling to know that although the road to migration knowledge has many ruts, the path is traversable by a trained demographer.

Entry Into the United States

Many forces were responsible for sending Europeans from their land and bringing them into the United States. The unprecedented rise in European population was for some groups cataclysmic. From a population of 140 million in 1750, Europeans grew to about 190 million in 1800, 270 million in 1850, 400 million in 1900, and 450 million in 1950 — a growth that would have been even more rapid were it not for the emigration of perhaps 100 million Europeans to other continents. Where one person stood in 1750, two attempted to secure footing in 1850, and three in 1950. From this simple reckoning, and the fact that land cannot be stretched, one may deduce that either farmers must grow more food per acre or factory workers must produce enough to purchase from people of other continents the additional food necessary to fill the additional digestive tracts — or migration must take place.

Peasants' sons, finding no room in the fields or the village, migrated first to European cities in search of a livelihood and then, in many cases, on to America and other less crowded lands. Not that this movement was voluntary; far from it. But population and economic pressure impelled the old-world peasants out of their homes — and for those who eventually reached America, the trip was the most momentous experience of their lifetimes.

Peasants pushed from their farms first had to reach the seaport without enough money over a route they had never before traveled. Many had to beg for food along the way; usually they had to walk, plodding tiredly the dusty roads in summer or exposed to the chill winds of winter, and often tasting "the thin soup of charity." Those whose energy and initiative were equal to the heavy payment exacted by hunger, sickness, and an uncertain future struggled through to reach the unfamiliar and intimidating streets of the port cities. Once there, they gave up their dwindling resources to avaricious brokers and captains for the privilege of ocean passage on ships offering nonexistent sailing schedules, month-long crossings, rudimentary bathing and toilet facilities, steerage accommodations partitioned into "cabins" measuring ten by five by three feet, virtually no ventilation or heating, and the threat of cholera, dysentery, and "ship fever," which may have been anything. Harvard University historian Oscar Handlin reports that normal mortality during a crossing was about 10 percent, reaching close to 20 percent in 1847, a year in which on Grosse Isle near Quebec ten thousand Irish immigrants died, "three thousand so alone that their names were never known."[4]

The newly arrived farm emigrants reached for a new life and an immediate living within the factory system, for few of them could afford to buy or even work a farm in America. Instead they took unskilled jobs offered by the labor boss, an earlier immigrant who had learned English and met the incoming ships. There was periodic unemployment, pay was low and irregular, the new folkways were unsettling, and yet somehow enthusiasm prevailed. Life in the new land was often hard, but still not so hard as it might have been had a man remained with three brothers to divide the small farm of their father.

The result of all this movement was that immigrants, first from northwest Europe (the "old immigrants") and after 1880 from southern and eastern Europe (the "new immigrants"), came to the United States in large numbers, amounting since the initiation of federal record-keeping in 1820 to about 46 million persons, of which probably 35-40 million remained permanently — totals which make the United States the greatest immigrant-receiving nation in the history of the world. Official records show erratically increasing annual numbers of immigrants, with high points in 1850-1854 (probably resulting from the potato famine in Ireland and unrest in Germany), 1870-1873 (when laborers were brought in to build railroads through the west), 1880-1884 (another famine in Ireland and trouble in Germany), 1903-1914 (when American industrial expansion attracted unskilled and semi-skilled workers), and 1920-1924 (the resumption of immigration after World War I); low numbers of immigrants entered in 1861-1862 (because of the Civil War and economic depression), 1876-1879 (another depression in the United States), 1897-1898 (more hard times), 1915-1919 (World War I), and 1932-1945 (restrictive laws, a worldwide depression, and World War II). The peak period by far was the decade immediately preceding World War I, when the number of entrants surpassed a million in each of six years — 1905, 1906, 1907, 1910, 1913, and 1914 — the maximum being 1,285,000 in 1907. Following enactment of restrictive legislation in 1921-1924, immigration fell to annual levels of 300,000 and below, dipping to nadirs of 23,000 in 1933 and 24,000 in 1943 and never reaching 100,000 in any year during the 1930s. From 1955 to 1965 some 250,000 to 300,000 aliens were admitted annually.[5]

Since 1965 new legislation has loosened up the immigration requirements and raised the annual average to about 400,000 immigrants by the mid-1970s. In 1973 the largest numbers were born in Mexico, 70,000; the Philippines, 31,000; and Cuba, Korea, and Italy at 22-24,000.[6] These official statistics do not fully report the number of entrants, for there are many illegal border crossings. Most illegal entrants supposedly are caught and deported (usually to Mexico, where nine-tenths of them originate), but many remain undiscovered. In every year of the 1970s the number of illegally entered aliens discovered by the Immigration and Naturalization Service has exceeded the number of legal immigrants.[7] The President's Commission on Population Growth and the American Future estimated in 1972 that there were one to two million illegal aliens residing in the United States, mostly men looking for jobs.[8]

The history of American immigration is shown in Figure 3. Of the total of 46 million official admissions in the last century and a half, 8.8 million entered in 1901-1910. In the 1930s, not only did few people arrive, but it was the only decade in United States history in which more people left than entered the country. Net outward moves occurred in the years 1932 through 1935.

Despite all these 46 million officially recorded immigrants, plus uncounted millions of illegal immigrants, migration has never, in the history of the United States, contributed as many persons to national growth as natural increase. Even in the peak immigrant-receiving decades of the 1880s and 1900s, natural increase outnumbered net migration by three to two. In other decades, it was simply "no contest."

The 1970 census reported 34 million residents of foreign stock (foreign-born or having one or both parents foreign-born), of which the largest numbers were, in order, Italian, German, Canadian, British, Polish, Mexican, Russian, and Irish.

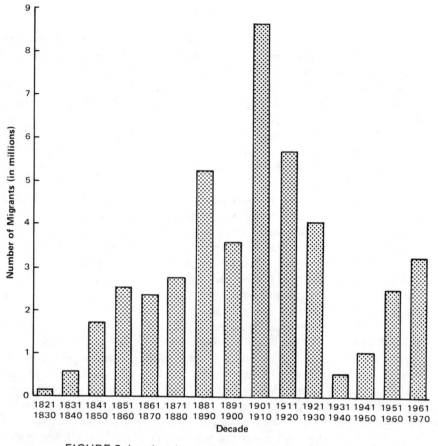

FIGURE 3. Immigration to the United States, 1821-1970

Source: U.S. Department of Justice, *1973 Annual Report of the Immigration and Naturalization Service* (Washington: Government Printing Office, 1974), p. 25.

Among them, 9.6 million were foreign-born (a decided decrease from the 14.3 million peak in 1930), of which one-seventh were from Italy. Both foreign stock and foreign-born are most frequent in New England and New York (where the proportion of foreign stock in 1970 was almost one-third and the foreign-born neared 10 percent); in contrast, fewer than one percent of the inhabitants of many southern states were born outside the United States, and five southern states are comprised of fewer than 2 percent residents of foreign stock. Whatever "melting" is taking place occurs principally in the West and Northeast, hardly at all in the Southeast, and very little in the Southwest.

The Brain Drain

A new hypothesis of melting has attracted considerable attention since the coining of the term *brain drain* in 1962: brainy people move toward attractive salary, interesting work, and pleasant living. As these desiderata are most frequently available in highly developed countries, that is where the highly trained, well-educated people migrate. In principle, there is nothing wrong with this, except that the places they leave are precisely the underdeveloped-but-making-every-effort-to-develop nations that most need their intellectual abilities and technological know-how. When an engineer leaves India for England, he benefits himself and his family considerably, the United Kingdom slightly, and India not at all.

In fact, the brain drain is not a new phenomenon, but rather a continued story that began in ancient times. As long as men have been able to change their residences, they have chosen to move toward opportunity, whether it be economic or intellectual, power or entertainment. The lures of ancient Athens, medieval Rome, nineteenth-century Paris, early-twentieth-century New York, and late twentieth-century Los Angeles are all well known. Equally familiar is the boredom of the boondocks. "Lots of bright people come from Ozark Junction — and the brighter they are, the faster they come."[9]

Circularity seems to be "the name of the game." The more intellectually gifted Pakistanis move to the United States, the more they send messages home relating opportunities and extending invitations; this results in even more of their compatriots leaving the home country in which they are so badly needed but so poorly paid, and moving to the United States which welcomes them luke-warmly but offers a higher level of living. In Pakistan, the absence of these technologists and scholars does nothing to promote economic development, and because the national developmental retardation continues and salaries remain low, other scientists are motivated to leave their "have-not" origins for the greener pastures of the "have" countries.

There is some exchange. Developed countries invite promising students to study and then return home as accomplished experts. And aid programs from industrial nations send their own experts to developing countries in an effort to build self-sufficiency into nations that otherwise could not "go it alone." Sometimes the high cost of living in an industrial country joins a lack of demand for high-level employees to push natives of developing nations back home, where they earn less but have more prestige and enjoy life more. But the net movement of trained manpower remains, as it has throughout human history, from the over-manned but under-educated developing areas to those cities and countries where the action is and where the rewards are most plentiful.

Immigration Restrictions

The fact that the number of foreign-born residents is decreasing is indicative of drastic changes in national immigration legislation over the past half century. From a traditional policy of admitting all aliens unless some individual flaw (such as a criminal record or mental illness) was discovered, the United States has been shifting to the policy that no alien shall be admitted unless there is some justification supporting his entry, although it has not yet and perhaps never will reach the extreme of barring all (or virtually all) aliens.

Restrictive laws date from the late nineteenth century, notably the Chinese Exclusion Act of 1882, the Gentlemen's Agreement with Japan of 1907, the Asiatic Barred Zone of 1917, the National Origins Quota Acts of 1921-1929, the McCarran-Walter Act of 1952, and its amendment in 1965; the years 1965 to 1968 constitute a transitional period of gradual supersession of the 1952 act by the 1965 amendment. Responding to an anti-foreignist popular sentiment expressed in vigorous and often abusive language by such militant Protestant organizations as the Know-Nothing Party of the 1850s and the Ku Klux Klan since 1915, these laws have been lauded as "keeping our doors ajar to worthy aliens and preventing the unworthy from approaching"[10] and attacked for being hostile to aliens: "Prospective immigrants must prove that they are not the bearers of contagious opinion, and even transient visitors are feared."[11]

Current United States Laws

The current laws are those enacted in 1952 and 1965. The two salient features of the Immigration and Nationality Act of 1952 are the refusal to admit naturalized citizens to all of the privileges of native-born citizens, and the continuance of national quotas begun in 1921. Under the latter provision, each country is granted a maximum number of annual immigrants, on the principle of holding a mirror before the American populace: each country's limit is determined by the proportion of present inhabitants of the United States originating from that country. In this fashion, assuming that each nation filled its annual quota every year, the ethnic composition of the United States would remain constant.

> The basic policy of the system is to grant to each group its fair share — no more and no less — of the permissible volume of annual quota immigration. Any other distribution of the quotas would, indeed, be discriminatory. One who objects to such an equitable distribution of immigration quotas must object to the ethnic composition of our population and must wish to alter it in favor of some particular group or groups.[12]

Of the 1952 total annual quota of 154,000 immigrants, 149,000 were allotted to Europe and 5,000 to the rest of the world; Great Britain alone was accorded 65,000. But not that many British wish and are able to enter: during 1953-1962 Great Britain used only 37 percent of its allotment, whereas nations given the minimum allotment of 100 — and also several other countries — used their entire amount. Thus these restrictions have failed to maintain the ethnic status quo, a circumstance which encourages some persons to advocate additional restrictions or at least to support this present "bulwark of our national solvency" and racial composition: "Our liberty and our free society, based upon a balance of the numbers and kinds of people in our country, can be drowned in a matter of years by a human tidal wave if the restrictions of the McCarran-Walter Immigration and Nationality Act of 1952 are destroyed."[13]

Opponents of the 1952 act contend that it is "the child of iniquitous prejudice and hysterical fear," giving "needless offense to many of our citizens and to the people of other countries," perpetuating a spirit of suspicion of immigrants, and rejecting the notion that the United States should accept all nationalities of people.[14] Although modified by the Displaced Persons Acts of 1948 and 1950 and the Refugee Act of 1953 and qualified from the start by not applying to nations of the Western Hemisphere and members of certain groups (for example, ministers), the national quota system remained in force until 1968 despite opposition from Presidents Truman, Eisenhower, Kennedy, and Johnson. In a 1965 message to Congress, President Johnson declared the national origins system "incompatible with our basic American tradition" and urged its replacement by a system assigning priorities on bases of occupational skills and family ties without regard for home country. "We must open opportunity to those in other lands seeking promise in America through a new immigration law based on the work a man can do . . . not on where he was born or how he spells his name."[15]

The 1965 law ended the national origins quotas by 1968 but did not eliminate the restriction of immigrants. The new legislation established a total quota of 290,000 immigrants annually, of which 120,000 are set aside for nations of the Western Hemisphere (previously these nations had not been subject to any quotas); the 170,000 annual quota for non-Western countries is slightly larger than the 154,000 permitted under the 1952 statute. Instead of national quotas, entrants are admitted on a first-come, first-served basis (although with an annual maximum of 20,000 from any single country) modified by family and occupational priorities. Principal beneficiaries of this abandonment of the country-by-country limits are immigrants from southern European, Asian, and African nations where former ceilings (frequently a token 100 persons a year) were far smaller than the numbers of people who wanted to enter the United States. The 1965 law set up preference categories, giving highest priority to children, spouses, and parents of United States citizens, and next highest priority to professional people and workers having occupations of which there is a shortage in the United States; refugees from communism or racial or religious persecution are also accorded preference. The 1965 law also does away with the rule that immigrants of Asian or Pacific extraction are charged against the quota of their ancestral lands even if they were born in Europe or elsewhere. The measure retains previously enacted safeguards against admission of people deemed undesirable for reasons of health, criminal records, poverty, or politics.

This latest law has not altered drastically the total number of immigrants, for the increase in the total quota almost equals the number of nonquota entrants previously admitted. The most distinguishing property of this legislation is the relatively even-handed treatment accorded potential immigrants from all countries, accepting newcomers according to their family ties and presumed occupational usefulness to the United States. No longer do northern European countries receive four-fifths of the annual allotments.

Whichever way immigration laws tend in the future, their application will probably seem, as in the past, capricious. Laws are overlapping, inconsistent, and internally contradictory, and thus subject to erratic policy changes and idiosyncratic interpretation by administrators. As Walter Hamilton quipped: "The legislature giveth and the legislature taketh away; blessed be the name of the legislature."

Motives and Directions

Whatever may be the direction and effectiveness of immigration and emigration laws — both of which show increasingly restrictive tendencies in most nations — the individual contemplating a move, either between countries or within a country, has his own reasons for going. Sometimes the motives are objective, sometimes subjective; sometimes simple but more often complex; sometimes known but frequently only partially understood. These incentives may operate either to push a person out of his present area (in which case he must decide where to go) or pull him into a new area (he then must decide whether to move at all). The individual makes an informal and often emotionally loaded comparison of his present residence with several potential other residences, an evaluation which easily becomes complex.[16]

For most people, migration is an act of courage. Since courage is not a universal trait, and since pressures and motives vary tremendously from individual to individual, those who migrate are not necessarily similar to those who do not. Compared with nonmigrants, persons who move tend more often to be young adults, male, and above average in physical condition, education, occupational skills, and ambition. International moves are additionally influenced by political and religious incentives, although both have been overemphasized by journalists and public school teachers anxious to promote the nationalistic conviction that the receiving country is vastly superior to all others. While some people did move to the United States in an attempt to secure religious or political tolerance, and a considerably smaller number actually practiced tolerance after their arrival, economic stimulus nearly always has been the major single motivation. There are migrants whose motives and directions are difficult to classify, and some seem to have an inner compulsion to keep on the move; their migration resembles the Brownian movement of minute solid particles suspended in a liquid, impelled hither and thither by the bombardment of the molecules.

Adjustment and Integration

Movement on this scale is bound to have serious repercussions, some good and some bad, affecting both the migrant and the sending and receiving areas. For example, where imbalances exist between the labor supply and the job supply, migration can be a corrective factor, improving the lot of the worker and his family and relieving unemployment in one region and underemployment in the other.

When a move carries a person from one culture to another, as often happens to international migrants, the newcomes may experience deep and prolonged disturbances, including especially a loss of confidence in his judgment because he is not yet sure of the social norms of the new group. An immigrant thus described his first years in the United States: "Whenever I decided on the spur of the moment I found myself out of sympathy with my environment. I did not feel as they felt and therefore I felt wrongly according to their standards. To act instinctively in an American fashion and manner was impossible, and I appeared slow and clumsy. The proverbial slowness of foreigners is largely due to this cause."[17] But in time these difficulties may be surmounted, and in many immigrants they never occur at all.

Not only the newcomer but also the native residents may be disturbed. Anti-foreign attitudes prevail in most countries, and when something occurs to inflame them, these attitudes may burst forth in violence such as the anti-Irish riots that occurred in New York in the 1850s or in the street mugging of Pakistanis and blacks in London in the 1970s. A 1971 sample survey in France disclosed uneasy acceptance of immigrants on the part of most segments of the French population, the only group with favorable attitudes toward foreigners being persons of high levels of education, implying that "knowledge and reflection temper instinctive reactions."[18]

Internal migration usually poses smaller obstacles to adjustment than international migration. But for certain internal migrant groups, acceptance in the new residence may be obstructed by cultural differences and local prejudices; blacks, Okies, Jews, American Indians, and other minorities are frequently rejected visibly and even ostentatiously. Sometimes the minority members themselves have difficulty controlling their own prejudices and imagine insults where none were intended. Competition for jobs and the supposed impact of minorities on local property values complicate the situation.

Chicago, New York, Los Angeles, and other American metropolises are the end-points of migration of rural southerners, categorized by older residents and police as clannish, dirty, suspicious of authority, and knife-happy. In turn the migrants are proud of their Anglo-Saxon heritage, spirit of independence, family solidarity, and religious fundamentalism. These bumptious native white Protestants form disorderly and delinquent minorities giving far more trouble, say many policemen, than the blacks, Orientals, Catholics, and foreigners they consider to be inferior.

Black Migration

One of these groups, the black population, is large (one-ninth of the national population), growing faster than the country as a whole, moving about relatively more frequently than the whites, and steadily recovering from a century-long condition of social discrimination — a set of facts that may be interrelated. Black migration may affect the pattern of race relations. Given their occupational and educational disadvantages, blacks are particularly vulnerable to unemployment in periods of recession and depression. By moving towards opportunity, they can improve their economic position. Moves into major urban centers, which generally offer a wider range of opportunity, should help to improve the educational and occupational level of the black population.

Such moves may also influence the acceptability of blacks by whites; studies of intergroup relations hint that prejudice decreases with increasing amounts of personal contact. Insofar as blacks migrate into areas that heretofore have been exclusively or principally white, both segregation and discriminatory attitudes may decline (though opponents of this view argue that overt conflict may increase). Invasion of white areas may create immediate conflict, but it could culminate in an eventual overall reduction of intergroup friction. A few scholars have suggested that as blacks move away from the South, racial tensions there will decrease; this dispersal hypothesis, however, has not been substantiated so far by empirical observations. Black movement out of the South will certainly spread out the nonwhite population nationally; the percentage of blacks in each state should thus become more uniform than at present. At the least, the high proportion of blacks in Mississippi, South Carolina, and other states of the deep

South should decline to fractions that may present less of a threat to the white majority. Also, blacks stand to gain by avoiding the traditionally discriminatory mores and folkways of the South.

Reasoning of this sort prompted Gunnar Myrdal, the author of the foremost study of race relations in the United States, to suggest a migration policy for blacks. He proposed a labor information service and a federal program of assisting blacks to get to the places where their employment opportunities are greatest, including particularly the possibility of encouraging southern blacks to settle in the smaller northern cities where the black population is small or nonexistent.[19]

A Look at the Future

Most nations are enacting increasingly restrictive migration laws, and persons hoping for removal or reduction of these limitations seem likely to be disappointed. In response, some writers advocate a strong international authority promoting migration; while some migration effort is expended through the International Labour Office, it arouses dissatisfaction on three counts: it is officially and essentially a labor rather than a migration organization; its powers are advisory only; and it lacks sufficient funds and manpower to perform the needed functions. Hence the I.L.O. is unable to do the two jobs than an international migration authority might do: to supply accurate and detailed information about employment opportunities and levels of living in various areas to potential migrants at no cost, and to try to liberalize emigration and immigration restrictions.

Except for the European movement to the Americas and Oceania, international migration has to date had little influence on the distribution of people throughout the world, for the reason that natural increase is normally far larger than the number of migrants. Nor is this fact likely to change in the near future. Nations faced with a pressure of population growth against available resources can expect little relief from emigration; what other nation or nations would accept India's annual increment of fifteen million, let alone China's fifteen million − or for that matter, the three to four million annual growth of Bangladesh or Indonesia? Thus, except for very small nations, emigration cannot serve even as an effective palliative for growing pains, and the only permanent solution seems to lie in economic development coupled with control over natural increase − aided in some countries by internal redistribution of population, for internal migration exerts an impact on production, unemployment, and education.

As for the United States, existing streams of internal migration seem almost certain to deepen and widen, including the westward flow, the rural-to-urban flow, suburbanization, the flight of blacks from the South, and interurban migration. Noneconomic motives should become increasingly important as larger numbers of people in this affluent nation can afford the luxury of living not where they have to in order to make a living, but where they want to be to enjoy their favorite weather, scenery, and forms of recreation.

Migratory currents, however, are subject to large and only partially predictable fluctuations and even reversals, making migration the most difficult of the three basic demographic variables to forecast. Unforeseeable economic, political, and legislative events are capable of inducing abrupt alterations in streams of migration, both internal and international. On the other hand, mortality changes can be foreseen more accurately, for there is a basic minimum mortality lending stability to death rates, and since all societies ordinarily strive consistently to minimize the frequency of sickness and death, mortality rates depend relatively little on the vicissitudes of fortune and fashion. Intermediate in predictability is fertility, which is more responsive to alterations in attitudes and conditions of life than mortality, but not so much so as migration, which of the three variables comes closest to being voluntary for most people. Although circumstance may influence the numbers of births, procreational attitudes tend to be modified slowly; hence large changes in the birth rate rarely occur in less than a generation, a fact lending confidence to estimates of natality over a decade or two. In any nation, both fertility and mortality — and, to a far lesser degree, migration — are powerfully affected by the age, sex, and other stable and somewhat predictable attributes of the inhabitants.

NOTES

[1] George W. Pierson, "The M-Factor in American History," in Franklin D. Scott (ed.), *World Migration in Modern Times* (Englewood Cliffs, N.J.: Prentice-Hall, 1968), pp. 51-57.

[2] Ralph Thomlinson, "Methodological Needs in Migration Research," *Population Review,* Vol. VI, No. 1, January 1962, pp. 59-64.

[3] Ralph Thomlinson, "The Determination of a Base Population for Computing Migration Rates," *Milbank Memorial Fund Quarterly,* Vol. XL, No. 3, July 1962, pp. 356-366.

[4] Oscar Handlin, *The Uprooted* (Boston: Little, Brown and Co., 1951), pp. 39-55.

[5] U.S. Department of Justice, *Annual Report of the Immigration and Naturalization Service: 1962* (Washington: Government Printing Office, 1963), p. 18.

[6] U.S. Department of Justice, *1973 Annual Report of the Immigration and Naturalization Service* (Washington: Government Printing Office, 1974), p. 3.

[7] *Ibid.,* p. 9.

[8] Commission on Population Growth and the American Future, *Population and the American Future* (Washington: Government Printing Office, 1972), p. 115.

[9] Robert C. Cook, "The 'Brain Drain': Fact or Fiction?," *Population Bulletin,* Vol. XXV, No. 3, June 1969, p. 57.

[10] Robert C. Alexander, "A Defense of the McCarran-Walter Act," *Law and Contemporary Problems,* Vol. XXI, No. 2, Spring 1956, p. 400.

[11] Alan Barth, *The Loyalty of Free Men* (New York: Viking Press, 1951), p. 193.

[12] Alexander, *op. cit.,* p. 387.

[13] American Committee on Immigration Policies, "Our Immigration Laws Protect You, Your Job, and Your Freedom" (Washington: 1964).

[14] Louis J. Jaffe, "The Philosophy of a New Immigration Law," *Law and Contemporary Problems,* Vol. XXI, No. 2, Spring 1956, pp. 358-375.

[15] Lyndon B. Johnson, State of the Union Message, January 4, 1965.

[16] Ralph Thomlinson, "A Model for Migration Analysis," *Journal of the American Statistical Association,* Vol. LVI, No. 295, September 1961, pp. 675-686.

[17] Robert E. Park and Harold A. Miller, *Old World Traits Transplanted* (New York: Harper & Brothers, 1921), p. 56.

[18] Alain Girard, "Attitudes des Francais à l'égard de l'immigration étrangère: enquête d'opinion publique," *Population,* Vol. XXVI, No. 5, September-October 1971, pp. 827-863.

[19] Gunnar Myrdal, *An American Dilemma* (New York: Harper & Brothers, 1944), pp. 198 and 387.

Photo by William L. Thomlinson

Men do the work of horses or fork-lift trucks
in Calcutta, India.

PART V. CORRELATES AND REMEDIES

An office seeker was asked by a belligerent listener at the end of his speech: "How do you stand on gambling?" He replied quickly: "I'm okay on that one. Are there any other questions?"

> *(Gilbert Geis, Not the Law's Business?, National Institute of Mental Health, Washington, 1972, p. 260.)*

Euphemism is the language of public policy.

> *(Charles F. Westoff, "The Commission on Population Growth and the American Future: Its Origins, Operations, and Aftermath," Population Index, Vol. XXXIX, No. 4, October 1973, p. 498.)*

Chapter 11.   The Structure of Population

EVERY population has both movement and structure. Movement or change occurs through births, deaths, and migration. Structure refers to the composition or characteristics — age, sex, race, nativity, religion, family, literacy, education, occupation, income, and so forth. These characteristics are pervasive cultural elements; all known societies set up differential rules governing the activities of males and females, young and old, and so on, usually supported by a biological rationale.

Sex Roles and Ratios

Most important of all demographic characteristics, partly because of physiological differences and partly because of the central functions they fulfill in continuance of the culture, are age and sex. "Arapesh women regularly carry heavier loads then men 'because of their heads are so much harder and stronger.' In some societies women do most of the manual labor; in others, as in the Marquesas, even cooking, housekeeping, and baby-tending are proper male occupations."[1]

In Western culture, Henry Adams noted a similarity of behavior between twelfth-century men and women, constituting a reversal in their way of thinking in comparison with his own nineteenth-century upbringing.

> The rule that such and such feelings or acts are permitted to one sex and forbidden to the other was not fully settled. . . . Men had the right to dissolve in tears, and women that of talking without prudery. . . . If we look at their intellectual level, the women appear distinctly superior. They are more serious, more subtle. . . . The women seem to have the habit of weighing their acts, of not yielding to momentary impressions.[2]

From a universal surplus of male babies over female babies amounting at birth to about 105 male to 100 female, the higher male mortality in the United States creates a progressive decline in the excess of males until age 18, when the two

192

sexes are approximately equal in number. From then on, the ratio of males to females steadily decreases, making it increasingly easy for men and difficult for women to find spouses — an imbalance in marital opportunity which becomes severe at older ages.

The sex ratio in the United States declines not only with age, but also through time. It has been declining throughout the twentieth century, going from 104 in 1900 to 97 in 1960 to 95 in 1970. Moreover, these ratios will become even lower in the future. For men, of course, the future may not seem so bleak.

Aging and Younging

One of the most striking changes in both United States and world population is aging: from a world proportion of an estimated 5 percent in 1970, persons over 65 years of age are expected to increase to 6 or 7 percent by the year 2000; in industrial nations, this percentage should rise from the current average of 9 to more than 11. The manner in which this dramatic change is taking place is shown by the population pyramids of Figure 4. The broad base and sharply sloping sides of Costa Rica's pyramid exemplify the traditional age distribution: the high fertility guarantees large numbers of children, and a high but declining mortality rapidly depletes the quantity of older persons. By contrast Sweden has a small fertility and a high survival rate — tendencies characteristic of the more advanced nations — and therefore a much older median age and a lower total proportion of people in dependent ages. The United States is intermediate; following a century of declining birth and death rates, the post-World War II rising birth rate and relatively unchanged death rate produced increased proportions of young people. The indentations in these United States and Sweden age-sex trees at ages 20-34 are consequences of the low natality rates during 1930-1944; also, Swedish fertility declined during the most recent decade.

The United States population is both aging and "younging." While the dominant trend throughout the nation's history has been one of aging, the temporary upsurge of fertility after World War II added a younging tendency. The 1960-1970 result of this combination of trends was a higher proportion of persons in both the youngest and oldest ages and decreasing proportions in the ages 30-39. This property of growing fastest at the two extremes of the age scale is new in United States history: the first census ever to record a decrease in the median age was in 1960. In the twentieth century the median age has changed as follows: 1900, 22.9 years; 1950, 30.2; 1960, 29.5; and 1970, 28.1.

This increase in both the aged and the very young is creating an increasing dependency ratio, which means that the working ages have larger numbers of "senior citizens" and children to support. The number of persons under 20 per

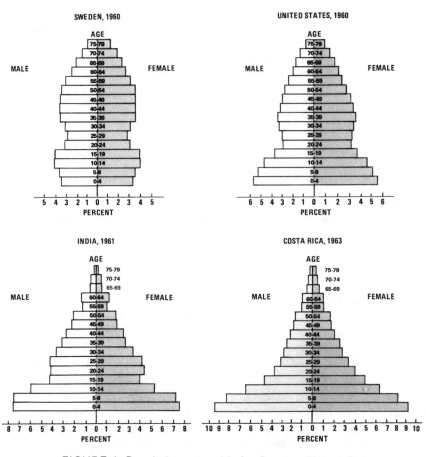

FIGURE 4. Population pyramids for Sweden, United States, India, and Costa Rica.

Source: Henry S. Shryock and Jacob S. Siegel, *The Methods and Materials of Demography* (Washington, D.C.: Government Printing Office, 1971), p. 240.

100 persons aged 20 through 64 decreased from 117 to 1850 to 86 in 1900, 59 in 1950, and thereafter increased to 72 in 1970. The number of persons aged 65 or more per 100 persons aged 20 to 64 increased from 6 in 1850 to 8 in 1900, 14 in 1950, and 19 in 1970. Increased numbers of young people provide a larger potential supply of juvenile delinquents, and greater numbers of aged enlarge other problems, notably use of leisure among the retired, family re-

sponsibility for the elderly, insurance and medical care, and problems of mental health.

This enlargement of the proportion of aged is not unique to the United States; it is common to all industrial nations. In fact several years ago the French national railroad system had fewer permanent active workers on the payroll than it had retired pensioners (but many workers retired before age 65), and countries like France, Sweden, and the United Kingdom may one day have 20 percent of their population older than 65. In these nations as in the United States, increasing attention is being paid to the question of how retired people shall use their leisure time and, if possible, how to make them feel wanted and useful despite the pervasive "youth cult." Not only do the years after retirement lengthen, but also the "empty nest" period is enlarging as children marry early and often leave home before their parents reach the age of 50.

Minority Groups

After the Emancipation Proclamation of 1863, blacks at first increased more slowly than whites, but in recent decades this trend has reversed. From an estimated 14 percent of the population in 1860, blacks declined to 10 percent in 1930, from which their natural increase brought them to 11 percent in 1970 — and a total of 23 million persons. It is probable that this percentage will climb further before the black birth rate drops to that of the whites. By the end of the century blacks may again reach 14 percent, and by the mid-twenty-first century they may constitute as much as 20 percent of the national populace — approximately the proportion of blacks at the founding of the United States. In redistributing themselves away from the South, blacks have gained a life expectancy and levels of education, occupation, and income slightly closer to those of whites.

Other racial minorities totaled a mere 1.4 percent in the 1970 census, which counted 793,000 American Indians, 591,000 Japanese, 435,000 Chinese, 343,000 Filipinos, and 720,000 other or unknown. Nearly all are predominantly urban, except for the Indians.

Each group tends to cluster in certain states. Nearly one-half of all Indians live in Oklahoma, Arizona, California, and New Mexico; totals range from 98,000 in Oklahoma to 229 in Vermont. Hawaii and California each has over 200,000 Japanese, whereas no other state has more than 20,000, and Vermont again brings up the rear with 134. The 170,000 Chinese in California are more than double the 81,000 in New York; only five states have more than 10,000, and South Dakota has only 163 (Vermont has 173). California and Hawaii together contain 232,000 Filipinos, leaving no other state with more than 14,000 and Vermont with only 53. Taking all racial groups together except the whites and blacks, their dominance in Hawaii is striking: 60 percent of the population of Hawaii is neither black nor white, as compared with 18 percent in Alaska, less than 10 percent in all other states, and a feeble 0.2 percent in Vermont and five southeastern states.

The distribution of blacks is less uneven. The 1970 census shows nine states to have over one million blacks — five in the South, three in the North, and California; New York leads with 2,169,000. Only one state has fewer than a thousand black residents: once again, Vermont, with 761. The picture is different by percentages, the six states that are more than 20 percent black all being in the South. No state has a black majority, although Mississippi achieves 37 percent. Lovers of consistency will be delighted to know that the two states having only 0.2 percent of their population black are South Dakota and Vermont. Other states under 1.0 percent are New Hampshire, Maine, and six states near South Dakota.

Not all minorities are racial, the most notable nonracial group being the 9 million persons of Spanish origin, of which 59 percent originated in Mexico. Seven-eights of all Mexican-Americans live in the four states bordering on Mexico (Texas, New Mexico, Arizona, and California) or the adjacent state of Colorado. Persons of Puerto Rican origin live principally in New York and New Jersey, and the cluster of Cubans in and near Miami, Florida, is familiar to newspaper readers. Spanish-origin families tend to have larger families than the national norm, and individuals have lower-than-average educational level, income, occupational status, and ability to speak English. Most are of foreign stock, and nearly all are better off financially then their relatives in Mexico or other Latin American countries.

The indigenous population of American Indians has fared less well. The long tradition of broken treaties and inhuman treatment is now giving way to city-ward relocation and scanty job training. Illiteracy has dropped from an estimated 55-60 percent in 1900 to about 10 percent in 1970, but Indians remain the least literate group in the nation. Many Indians continue their reservation life, although their rate of natural increase is so large that soon the reservations will not be able to hold them. What will happen then to these "wards of the government" no one can foretell, though we can be sure that the conversion of their value systems to time- and money-conscious ways of thinking will require considerable effort and personal reorientation. The once properly designated "vanishing Americans," who declined from a pre-Colombian population of a million to a quarter of that size at the end of the nineteenth century, have now recovered to the extent of being probably the fastest growing segment of the American population.

Although the decennial census makes no religious identification, nonetheless demographers know that about two-thirds of United States adults are Protestant (about half of whom are Baptist or Methodist), and about one-fourth are Roman

Catholic, leaving only a small remainder to be classified as Jewish, agnostic, atheistic, or other.

Since World War II church membership has increased, although in the mid-1960s there were portents of a decrease. Considerable doubt exists whether this religious revival represents true religious feeling or whether it constitutes enrollment in another social club. In the 1960s the First Baptist Church of Dallas, with twelve thousand members, developed a staff of fifty, a Sunday school of eighty-seven departments and over six hundred classes, a seven-story parking and recreational building containing a gymnasium, four bowling lanes, and a skating rink, and an operating budget exceeding a million dollars. Modern churches combine features of social welfare agencies, psychiatric clinics, and country clubs.

Regional Characteristics

Aside from age, sex, and race a number of other characteristics exert important influences on attitudes and behavior. Table 11 provides state figures for age, race, nativity, household size, and education. Many notions can be drawn from this table; here are some samples.

Few states vary far from the national average of 34 percent children, but in Utah and New Mexico, 4 of every 10 persons are under age 18. Alaska, Hawaii, and Nevada have the smallest percentages of aged (at a remarkable 2.3, 5.7, and 6.3 percent, respectively), whereas Florida is far to the other extreme with 14.6, well beyond the 12.4 percent of the next-oldest states. The distribution of blacks and other nonwhites varies tremendously, ranging from less than one percent in the three states in the northeast corner all the way to 37 percent in Mississippi and 61 percent in Hawaii (the District of Columbia is a special case, being entirely urban).

Foreign-born residents are in greatest proportion in New York, amounting to one out of every nine persons, but are so scarce in the South as to number only one person of 200 in several states. Household size, like youth, is fairly uniform, except for Hawaii and Alaska. The national educational norm of 12 years completed also is remarkably uniformly spread about the country, although Kentucky and a few other southern states manage to dip below par.

TABLE 11

SELECTED BIOLOGICAL AND SOCIAL CHARACTERISTICS BY STATE, UNITED STATES, 1970

State	Percent under age 18	Percent age 65 and over	Percent black and other nonwhite	Percent foreign born	Persons per household	Median years of school completed, age 25 and over
United States	34.3	9.9	12.5	4.7	3.11	12.1
New England						
Maine	34.7	11.6	0.7	4.3	3.16	12.1
New Hampshire	34.5	10.6	0.6	5.0	3.14	12.2
Vermont	35.3	10.7	0.4	4.2	3.21	12.2
Massachusetts	33.0	11.2	3.7	8.7	3.12	12.2
Rhode Island	31.7	11.0	3.4	7.8	3.07	11.5
Connecticut	33.7	9.5	6.5	8.6	3.16	12.2
Middle Atlantic						
New York	32.0	10.8	13.2	11.6	3.01	12.1
New Jersey	33.3	9.7	11.4	8.9	3.17	12.1
Pennsylvania	32.6	10.8	9.0	3.8	3.10	12.0
East North Central						
Ohio	35.1	9.4	9.4	3.0	3.16	12.1
Indiana	35.4	9.5	7.2	1.6	3.14	12.1

198

TABLE 11 (Continued)

SELECTED BIOLOGICAL AND SOCIAL CHARACTERISTICS BY STATE, UNITED STATES, 1970

State	Percent under age 18	Percent age 65 and over	Percent black and other nonwhite	Percent foreign born	Persons per household	Median years of school completed, age 25 and over
Illinois	34.2	9.8	13.6	5.7	3.09	12.1
Michigan	36.6	8.5	11.7	4.8	3.27	12.1
Wisconsin	35.8	10.7	3.6	3.0	3.22	12.1
West North Central						
Minnesota	36.3	10.7	1.8	2.6	3.20	12.2
Iowa	34.5	12.4	1.5	1.4	3.05	12.2
Missouri	33.2	12.0	10.7	1.4	2.98	11.8
North Dakota	36.6	10.7	3.0	3.0	3.25	12.0
South Dakota	36.2	12.1	5.3	1.6	3.18	12.1
Nebraska	34.2	12.4	3.4	1.9	3.02	12.2
Kansas	33.2	11.8	5.5	1.2	2.97	12.3
South Atlantic						
Delaware	36.0	8.0	14.9	2.9	3.23	12.1
Maryland	35.2	7.6	18.5	3.2	3.25	12.1
District of Columbia	29.6	9.4	72.3	4.4	2.72	12.2

TABLE 11 (Continued)

SELECTED BIOLOGICAL AND SOCIAL CHARACTERISTICS BY STATE, UNITED STATES, 1970

State	Percent under age 18	Percent age 65 and over	Percent black and other nonwhite	Percent foreign born	Persons per household	Median years of school completed, age 25 and over
Virginia	34.2	7.9	19.1	1.6	3.20	11.7
West Virginia	33.3	11.1	4.1	1.0	3.12	10.6
North Carolina	34.6	8.1	23.2	0.6	3.24	10.6
South Carolina	36.9	7.4	30.7	0.6	3.39	10.5
Georgia	35.8	8.0	26.1	0.7	3.25	10.8
Florida	31.1	14.6	15.8	8.0	2.90	12.1
East South Central						
Kentucky	34.6	10.5	7.4	0.5	3.17	9.9
Tennessee	33.8	9.8	16.1	0.5	3.15	10.6
Alabama	35.8	9.5	26.4	0.5	3.25	10.8
Mississippi	38.1	10.0	37.2	0.4	3.39	10.7
West South Central						
Arkansas	34.1	12.4	18.6	0.4	3.05	10.5
Louisiana	38.1	8.4	30.2	1.1	3.37	10.8
Oklahoma	32.7	11.7	10.9	0.8	2.90	12.1
Texas	35.7	8.9	13.2	2.8	3.17	11.6

TABLE 11 (Continued)

SELECTED BIOLOGICAL AND SOCIAL CHARACTERISTICS BY STATE, UNITED STATES, 1970

State	Percent under age 18	Percent age 65 and over	Percent black and other nonwhite	Percent foreign born	Persons per household	Median years of school completed, age 25 and over
Mountain						
Montana	36.5	9.9	4.5	2.8	3.10	12.3
Idaho	36.9	9.5	1.9	1.8	3.17	12.3
Wyoming	36.1	9.1	2.8	2.1	3.09	12.4
Colorado	35.1	8.5	4.3	2.7	3.08	12.4
New Mexico	40.0	6.9	9.9	2.2	3.43	12.2
Arizona	36.4	9.1	9.4	4.3	3.20	12.3
Utah	40.0	7.3	2.6	2.8	3.46	12.5
Nevada	34.8	6.3	8.3	3.7	2.99	12.4
Pacific						
Washington	34.0	9.4	4.6	4.6	2.98	12.4
Oregon	33.4	10.8	2.8	3.2	2.94	12.3
California	33.3	9.0	11.0	8.8	2.95	12.4
Alaska	39.9	2.3	21.2	2.6	3.52	12.4
Hawaii	35.7	5.7	61.2	9.8	3.59	12.3

Source: U.S. Bureau of the Census, *1970 Census of Population,* "General Population Characteristics," PC(1)-B1; and "General Social and Economic Characteristics," PC(1)-C1 (Washington, D.C. Government Printing Office, 1972), p.292 and p. 468

Marriage and Divorce

The proportion of the population in the United States who ever marry is very great — almost 95 percent. The percentage of single persons in the age group 45-54 in the United States hovers about 8, as compared with 3 in India, 10 in France, 17 in Sweden, and a whopping 28 in Ireland, where deferral of marriage, which serves to control the birth rate, is carried to an unusual extreme in response to depressing economic and social conditions. The median age at first marriage in the United States is 23 among men and 21 among women — a decline from 26 and 22 at the turn of the century.

All this marrying plus a larger population and an increasing tendency toward residential separation of the generations has resulted in a considerable increase in the number of households (a household is a group of related or unrelated persons sharing living quarters and functioning as an economic unit) from 43 million in 1950 to 64 million in 1970 and 68 million in 1973 — an increase calling for extensive construction of new houses and apartments by a building industry which has justifiably established a reputation as one of the most sluggish and laggard industries in the nation. Since the household is the basic consumer unit, it is vitally important to manufacturers and retailers of milk, bread, automobiles, television sets, encyclopedias, and backyard swimming pools. More households mean expanded markets and busier factories; unfortunately they also contribute to shortages of certain services and commodities.

Not only the numbers but also the functions of American families are changing. While keeping the functions of procreation, child-rearing, status ascription, and affection, the family has largely (though not entirely) lost its former penetrating impact in the fields of education, recreation, religion, employment, and civic affairs. Clarification of this loss of functions is achieved by comparing the present limits of family influence with its areas of direct involvement a century ago. Americans no longer manufacture things as a family unit, fathers do not teach their sons their occupational skills, worship is rarely conducted in the home with a formal ceremony led by the father, leisure-time activities are individualized as each person goes off to his own interest group, marital vows are taken less seriously and marriages are more frequently dissolved, schools have taken over much of the home economics teaching of the mother, the family does not often act as a solid political unit, and parents have decreasing authority over their children. Only the personal functions remain strong — and there are sociologists who claim that personal functions alone will not sustain an institution.

The United States marriage rate is among the highest in the world, and its divorce rate also vies for world supremacy, though having to yield the highest ranking to Egypt. International comparison of divorce rates is very difficult, however, for regulations vary and legal fictions abound — for example, annulment, which is a judicial declaration that a marriage was void from the beginning, and therefore presumably that the marital partners had inadvertently been living in sin (the children, however, are not thereby proclaimed illegitimate). English and American divorce laws operate on the principle that divorce is granted to one spouse as a punishment for the wrongdoing of the other, but if both agree that they cannot get along with each other, the fact must be concealed legally because "collusion" is not permitted. This "contest theory" of divorce insists that one person must have clean hands, whereas the other must appear guilty. Note the word "appear"; actual guilt is not needed as long as the appearance will stand up in court. But it is obvious that the law is frequently used to accomplish the exact opposite of what it ostensibly supports. Perjury is so common that one might say that for each divorce granted there are two liars (the client and the lawyer) and two accomplices (the spouse and the judge). Most divorces are in fact not contested. Absurdity reached a height unusual even for the law in the case of the divorce granted upon testimony of the wife's sister that she saw the husband in bed in a hotel room with a blonde woman she did not recognize — but one wonders how she could fail to recognize the brunette wife and sister she had known from childhood, even though the wife-other woman was wearing a wig to save the cost of hiring a co-respondent.

Whatever is done about the law, the United States divorce rate has been increasing for a century and seems likely to continue its rise. This increased rate of marital dissolution is counterbalanced, however, by decreased numbers of marriages broken by death, as well as by the increasing tendency for divorced and widowed persons to remarry.

Educational Enrollment and Attainment

School enrollment also is rising. In October 1973 there were 59 million enrollees in schools of all levels, of which 15 million were in high school and 8 million in college.

The United States is one of the few countries economically secure enough to afford having a major portion of its adolescent and young adult labor supply thus removed from productive employment — a luxury advantageous for the long-run advancement of the country. The more people who pass through the educational system, the more we open up prospects of intellectual and technical expertise.

Educational achievement is improving, for among the population aged 25 years or older, the median years of school completed increased from 9.3 years in 1950 to 10.6 in 1960 and 12.1 in 1970. Both white and nonwhite residents of metropolitan areas attain more schooling than their counterparts in smaller communities, and the West has a somewhat better record than the Northeast and Midwest, which in turn are considerably above the South. Years of schooling fail to indicate how much one learns, but from other evidence it seems that differences in knowledge are in the same direction and if anything even greater, for teachers' salaries and average annual expenditures per pupil are high in New York and California and low in Mississippi and nearby states. A 1962 study comparing men aged 20 to 64 with their fathers also reveals substantial upward educational mobility: in one generation, high school graduates increased from 24 to 55 percent, college attendance improved from 10 to 26 percent, and median school years completed rose from 9.2 to 12.2.[3]

If present trends continue, by 1985 one-fifth of the men and one-tenth of the women 25 years of age and older will have completed four years of college, and the number of college graduates will rise from 8 million in 1960 to 20 million.[4] This commendable achievement, if continued, may in time make college graduation an accomplishment to be taken for granted by employers and hence something of a necessity for job-seekers, putting the poorly educated person at a further disadvantage.

College Education

Whatever else results from completing various levels of education, it seems certain that two present advantages of education will remain. Primarily, education puts a person more in touch with the intellectual phenomena of the world, more able to understand the causes and consequences of the events that take place around him, more appreciative of music, science, and literature — or, if he takes specialized courses, more attuned to accounting or airplane design or underwater archaeology.

A second benefit is money. A 1973 census bureau study showed that each level of education brought increased income. Among men aged 25 years or more, elementary school graduates earned a median income of $6,800 a year, high school graduates made $10,400, college graduates received $15,300, and those with some graduate training made $17,300. Over a lifetime, earnings from age 18 to death totaled an average of $345,000 for elementary school graduates, $479,000 among high school graduates, $711,000 for college graduates, and $824,000 for men who had completed at least one year of graduate work.[5] The message should be clear: if you want money, one way to get it is through further education. Of course, these averages hide gross variations: some college graduates fail to make a living, and some grade-school drop-outs become millionaires. But next to high intelligence, driving ambition, and the ability to work longer hours than the guy next door, another year of school may get the best results.

On the college level, the reputation of the diploma is determined by the amount of learning that people believe it represents; consequently, there are both practical and intellectual reasons for choosing a first-rate college. The quality of a university depends on many things, and no one institution is first in everything. Yet there are carefully researched statistics reporting the accomplishments of graduates, the quality of professors, and the amplitude of library and other facilities. A multidimensional rating scale developed by the author for 1948 through 1974 yields the following ranking of American institutions of higher learning:

1. Harvard University (Massachusetts)
2. University of Chicago (Illinois)
3. University of California, Berkeley
4. Columbia University (New York)
5. Princeton University (New Jersey)
6. Yale University (Connecticut)
7. University of Michigan, Ann Arbor
8. Massachusetts Institute of Technology, Cambridge
9. University of California, Los Angeles
10. California Institute of Technology, Pasadena
11. Stanford University (California)
12. University of Wisconsin, Madison
13. Cornell University (New York)
14. University of Pennsylvania, Philadelphia
15. Oberlin College (Ohio)
16. Swarthmore College (Pennsylvania)
17. University of North Carolina, Chapel Hill
18. Johns Hopkins University (Maryland)
19. Brown University (Rhode Island)
20. University of Washington, Seattle

Of these 20, nine are in the Northeast, five in the West, four in the Midwest, and only two in the South.

Achieving World Literacy

An American high school student selecting a college is fortunate, for already he is far beyond the educational level that anyone could reasonably expect if he — and especially she — lived in a developing country. In much of the world, learning how to read and write is a commendable accomplishment, for even today only about two-thirds of the people of the world know how to read simple sentences in any language, and in Africa and southern Asia, a majority of adults cannot write or read. In some countries, the proportion literate is as low as one person in ten.

Yet these static statistics, however far from flattering they may be, understate the problem, for the number of illiterates in the world is growing larger. In view of all the efforts that are being expended on teaching the world's peoples how to read, such a result is perturbing. To look at the bright side, the percentage of illiterates in the world is decreasing; unfortunately, the world's population is increasing faster than illiteracy is decreasing. Evidently this is an *Alice in Wonderland* situation in which one keeps even by running, gains only by sprinting twice as fast, and loses ground if one merely walks.

How can we do better? One obstacle is that farmers traditionally repulse the notion of taking their children away from the hoe to attend school. But this conviction is changing, as parents in all nations come to recognize that the road to prosperity is paved with alphabet blocks. Similarly, governments now see that no investment pays off better in the long run than does money spent on schools; regrettably, some leaders are compelled to feed their people today, build houses tomorrow, and pave roads on Thursday; the next generation is a long way off.

Nonetheless, the next generation will arrive. And a reasonable proportion of the children must go to school if the nation is not to founder. The problem is how to send increasing proportions of children to school, especially as a high birth rate ensures that there are more children every year. This dual demand on the educational system has been studied by Gavin Jones from his experience in several developing countries, and the conclusions are not encouraging: for a typical developing nation, it is difficult to increase the proportion of children attending school unless fertility declines fairly rapidly, and if fertility does not decline at all, the costs of providing schooling for additional children become almost impossible to bear.[6]

Work and Leisure

In the United States the labor force is changing regarding the number of jobs, ages of workers, number of working women, length of the work week, income, and various folkways. Some economic statistics from the 1970 census are supplied in Table 12. In most states, there are three nonworkers for every two workers. Unemployment varies from 2.7 percent in Nebraska, which is about as low as unemployment rates get, to 9.2 percent in Alaska, which means that one of every eleven work-seekers is disappointed. The percentage of workers who are in manufacturing tells something of the economic base of each state: when, as in Nevada, Wyoming, and New Mexico, that proportion is below 7 percent, it is clear that the state's workers engage primarily in farming or other extractive activities. Although the ratio of white to blue collar persons has a long-run rising trend, it still is about 50-50. Incomes in Mississippi and Arkansas are a thousand dollars below those of any other state, including even Alabama; on the other hand, people in Alaska do rather well. One-tenth of the nation's families have incomes below the officially designated poverty level, and these low-income families are even more numerous in southern states. There should be some comfort in Mississippi, however, for it costs less to live there.

The work week has shortened from an average of 70 hours in 1850 and 60 in

1900 to 40 hours in 1950 and 37 in 1970, and 35- and even 30-hour weeks are now to be found. Although at first glance this appears to be an unalloyed benefit, the question of what to do with the resultant leisure time is coming to be regarded as a problem. An ironic circumstance is that some wage-earners are taking advantage of the shorter working hours to obtain additional employment. Consider a day in the life of such a man: from nine to five he works in the office; at quitting time he races to his car and inches through rush-hour traffic to his evening job at the Texaco Station or Sears Roebuck; on week-ends he sells swimming pools. By giving up most of his leisure time the moonlighter is able to drive a Buick instead of a Chevrolet and to keep up the payments on a magenta refrigerator with revolving shelves, plus a power mower to save time in cutting the lawn.

The blessings of leisure are not enjoyed equally by all segments of the population: children and the aged share copious leisure time, sometimes even complaining that they have too much of it. Men who have organized their days around work for all their adult lives often lack enough avocational interests to keep from suddenly feeling old; the tale of the heretofore healthy man who has a heart attack a few months after retirement has become a cliché. More than a century ago Charles Lamb wrote of being overwhelmed by retirement: "Let me caution persons grown old in active business, not lightly, not without weighting their own resources, to forego their customary employment all at once, for there may be danger in it." In addition to being unable to amuse ourselves all day long, Americans are beset by moral qualms, often regarding enjoyment for its own sake as improper and perhaps even degenerate. Interiorization of the Portestant Ethic compels us to justify recreation by insisting that it makes us work better when we return to that more worthwhile pursuit; people should be refreshed *for* work, not *from* work. "The puritan treats himself as if he were a firm and, at the same time, the firm's auditor. . ., Leisure is defined as a permissive residue left over from the demands of worktime. . . . For the prestige of work operates as a badge entitling the holder to draw on the society's idleness fund."[8] If leisure is a problem now, what will life be like when automation takes over?

Americans still cling to the folkway traditional to their own culture, but not to all others, that all able-bodied men must have gainful occupations in order to be considered respectable; full-time coupon clippers are ostentatiously pitied because they have never had to buckle down to work in order to keep from starving, and therefore they do not really know the value of a dollar. Many rate a man in terms of how much money he can earn: a $20,000-a-year man is twice as good as a $10,000-a-year man. Adolescents are socialized to this principle by their parents and peers, and money is often cherished more for its evaluative function ("How good am I? Why, $24,000 good, that's how good!") than for the necessities and luxuries it can buy.

TABLE 12

SELECTED ECONOMIC CHARACTERISTICS BY STATE, UNITED STATES, 1970

State	Nonworker-worker ratio	Percent of civilian labor force unemployed	Percent of employed persons in manufacturing	Percent of employed persons in white collar	Median family income in dollars	Percent of families with income less than poverty level
United States	1.45	4.4	25.9	48.2	9,590	10.7
New England						
Maine	1.50	4.2	31.6	40.7	8,205	10.3
New Hampshire	1.35	3.5	35.5	44.6	9,698	6.7
Vermont	1.50	4.1	23.9	46.2	8,929	9.1
Massachusetts	1.33	3.8	29.2	52.7	10,835	6.2
Rhode Island	1.25	4.0	35.1	45.2	9,736	8.5
Connecticut	1.29	3.5	34.8	52.5	11,811	5.3
Middle Atlantic						
New York	1.43	4.0	24.2	55.2	10,617	8.5
New Jersey	1.35	3.8	32.0	52.7	11,407	6.1
Pennsylvania	1.47	3.7	34.1	45.1	9,558	7.9
East North Central						
Ohio	1.48	4.0	35.6	45.4	10,313	7.6
Indiana	1.43	4.1	35.9	42.1	9,970	7.4

TABLE 12 (Continued)

SELECTED ECONOMIC CHARACTERISTICS BY STATE, UNITED STATES, 1970

State	Nonworker-worker ratio	Percent of civilian labor force unemployed	Percent of employed persons in manufacturing	Percent of employed persons in white collar	Median family income in dollars	Percent of families with income less than poverty level
Illinois	1.37	3.7	30.3	49.1	10,959	7.7
Michigan	1.52	5.9	35.9	44.9	11,032	7.3
Wisconsin	1.45	4.0	31.0	43.3	10,068	7.4
West North Central						
Minnesota	1.44	4.2	21.1	48.5	9,931	8.2
Iowa	1.46	3.5	20.0	42.9	9,018	8.9
Missouri	1.46	4.2	24.4	46.9	8,914	11.5
North Dakota	1.70	4.6	4.7	42.5	7,838	12.4
South Dakota	1.56	3.7	7.4	41.1	7,494	14.8
Nebraska	1.41	2.7	13.7	44.4	8,564	10.1
Kansas	1.40	3.9	17.4	47.8	8,693	9.7
South Atlantic						
Delaware	1.41	3.8	29.7	51.0	10,211	8.2
Maryland	1.35	3.2	19.5	55.8	11,063	7.7
District of Columbia	1.11	3.8	4.9	57.9	9,583	12.7

TABLE 12 (Continued)

SELECTED ECONOMIC CHARACTERISTICS BY STATE, UNITED STATES, 1970

State	Nonworker-worker ratio	Percent of civilian labor force unemployed	Percent of employed persons in manufacturing	Percent of employed persons in white collar	Median family income in dollars	Percent of families with income less than poverty level
Virginia	1.38	3.0	22.4	49.0	9,049	12.3
West Virginia	1.98	5.1	23.2	40.4	7,415	18.0
North Carolina	1.34	3.4	35.5	38.6	7,774	16.3
South Carolina	1.42	3.8	36.2	37.3	7,621	19.0
Georgia	1.41	3.2	27.2	43.7	8,167	16.7
Florida	1.56	3.8	14.1	49.8	8,267	12.7
East South Central						
Kentucky	1.70	4.6	25.6	40.2	7,441	19.2
Tennessee	1.51	4.4	30.6	41.5	7,447	18.2
Alabama	1.67	4.5	28.6	40.7	7,266	20.7
Mississippi	1.82	5.0	25.9	38.6	6,071	28.9
West South Central						
Arkansas	1.73	5.7	26.1	39.0	6,273	22.8
Louisiana	1.86	5.4	15.9	45.2	7,530	21.5
Oklahoma	1.52	4.2	15.8	47.9	7,725	15.0
Texas	1.48	3.6	18.5	48.5	8,490	14.6

TABLE 12 (Continued)

SELECTED ECONOMIC CHARACTERISTICS BY STATE, UNITED STATES, 1970

State	Nonworker-worker ratio	Percent of civilian labor force unemployed	Percent of employed persons in manufacturing	Percent of employed persons in white collar	Median family income in dollars	Percent of families with income less than poverty level
Mountain						
Montana	1.56	6.2	9.7	45.3	8,512	10.4
Idaho	1.53	5.2	14.7	43.1	8,381	10.9
Wyoming	1.46	4.8	6.4	46.4	8.943	9.3
Colorado	1.39	4.2	14.6	53.9	9,555	9.1
New Mexico	1.80	5.7	6.8	51.5	7,849	18.5
Arizona	1.62	4.2	15.6	51.2	9,187	11.5
Utah	1.58	5.2	14.5	51.9	9,320	9.1
Nevada	1.21	5.4	5.2	47.1	10,692	7.0
Pacific						
Washington	1.40	7.9	21.6	50.7	10,407	7.6
Oregon	1.45	7.0	21.4	48.3	9,489	8.6
California	1.37	6.3	21.6	54.4	10,732	8.4
Alaska	1.28	9.2	7.1	55.3	12,443	9.3
Hawaii	1.22	3.0	10.9	49.9	11,554	7.6

Source: U.S. Bureau of the Census, *1970 Census of Population,* "General Social and Economic Characteristics: United States Summary," PC (1) - C1, (Washington D.C. Government Printing Office, 1972, p. 469.

211

Women Who Work

A mainstream 1970s movement is women's liberation. Among other things, women demand to work on exactly equal bases with men, whether it be on high-rise structural steel or in professional tennis. Never in the history of the United States have all employers given equal opportunities to women, but they are coming to do so now.

Women are entering the job market in much larger quantities than in their mothers' and grandmothers' times. Today women constitute about one-third of the labor force, and more than half of female workers are married, as against one-seventh in 1890. Two other trends also emerging are a considerable increase in gainful work by mothers of children under 18, and greater acceptance of women in supervisory positions.

Systems of work are cultural and vary tremendously from one society to another. In most societies, nearly all adult males are expected to work. But the expectations regarding females are extremely varied. In industrial nations, many women work, often in order to help pay the rent on their city apartment. Predominantly agricultural countries, however, vary so much that generalization is impossible.

Countries in the Orient often have high rates of participation of women in the labor force. In Thailand, women farm, sell truck tires, and manage restaurants; often they also manage the family finances, handing out daily allowances to their husbands. A 1969 Thai government survey reported that 73 percent of all women of age 15 or older were in the labor force — that is, either working or trying to find work.[9] For ages 30 to 49, this percentage rose to 81[10] despite the fact that Thai women tend to continue to bear children through the end of their childbearing ages.

Female labor force participation rates are lower in Latin countries, but the extreme probably occurs in the Arab Middle East, where women rarely work at all outside the home. In some Muslim nations, women are still kept in purdah, requiring their husband's permission to go out, veiling themselves from head to foot except for the eyes and sometimes the nose. Traditional Muslim females are told to marry early and to satisfy all demands of their husbands and male children, which more or less compels them to stay at home. Farm women certainly work, first for their fathers and later for their husbands, but they are not "employed" and earn no salary. Only 8 percent of all nonagricultural jobs are held by women in Egypt and Syria; in Iraq, the percentage is 6.[11]

In the United States, increasing proportions of women are entering the labor force, and the traditional division of labor — certain jobs only for men, others only for women — is breaking down. The United States is heading toward equality of work, but whether women will soon come to hold 50 percent of all jobs is uncertain — and whether as many women as men will be in executive and supervisory positions is still more uncertain.

212

Income and Poverty

The median family income in the United States in 1972 was $11,100, nearly triple the median in 1952. However, rising consumer prices during this period ate up two-fifths of the gain, so that only three-fifths of the increase in dollar income could be converted into real income. Income is related to region of residence (highest in the West and lowest in the South), urbanization (lowest in farm families), age of head of family (highest at age 45), occupation (highest for physicians and bankers and lowest for laborers and service workers), and sex (lower for women).

The most attention-grabbing differential is that between whites and blacks. In 1972, white families averaged earnings of $11,500, but black families only made $6,900. Twenty years earlier, these medians were $4,100 among whites and $2,300 among nonwhites (who are nine-tenths black; unfortunately, separate data for blacks were not available for 1952). Although black incomes have risen slightly faster than those of whites, they remain far behind, averaging only about 60 percent of white incomes. This differential, as might be assumed, is greatest in the South.

Demographic properties frequently characterizing poor families are: head of family over 65 years of age, elementary school education only, nonwhite, unemployed, southern, rural farm, unskilled, frequently sick or disabled, and high fertility. After President Johnson pledged "unconditional war on poverty" in his State of the Union message on January 8, 1964, incomes below specified levels (which change from year to year and vary also according to family size) were declared too low. In 1972 some 24 million persons earned less than the officially determined minimum — a large number for a land of plenty. Table 12 shows variations among states as reported in the 1970 census. All too frequently, the poor are black: 29 percent of black families fell below the poverty line in 1972, as opposed to merely 7 percent of white families. While national leaders battle against poverty, we would do well to listen to the advice given by Pericles in 431 B.C.: "As for poverty, no one need be ashamed to admit it; the real shame is in not taking practical measures to escape it."[12]

Unfortunately the future is discouraging, because poverty families have exceptionally high fertility, thereby adding to their present financial woes and making it unlikely that their children will have the kind of upbringing that might ease their escape from the poverty environment. Not only individuals and families suffer from this combination of low income and high childbearing, but the nation suffers because its next generation is being so heavily supplied by these families, who are the least able to provide the material things that children need: good food, adequate housing, health care, sufficient education, and a chance at the kind of occupation that would provide enough salary to climb out of the poverty pit. This does not mean that children of poverty-level parents with large families are doomed to perpetuate a family tradition of insolvency;

what it does mean is that such children will have a harder (though not impossible) time making the grade to a comfortable existence.

NOTES

[1] Ralph Linton, *The Study of Man* (New York: D. Appleton-Century Co., 1936), pp. 116-117.

[2] L. Garreau, "Etat social de la France au temps des Croisades," 1899; quoted in Henry Adams, *Mont-Saint-Michel and Chartres* (New York: American Institute of Architects, 1913; republished New York: Doubleday Anchor, 1959), p. 216.

[3] U. S. Bureau of the Census, "Educational Change in a Generation: March 1962," *Current Population Reports*, Series P-20, No. 132, September 22, 1964.

[4] U. S. Bureau of the Census, "Projections of Educational Attainment in the United States: 1965 to 1985," *Current Population Reports*, Series P-25, No. 305, April 14, 1965.

[5] U. S. Bureau of the Census, "Annual Mean Income, Lifetime Income, and Educational Attainment of Men in the United States, for Selected Years, 1956 to 1972," *Current Population Reports*, Series P-60, No. 92, March 1974, pp. 2 and 6.

[6] Gavin W. Jones, "Effect of Population Change on the Attainment of Educational Goals in the Developing Countries," in Roger Revelle (ed.), *Rapid Population Growth* (Baltimore: Johns Hopkins Press, 1971), pp. 315-367.

[7] Charles Lamb, "The Superannuated Man," *The Last Essays of Elia* (London: 1833).

[8] David Riesman, Nathan Glazer, and, Reuel Denney, *The Lonely Crowd* (New Haven: Yale University Press, 1950), pp. 145 and 329.

[9] Ralph Thomlinson, *Thailand's Population: Facts, Trends, Problems, and Policies* (Bangkok: Thai Watana Panich Press Co., 1971; republished Winston-Salem, North Carolina: Wake Forest University, 1972), p. 39.

[10] Nibhon Debavalya, "Labor Force Composition of Thailand," *Journal of Social Sciences*, Vol. VIII, No. 1, January 1971, pp. 146-148.

[11] Nadia Haggag Youssef, *Women and Work in Developing Societies* (Berkeley: International Population and Urban Research, University of California, 1974), p. 20.

[12] Pericles, "Funeral Oration," in Thucydides, *History of the Peloponnesian War*, Vol. II, Chapter 40, c. 410-400 B.C.

Chapter 12.   National Policies

POOR people and impoverished lands stand to gain if they can successfully face "the world's second problem:"[1] keeping the sizes of families and nations sufficiently under control to permit enhancement of the pleasures that people are able to draw from their surroundings. But the enemy in this struggle must be recognized for what it is: not sheer quantity, but rather the rate of growth. And from the simple arithmetic of births minus deaths and the information in the preceding chapters, it is evident that the culprit responsible for this population explosion is not a higher fertility but a lowered mortality.

Still, this is a culprit we welcome, for with lower mortality comes release from the traditional daily expectation of death to oneself or one's fellows. Reduced mortality is central to a higher standard of living, which superficially means more and better food and appliances and trinkets, but which more importantly means more of the truly good things of life: health, knowledge, and freedoms of various kinds. So we certainly would be cutting off our nose to spite our face if we gave up lower mortality in order to remove the threat of overrapid increase.

That leaves fertility and migration as objects for national manipulation. Encouraging outward migration to other nations is more humane and politic than raising the death rate, but it is almost as unlikely a solution. For where would the emigrants go? Most prospective countries of destination are unreceptive, since many if not most of them are also worried about their own natural increase. And migration to outer space is not yet feasible either, for the blasting off to other planets or solar systems of only a single day's world increase is nothing more at present than science-fiction conjecture. While we are being fanciful and considering outward world migration, it might be well to point out the possibility of creatures from other worlds migrating here, thereby making demographic if not other matters far worse. To return to earthlings, the only remaining demographic solution (although nondemographic means are also available) is to decrease fertility, which is precisely what most contemporary national policies are attempting.

The Demand for Action

The unprecedented rate of population increase is bringing about two additional remarkable phenomena of our times — a growing inclination of private citizens to talk about manipulating the birth rate, and the institution of antinatal policies by national governments. Aversion toward such policies may stem from a conviction that growth is inherently desirable or from a belief that it is sacreligious to tamper with the mystery of the creation of life. It is now difficult to support the first view; hence current opposition to antinatal policies originates most often in religious beliefs — although adherents to those beliefs are not always willing to acknowledge their basis. Rather than relying straightforwardly on religious dogma, many persons seem to feel a compulsion to invent biological, economic, or geographical justifications. But if birth control is contrary to God's wishes, it should not be necessary to add the argument that science will surely find a way out of the bottleneck of humanity's numbers. Yet many of us seem to feel obliged to demonstrate that the alternative we perfer for fundamental religious reasons is also the most practical alternative; views that are supported by religious conviction must be efficient or economical.

Turning 180 degrees from the notion that in numbers there is divine grace and political strength to the idea that this growth is enchanted fruit, governmental and opinion leaders are spawning depressive population policies at a great rate. Although they have three demographic variables to choose from, the increasingly consistent trend is toward promoting birth control. Weapons are many: religious, technological, medical, social, and economic. Criticizing the popular Christian notion that sex is inherently evil, Bishop Pike pointed out that the American Episcopal Church deleted from the marriage office the statement: "With my body I thee worship," and complained that the "puritan pietistic atmosphere is such that we lost that fine direct statement about the goodness of sex in this relationship."[2] India's Prime Minister Nehru announced that one advantage of electrification might be the facilitation of other indoor sports than sex, and a former governor general of Ceylon advised introduction of electric lighting to counter population growth, quoting the ancient Chinese proverb: "He who goes to bed early to save candles begets twins." IUDs, sterilization, and abortion have been widely espoused in underdeveloped nations having low levels of literacy and income, the first two because they offer the advantage of a one-time procedure, and none of the three demanding much foresight or interference with the sexual act. Deferral of marriage by five years or a 15 percent decrease in the proportion marrying would probably cut the birth rate in countries like India by about 20 percent,[3] but the marriage practices of any society are closely bound up with other aspects of its culture and hence are not easy to alter.

The strongest of these anti-natality efforts are directed toward inhabitants of the have-not countries. The more fortunate underdeveloped areas are attempting to raise their level of living from subsistence to something approaching the freedom from want and even the luxury that is taken for granted in the United States; the less fortunate nations are trying to keep people alive, healthy, reasonably happy, and free from the constant nagging threat of undernourish-ment or starvation. These struggles for improvement amount to efforts to change the population-resources and population-real income ratios.

Three major policies are available and practicable in areas where population rise threatens to destroy the hope of a rising level of living: increasing agricul-tural productivity, industrializing, and decreasing fertility. Some nations are attempting all three; certainly no one alone is likely to suffice. To raise the living level of all people to that of the Western world will probably demand both adoption of family planning and enlargement of present production of food and industrial goods. This three-pronged program requires capital, firm leadership, and citizen co-operation — all of which are difficult to secure. The president of the International Bank for Reconstruction and Development said somberly: "Population growth threatens to nullify all our efforts to raise living standards in many of the poorer countries. We are coming to a situation in which the optimist will be the man who thinks that present living standards can be maintained. The pessimist will not look even for that."[4]

In the United States several state governments are concerned over urban sprawl — which inspired, for example, the California Environmental Quality Study Council to urge in 1970 a redistribution of the state's population by making sparsely populated areas more attractive to industry and people. Unoffi-cially, the California Depopulation Commission encourages people to settle elsewhere. To this end, Caldepop has proclaimed a "Florida Appreciation Month," planned a brochure called "Happiness in the Hollow States," endorsed the slogans "Progress Smogress" and "It's In To Stay Out," and commended Dean Martin for his moving rendition of "Goin' Back to Houston."

Zero Population Growth

The most attention-getting effort toward population control to date has been ZPG — Zero Population Growth, Inc. — which was founded in the United States in 1969 to advocate reduction of growth in every nation to zero as quickly as possible. In a critique of ZPG, one prominent demographer concluded that a vast majority of its recommendations are simply declarative, exhortatory, or propa-gandistic expressions of ideas that are well accepted among demographers. Hence demographers tend to agree in principle with ZPG's goals, although they disagree about the means or timing to achieve them. ZPG urges stability, rejects "growth mania," encourages discussions, supports increased research to improve contra-ception technology, calls for more birth control clinics and services, argues for repeal of archaic abortion laws, and favors elimination of all pronatalist implica-tions of tax and insurance laws. Says Paul Demeny, "Shorn of their rhetoric and stridency, I consider the action programs proposed by ZPG for the present United States situation entirely sound."[5] The main complaint from professional demographers is that ZPG is naive. But in promulgating a reform of national policy and placing its case before the entire national population, regardless of educational level, ZPG probably has been more effective as a result of its uncomplicated advocacy of an easily understood goal.

In 1972 some ZPG members broke away to form a less conservative organization called NPG — Negative Population Growth, Inc. Taking as their purpose the immediate adoption of action programs toward reduction of all national populations to one-half of their 1972 size, NPG does make ZPG seem unimaginative.

The success of the ZPG-NPG movement has been phenomenal, for the reason that it was an idea whose time had come. But there remains the problem of precisely how nongrowth is to be achieved. Some people advocate persuasion alone, whereas others favor government permission to have children, with law-violating mothers sterilized and non-permit children given to sterile couples. But the latter view espouses a Draconian dictatorship, bringing forth protestations against abandonment of the freedom to reproduce. Kingsley Davis wonders why Americans are so concerned about reproductive freedom.

> If having too many children were considered as great a crime against humanity as murder, rape, and thievery, we would have no qualms about 'taking freedom away.' Indeed, it would be defined the other way around: a person having four or more children would be regarded as violating the freedom of those other citizens who must help pay for rearing, educating, and feeding the excess children. The reason why reproductive freedom is still regarded as 'a basic human right' regardless of circumstances is of course that it accords with traditional sentiments and established institutions. These, it will be recalled, are pronatalist.[6]

The population problem thus is seen by Davis as a conflict between two desires: for families and children, and yet against runaway growth. Making this conflict even more of a conundrum is the hope of finding a solution that safeguards Americans' freedom to have five children if they wish. "In short, they want a miracle."[7]

Even if all couples immediately adopted the ZPG code, there still would be a natural delay before growth ceased. Because populations have a built-in stability as people pass through the age structure, total growth slows gradually even if everyone has only two children. Nongrowth must await the passage through the childbearing years of the larger-than-replacement numbers of children who are born before the two-child family becomes (if ever) universal, plus another generation while their children breed their own families. Although it seems at first that zero growth could be achieved as soon as all couples had only two children, nongrowth cannot be achieved until the number of couples is reduced. The Commission on Population and the American Future explained that "an average of two children per family would slow population growth, but would not stop it soon because the number of people of childbearing age is increasing. So even if family size drops to a two-child average, the resulting births will continue to exceed deaths for the rest of this century"[8] — and well into the next. The process of stabilization is complicated by the effect of the changing proportions of people of childbearing ages, as the Commission pointed out in its final report to the President and Congress.

Some called for zero growth immediately, but this would not be possible without considerable disruption to society. While there are a variety of paths to ultimate stabilization, none of the feasible paths would reach it immediately. Our past rapid growth has given us so many young couples that, even if they merely replaced themselves, the number of births would still rise for several years before leveling off. To produce the number of births consistent with immediate zero growth, they would have to limit their childbearing to an average of only about one child. In a few years, there would be only half as many children as there are now. This would have disruptive effects on the school system and subsequently on the number of persons entering the labor force. Thereafter, a constant total population could be maintained only if this small generation in turn had two children and their grandchildren had nearly three children on the average. And then the process would again have to reverse, so that the overall effect for many years would be that of an accordion-like continuous expansion and contraction.[9]

International Organizations

Efforts to solve population problems are made on several levels and by several types of organizations, the major ones being the United Nations and its sister agencies, various private organizations, and several national governments. The United Nations has long been fighting mortality — largely through the Food and Agriculture Organization and World Health Organization — and the International Labour Office and several *ad hoc* United Nations agencies helped World War II refugees and later helped other migrants. This extensive and continuing work on mortality and migration failed for some years to have a fertility counterpart, as there was heated controversy over whether the United Nations should extend technical assistance to family planning. The disagreement was largely between representatives of India, who favored widespread dissemination of information and supplies for many birth limitation methods, and those from Roman Catholic and Iron Curtain countries, both of which have consistently expressed hostility toward these efforts. Recently the Catholic representatives modified slightly their previously inflexible stance, thus opening a prospect of a slow advance toward an international family planning program. A breakthrough finally was achieved in the mid-1960s, after which action programs blossomed rapidly.[10]

The foremost international private organization having a strong action

219

orientation is the International Planned Parenthood Federation and its 79 national affiliates. Most of the efforts of other private organizations are directed toward research: the International Union for the Scientific Study of Population, the Ford Foundation, the Rockefeller Foundation, and The Population Council. However, research is increasingly turning toward action.

As parts of their foreign policy, a few of the more favorably situated nations have set up assistance programs for underdeveloped areas. Sweden has offered birth control information and supplies, although the budget committed by this small nation is diminutive by American standards. In a remarkable shift from its classic do-nothing policy, the United States decided in December 1962 to unobtrusively provide information and other assistance to nations requesting it. A further step was taken when President Johnson's 1965 State of the Union message to Congress acknowledged the "explosion of world population" and the need to deal with it.

Types of Policies

In dealing with the three basic variables, plus other demographic and semi-demographic factors, there are a number of possible kinds of action:

Mortality
    Pro: war
    Anti: health care and death control
Fertility
    Pro: births encouraged and rewarded, family subsidies given
    Anti: births discouraged or prohibited
    Neutral: Natal care and family subsidies not designed to encourage births
Migration
    Immigration
        Pro: unrestricted entry
        Anti: restrictive laws and quotas
    Emigration
        Pro: easy departure without qualification
        Anti: restrictive laws
    Internal redistribution
        Pro: encouragement or acceptance of movement across local boundaries
        Anti: curbs on relocation, insistence on movement to or from certain areas
Characteristics: regulations concerning religion, language, marital status, education, literacy, caste, occupation, or employment
Level of living: laws regarding food distribution, environmental pollution, resource depletion

Macrodemography: efforts to achieve optimum size, optimum growth, upper or lower limits of size or growth

Eugenics: laws promoting or discouraging attempts to alter the physical or mental quality of human endowment

Sometimes policies are permissive attempts to let each citizen do as he or she wishes; more frequently they try to encourage certain demographic tendencies (such as raising or lowering fertility); occasionally they bluntly tell citizens what they can or cannot do (move to a farm or have no more children). In any nation, either politicians' temptations to be king, or environmentalists' desires to limit humanity's drain on the earth's resources, or some other motivation may support a rigid requirement that each citizen do thus-and-so. Most policies attempt to influence rather than demand, and most follow the spirit of the time. But the temper of the time may change, as in the American publication in 1971 of a book on compulsory birth control, which would have been unthinkable a few decades earlier.[11]

Permitting voluntary action versus compelling residents to do as the government directs is a conflict that obviously applies to migration and fertility. But mortality, too, has its voluntary-coercion dichotomy. In addition to the familiar argument of whether or not a person is entitled to end his or her own life, there has been added the disagreement over euthanasia, a term derived from the Greek for "good death" to describe merciful killing (some would say, murdering) of terminally-ill persons who have no hope and sometimes crushing pain. Persons favoring coercion believe that life should be preserved as long as possible and at all costs, regardless of the wish of the sick person. Advocates of voluntariness argue that no one should be compelled to suffer agonizing pain or to become a vegetable, lacking control over bodily functions and unable to think — the definitive criterion, as some say, of being human. Indeed, the traditional medico-legal dependence on the heart function as a definer of life and specifier of the moment of death is yielding to preference for the brain. The questions are whether someone whose brain still functions can ask for and receive the release of death, and whether a mentally-deceased person should continue to have his blood circulated and breath renewed. And who should decide: a judge, a physician, the closest relative, or the person himself (by a statement made before the illness)?

National Programs

Attitudes toward national action are changing throughout the world. In the past, Western governments have had little involvement with population on the premises that the greatest welfare resulted from an attitude of laissez-faire in population as in other matters. What policies there were usually encouraged the maximum possible population growth, and since we have lived with this orientation for a long time, a preference for population increase might be considered inbred. Growth is believed to be natural — and any growth-retarding policy dangerous.

But when trouble brews, as in the threat of incipient decline of the 1930s, study groups are set up by governments that run scared. Sweden appointed population commissions in 1935 and 1941 to explore problems and propose solutions. In 1944 Great Britian established a Royal Commission on Population to examine facts and make recommendations. President Herbert Hoover's Research Committee on Social Trends included population in the topics covered within its fourteen published volumes,[12] and President Roosevelt appointed a committee on Population Problems;[13] although both committees turned in substantial documents, neither stimulated Congress to formulate national policies. But results were not always negative, for many nations instituted or extended family subsidy and other programs based on demographic findings. The strongest advocates of family subsidies from the government have been Roman Catholics, fascists, and communists; socialists, liberals, and Protestants have been inconsistent.[14] The result is that more than half of the world's countries now have some form of family subsidy.

European nations take varying stances on population control. Yugoslavia supplies contraceptive services as part of the national health service. Sweden offers extensive free maternal and child care, sex education, loans to get married, and other services absorbing a tenth of the national budget and intended to make parenthood as voluntary as possible in both directions. The government of Ireland, considering the country to be underpopulated, is trying to check emigration and reduce labor surpluses and underemployment. The Soviet Union's pursuit is a mixed approach of giving financial aid and honorary medals to mothers of large families while simultaneously legalizing abortion in 1955 and semiofficially recommending use of contraceptive devices supplied free in government pharmacies.

The Developing Nations

Since it is the underdeveloped countries that suffer most from population growth, it is there that the greatest attention is being directed. Sample surveys of population attitudes have become so numerous as to be characterizable as "the most substantial set of comparative social data ever collected across such a range of societies."[15] Public opinion and practices in developing countries in the 1960s have been summarized by the Population Council: practice family planning now, 5-20 percent; have some detailed information about reproduction and contraception, 10-40 percent; want no more children (of those with three or more), 40-60 percent; interested in learning about family planning, 50-70 percent; and approve of birth control, 65-80 percent.[16]

Given this permissive and mildly enthusiastic popular attitude toward birth control, a number of governments are undertaking action programs aimed at moderating their population increase. Before 1960 India and Communist China were the only nations to have adopted national family planning policies, but by 1964 they had been joined by Pakistan, Tunisia, Turkey, Ceylon, Korea, Thailand, Egypt, and Malaysia; other nations have since added their names to this antinatalist list.

Family planning programs can and do have either of two objectives: service or persuasion. That is, they can supply materials and information to those men and women who want them, or they can attempt to convince couples of the undesirability of having another child. To these two immediate goals can be added a third, long-term aim: a country can try to industrialize, urbanize, and raise the educational level, in the expectation that such modernization automatically will result in citizen attitudes favoring lower fertility. This long-run solution has considerable support, but nations faced with immediate problems are not content with long-range efforts. In addition, or instead, they spend money and devote time to either or both of the two direct objectives: getting pills and IUDs to the women, and persuading as many people as possible to use them.

The Problems of India

The prospect that things will get worse before they get better has motivated the Indian government to introduce a series of increasingly vigorous five-year plans attempting to reduce the birth rate while some hope for economic progress remains. Beginning with a small budget and mild attention to family planning in the First Five-Year Plan of 1951-1956, the policy-makers greatly increased the budget and made their discussion of birth control more emphatic with each new plan. In the Fourth Plan of 1969-1974, the "urgency and gravity of the situation" were empahsized.[17] This effort appears to have succeeded in lowering fertility somewhat: Simmons concludes that "we are justified in attributing most of the benefits of birth prevention to government investments in family planning."[18] The ratio of benefits to costs, according to elaborate calculations by Simmons, is extraordinarily high: in 1969-1970, each rupee invested in the program returned 40 rupees of benefits.[19] Such partial success notwithstanding, the Indian planners — like the Indian birth rate — still have a long way to go to reach the stabilization that they desire.

From Kashmir to Madras, from Bombay to Calcutta, on trains and rickshas, on buses and highway posters, in bazzars and villages, Indians see two symbols that have spread throughout the developing world from their origin in India: the inverted red triangle signifying family planning, and the "four happy faces" representing a planned family. In 1969 an elephant called Lal Tikon (Red Triangle) began traveling across the country, bearing a family-planning triangle on her forehead and using her trunk to dispense government-subsidized handbills and contraceptives. The Indian government also places announcements in newspapers, on the radio, and in movie theaters. These mass-media efforts aimed at the urban public are supplemented by nonmedia ads understandable to illiterate peasants. To interest illiterate farmers too poor to own a radio, two modes of information dissemination are practical: sending out field workers to talk directly with people of childbearing age, and placing signboards on walls of buildings and carts pushed by itinerant vendors. So numerous are these signs that observant foreign travelers come, within several days, to accept them as part of the landscape.

The government is trying to reach 90 percent of India's married population. The target is to reduce the birth rate from about 40 in 1970 to 25 by 1979 — or as quickly as possible. If achieved, that reduction would then produce a growth of about 1-1/2 percent a year. But as the Indian government has been trying to reduce natural increase since 1951 with little success, there is not much hope that the desired rates will be achieved by 1979 or a few years thereafter.

The Struggle in China

Family planning is encouraged in Communist China. Although according to Marxist ideology overpopulation is not possible in a properly organized state, national leaders have been compelled to recognize that each new pair of hands to hold a gun or plow or lathe is accompanied by a mouth to feed and a body to house and clothe. Thus divided in motive, Chinese government officials have wavered and vacillated — or, to put it more positively, they have never been as inflexible about family planning as the Soviet leadership and have tolerated minority and even divergent opinions in the press. Following the stunning results of the 1953 census, which revealed an even more huge and rapidly growing population than had been supposed, birth control was first pushed and then discouraged and then resumed. [20]

The Chinese have nevertheless made progress in lowering fertility, partly because of their emphasis, to a greater extent than in any other nation, on deferment of marriage. Before the Communists came into power, most Chinese girls were married by their mid-teens; today, few are married until well into their twenties. Childbearing therefore starts several years later.

The target is to reduce the national growth rate to one percent by the year

2000. But in view of the fluctuating policy since the Communists took over, the nation's demographic future is difficult to predict. Despite these vascillations, however, "the twenty years, 1949-69, saw the adoption and implementation of more explicit demographic measures than any other similar time-interval during China's past millenia."[21] Some measures were short-lived, and none is assured of lasting effect. Still, taken as a whole, the first twenty years of the People's Republic should "go down in history as the watershed in the management of China's demographic affairs."[22]

The overall effects of this new management are uncertain, although it seems clear that the rate of urban overcrowding has been retarded by such efforts as the 1953 "Directive on Dissuasion of Peasants from Blind Influx into Cities" followed by the 1954 "Joint Directive Concerning Implementation of Directive Advising Against Blind Influx of Peasants into Cities," and supplemented by the policy of moving people from the dense coastal strip to sparsely settled inland regions. Mortality as well as fertility appears to have been lowered by government activity.

Yuan Tien concludes his book on China's population policy by deploring the inaccuracy of past "wayward prophecies." Whatever the future holds, "China's ability both to care for its existing population and to affect population growth remains a very lively and irresistible issue."[23]

Programs in Other Countries

The government of Taiwan adopted an official population policy in 1968 but previously permitted extensive experimental work encouraging family planning. Results suggest that fertility is being altered substantially by the planned program.

South Korea's government-supported family planning program began in 1962 and also has been remarkably successful. As in Taiwan, Korea's program relies heavily on intrauterine contraceptive devices and pills, while also making use of traditional contraceptives. The target is to reduce natural increase from 2.2 percent in 1971 to 1.0 percent in the 1980s and 0.5 percent by 2000. As Korea represents one of the three foremost family planning success stories (the others are Taiwan and Japan), such objectives seem reasonable.

The most dramatic and successful attempt to decrease natality in any nation occurred in Japan, whose literate and highly motivated populace cut their birth rate in half in a decade (1947-1957) by using abortion, contraception, and other actions encouraged by the government and accepted by citizens as being in their own interest. But one must not generalize too quickly from Japan's experience, for Japan is unique in its rapidity of industrialization, this-worldly outlook, and levels of literacy and education. Japan's acceptance of the small family system seems to be just one aspect of a prevailing high level of rationalization of conduct and ambition to attain a higher standard of living; in demographic as in other respects, the Japanese, though starting later than the Europeans, have moved much faster toward the achievement of much the same goals: higher real income and possession of the luxuries of life.

Convinced until recently that their countries were underpopulated, Latin Americans are now abandoning that view and showing signs of instituting national policies to slow their growth. This emergent interest was first expressed in Chile, where concern over the "twin evils" of high birth and abortion rates prompted the government to set up a few birth control clinics, and in Peru, whose government established a Population and Development Center in 1965. As yet, however, most Latin American governments have contented themselves with permitting the operation of privately supported clinics, although several nations refuse to tolerate any kind of family planning center. As elsewhere, the major opponent of planned parenthood programs is the Roman Catholic Church, although many Catholic physicians and clergymen seem prepared to accept a birth control program provided that guarantees are given that only methods approved by the Church are mentioned. More liberal Catholic physicians and even priests are said to be advising parishioners to use contraceptive methods not accepted by the Vatican. The urban poor are well aware of the burden of large families, and as population increases, the demand for government services will probably increase as well, so that most Latin American nations may soon be supporting programs for dispensing information and possibly even distributing contraceptive supplies.

United States Government

Demographers have for some years seen the population rise in the United States as posing both economic and welfare problems and have been pointing out what the consequences may be if the American people do not continue to voluntarily lower their fertility. As in other countries, the only tolerable demographic manipulation is of migration and fertility, and since almost 90 percent of the increase results from fertility and only some 10 percent from migration, it is fertility control that deserves and receives the major attention.

Federal and local governments can take any of three positions regarding birth control: for, against, or neutral. To date most action has been restrictive by prohibiting or curtailing dissemination of information and sale of equipment. Promotion would consist of active efforts using government funds to persuade or compel people to adopt birth control; the extreme view has been expressed by biologist H. Bentley Glass that the time may come when married couples would need permits to have children, and normally no couple could qualify for more than two. Persons who believe that each individual should have complete freedom to determine the size of his family do not like either the existing restrictive legislation or this prospective compulsion, preferring instead the permissive approach of permitting open sale of devices and distribution of information, to be bought or listened to at the discretion of the individual.

Today federal and local governments are retreating from their traditionally restrictive stance to be more middle-of-the-road position. Some restrictions are kept, and yet tax-supported clinics are set up to dispense birth control advice — not that much propagandizing is done, as clinics generally wait for patients to come to them asking for information or supplies. State laws too have been changing: the last state to outlaw birth control clinics and prohibit dissemination of family planning information — Massachusetts — removed its ban in 1966. Quite a number of country and city health departments operate family planning clinics, catering especially to low-income families; local health departments lacking their own clinics often refer women to private clinics in the community.

The climate of opinion is changing fast. President Eisenhower avowed in 1959 that birth control is not a proper governmental responsibility or concern, but by 1963 he had so far changed his view as to state publicly that the federal government should supply birth control information upon request, adding in 1965 that foreign aid programs are crippled without "parallel programs looking to population stabilization" and that population growth has also "serious portents" for the United States: unless action is taken, the nation "will find itself in the curious position of spending money . . . providing financial incentive for increased reproduction by the ignorant, feeble-minded or lazy."[24] This fear that welfare income will lure irresponsible young women into repetitive production of illegitimate offspring has motivated many state legislators and local officials to install family planning services in their free public health programs. Other persons advocate the same action but for a different reason: upper- and middle-class families have access to family planning knowledge, but persons of lower economic and educational levels often feel they cannot afford contraceptive supplies and sometimes are grossly ignorant of birth control techniques. As recently as 1963 an Illinois public aid commissioner was forced out of office for proposing to offer fertility planning information and supplies to any welfare recipient with a child or a spouse; today just such a program is in effect, following authorization from the state legislature in 1965. On June 25, 1965, Lyndon B. Johnson became the first United States president to take a public stand in favor of birth control: "Let us act on the fact that less than $5 invested in population control is worth $100 invested in economic growth."

Government support of family planning is not without opponents. Many Roman Catholics feel that government funds should never be used to support such clinics, and others oppose publication of information on the subject.

Still a number of colleges do research on social and medical aspects of fertility, and the University of Chicago established in 1964 a cirriculum "designed to prepare students to take a leading role in organizing, administering, and evaluating family planning programs." One rags-to-riches millionaire industrialist, Joseph Sunnen, launched his own campaign, distributing Emko (meaning "happy woman" in Japanese), a spermicidal vaginal foam packaged in aerosol dispensers, without cost through community volunteers working door-to-door; the Emko program has been remarkably effective in the slum and blighted districts of St. Louis, Puerto Rico, New York, Los Angeles, and other American areas. Thus in both their public and private lives, Americans are increasingly active in attempting to narrow the gap between birth and death rates, of which the National Academy of Sciences said in 1963: "Other than the search for lasting peace, no problem is more urgent."[25]

The United States has slowly fumbled and bumbled itself in the direction of a national policy concerning population.[26] Let us look at the records of our chief executive officers: There was almost complete silence about population from the Presidency until Eisenhower, who in 1959 asserted that the government should have absolutely nothing to do with birth control; apparently he thought that maintaining restrictive laws limiting use of birth control was the same as having nothing to do with the subject. President Kennedy avoided overt references to family planning, but he did talk repeatedly about population problems, and he authorized United States assistance to countries experiencing demographic difficulties. President Johnson spoke frequently about population matters and continued the overseas assistance program. In 1969 President Nixon delivered a "Message to Congress on Population" in which he recommended the creation of a Commission on Population Growth and the American Future;[27] the following year such a commission was established by Congress.

Examining data and ideas supplied by hundreds of scholars and opinion leaders, the Commission and its staff published a final report in 1972 introduced by the statement: "We have concluded that, in the long run, no substantial benefits will result from further growth of the Nation's population, rather that the gradual stabilization of our population through voluntary means would contribute significantly to the Nation's ability to solve its problems."[28] Supplying seven pages of recommendations for reducing population growth by liberalizing laws restricting birth control, the report was well received by demographers but attacked by Roman Catholic priests as well as by President Nixon himself.

Nixon objected to reducing restrictions on abortion and to expanding the distribution of family planning services, especially to minors. The President's real desire appeared to be to quash the report entirely, but this proved impossible. Indeed, the report probably will stand for some years as a landmark in the history of American population policy.

The antiprofessionalism that has inhered in American population policy from its beginning continued in 1974 with President Nixon's nominees to the Commission for the Observance of World Population Year 1974. The twenty-person committee included only one demographer (retired) and no family planning expert, the majority being businessmen and civic leaders. Apparently the objective was to staff the Commission with the customary elitist-oriented quasi-representation of American society, for members included one athlete, one fireman, one college president, one youth coordinator, one mayor, one newspaperman, one former Cabinet member, one lawyer, one economist, two physicians, a few miscellaneous persons, and several company presidents varying from CBS and General Motors to Mrs. Paul's Kitchens. Knowledge of population clearly was irrelevant to membership. Given this roster, the Commission could hardly have been expected to provide authoritative statements about population facts or policy.

Are Antinatal Programs Succeeding?

A running debate has been taking place about the effectiveness of existing government fertility programs. Basically the argument concerns the sufficiency of concentrating program attention on the distribution of birth control information and supplies. On one side are those who believe in the effectiveness of supplying the public with means to control their fertility, thinking that if the means are readily available, safe, and cheap, then people will rush to use them; advocates of this position include Donald Bogue[29] and some Population Council and government personnel.[30] Opposed to this belief are Kingsley Davis, who argues that control of fertility is an enormous task which depends upon detailed knowledge of people's motivations in their socioeconomic context,[31] and Philip Hauser, who calls supply-oriented programs "simplistic," emphasizes the importance of the social milieu, and points out that significant changes in fertility behavior necessarily involve broad social change.[32]

The terminology should be clear: population policy and control are large topics encompassing many subtopics concerning mortality and migration as well as fertility. Fertility control and family planning are limited — but there is disagreement of their appropriate extent. Current programs often include only the provision of clinical services, and it is this restriction that causes many sociologists to regard them as incomplete.

Out of this background controversy there arose in 1969 a heated disagreement between Judith Blake of the University of California at Berkeley and three representatives of action-oriented agencies: Oscar Harkavy of the Ford Foundation, Frederick Jaffe of Planned Parenthood-World Population, and Samuel Wishik of Columbia University's public health program. Writing in the official journal of the American Association for the Advancement of Science, Blake argued that increasing government support of voluntary birth control for the poor and uneducated is irrelevant to the needs of ghetto dwellers and wastes federal funds:

> The problem of inhibiting population growth in the United States cannot be dealt with in terms of 'family-planning needs' because this country is well beyond the point of 'needing' birth control methods. Indeed, even the poor seem not to be a last outpost for family-planning attention. If we wish to limit our growth, such a desire implies basic changes in the social organization of reproduction that will make nonmarriage, childlessness, and small (two-child) families far more prevalent than they are now.[33]

Blake's "gloomy view" inspired many Letters to the Editor in *Science*, plus an article by the three aforementioned administrators, alleging that government support of family planning programs for the medically indigent is vital. The poor, argue Harkavy and his co-authors, do need to improve their access to and efficient use of birth control methods, and therefore the present government program is valuable to social welfare.[34] Blake replied in the form of a letter to *Science* which was later expanded into an article.[35] Far from dead, this controversy continues vigorously and may have a lively future.

Perfect Fertility Control

Without joining the argument, Udry and Bauman supply evidence indicating that perfect fertility control — by which is meant that every woman is able to have exactly the number of births she wants — might slow annual rates of growth in less developed nations to one percent instead of 2 or 3 percent.[36] In the United States, making physician-administered contraception available to all women probably would decrease unwanted fertility in low-income areas by 80 percent, and if sterilization were substituted for the pill and intrauterine devices, the effect would be even greater.[37] As residents of low-income areas form only a minority of the national population, however, cutting their fertility would not reduce national fertility greatly.

The government's five-year plan of 1971 for family-planning services is designed to "assist American couples to avoid unwanted pregnancies" and to "enable Americans to freely determine the number and spacing of their children" by placing primary attention on poverty-level families.[38] Underlying these twin goals is a conviction that an "unmet need" for birth control exists among certain American women. This unmet need is measured straightforwardly by counting the number of unwanted children: if a woman has more children than she wants, then her need for birth control information and supplies was not met. (Allowance should be made, however, for inefficiency in use of birth control techniques.) Several statisticians have estimated that such an unmet need is present among some five million American women[39] — although Blake and other scholars argue that this figure over-estimates the need.[40] Examination of interview data collected in seventeen metropolitian areas during 1969-1970 led

Bauman and Udry to conclude that if these five million women had adopted physician-administered contraception, there would have been 24 percent fewer unwanted births in the country.[41]

Reducing Growth Toward Zero

All factors considered, it seems unlikely that present programs will bring about zero growth in most countries. Hauser has observed that present family planning programs tend to reduce the birth rate to a plateau that is higher than desired.[42]

The historic fertility reduction in economically advanced nations resulted from individual decisions and efforts instead of government policies or programs. Birth rates declined even though people had only rather primitive birth control methods — and no government clinics. "In the economically advanced countries the birth rate declined even though the government, the church, the medical profession, and the 'establishment' in general were opposed to it. It remains to be ascertained whether in the less developed countries the birth rate can be significantly reduced when the government and the establishment in general has this as an objective."[43] Unless there is adequate motivation, even the most modern methods of contraception will not be effective. Whether there is sufficient incentive in a given country or socioeconomic group is not generally known; presently available evidence from interview studies implies that some persons are sufficiently motivated to restrict their fertility to replacement, whereas others are not. As yet we do not know just how many persons fall into each of these two categories.

Japan's unparalleled fertility decrease in the 1950s supports Hauser's point. According to Minoru Muramatsu, it was not the government but the citizenry that decided which way to go: "The government in general was not in a position to tell the people what to do but rather to follow the people and to help them accomplish their desire." The people's desires were channeled toward fertility reduction by various social forces accompanying modernization: "a high degree of literacy, universal education system, great interest of parents to give even better education to their children, effect of prolonged years of compulsory education after the war, enormous influence of newspapers and magazines and other reading materials, impact of the new Constitution which prescribed, among other things, equal inheritance by all children, and rising status of women."[44]

Conclusion

A fitting conclusion is to return to the first word of the subtitle of this book: *controversy*. Acknowledging that birth control is the most highly controversial

231

facet of the population problem as far as *non*demographers are concerned, we should realize that there is barely any controversy within the field. Professional demographers almost unanimously favor controlling fertility by whatever techniques science can offer. This near-unanimity has risen to the point where, foɪ example, a television network that wants to stage a pro-con discussion of birth control can easily find debaters for the affirmative but has a difficult time locating experts willing to take the negative. So we are left with the paradox that the greatest "Controversy over Population Control" is hardly a controversy at all.

NOTES

[1] Bernard Berelson, "The World's Second Problem: Population," *Oberlin Alumni Magazine*, Vol. LXI, No. 1, January 1965, pp. 4-8.

[2] James A. Pike, "The Ethics of Family Planning," in American Assembly, *The Population Dilemma*, Columbia University and Occidental College, Palm Springs, 1963, p. 12.

[3] National Academy of Sciences — National Research Council, *The Growth of World Population* (Washington: 1963), p. 20.

[4] Eugene R. Black, Address to the Economic and Social Council of the United Nations, New York, April 24, 1961.

[5] Paul Demeny, "Comment on Zero Population Growth," *Population Index*, Vol. XXXVI, No. 4, October 1970, p. 465.

[6] Kingsley Davis, "Zero Population Growth: The Goal and the Means," *Daedalus*, Vol. CII, No. 4, Fall 1973, p. 28.

[7] *Ibid.*, p. 29.

[8] Commission on Population Growth and the American Future, *Population and the American Future* (Washington, D.C.: Government Printing Office, 1972), pp. 20-21.

[9] *Ibid.*, p. 110.

[10] Richard Symonds and Michael Carder, *The United Nations and the Population Question: 1945-1970* (New York: McGraw-Hill, 1973), pp. 135-172.

[11] Edgar R. Chasteen, *The Case for Compulsory Birth Control* (Englewood Cliffs, N.J.: Prentice-Hall, 1971).

[12] Warren S. Thompson and P. K. Whelpton, *Population Trends in the United States* (New York: McGraw-Hill, 1933).

[13] National Resources Committee, *The Problems of a Changing Population* (Washington: Government Printing Office, 1938).

[14] William Petersen, *The Politics of Population* (New York: Doubleday and Co., 1964), p. 154.

[15] Bernard Berelson, "Sample Surveys and Population Control: Introduction," *Public Opinion Quarterly*, Vol. XXVIII, Fall 1964, p. 365.

[16] The Population Council, "National Family Planning Programs: A Guide," *Studies in Family Planning*, No. 5 (Supplement), December 1964, p. 2.

[17] George B. Simmons, *The Indian Investment in Family Planning* (New York: The Population Council, 1971), pp. 177-179.

[18] *Ibid.*, p. 120.

[19] *Ibid.*, p. 93.

[20] H. Yuan Tien, "Birth Control in Mainland China: Ideology and Politics," *Milbank Memorial Fund Quarterly*, Vol. XLI, No. 3, July 1963, pp. 269-290; and John S. Aird, "Population Policy and Demographic Prospects in the People's Republic of China," in Joint Economic Committee, Congress of the United States, *People's Republic of China: An Economic Assessment* (Washington, D.C.: Government Pringint Office, 1972), pp. 220-331.

[21] H. Yuan Tien, *China's Population Struggle* (Columbus: Ohio State University, 1973), p. 335.

[22] *Ibid.*, p. 338.

[23] *Ibid.*, p. 341.

[24] Dwight D. Eisenhower, statement prepared for hearings of the United States Senate Subcommittee on Government Operations to consider legislation permitting governmental distribution of birth control information both at home and abroad, June 22, 1965.

[25] National Academy of Sciences, *The Growth of World Population* (Washington, D.C.: 1963), p. 2.

[26] Phyllis Tilson Piotrow, *World Population Crisis: The United States Response* (New York: Praeger, 1973).

[27] Richard M. Nixon, "Presidential Message to Congress on Population," Washington, D.C.: July 18, 1969.

[28] Commission on Population Growth and the American Future, *Population and the American Future*, *op. cit.*, p. 4.

[29] Donald J. Bogue, "The Demographic Breakthrough: From Projection to Control," *Population Index*, Vol. XXX, No. 4, October 1964, pp. 449-454.

[30] R. T. Ravenholt, "AID's Family Planning Strategy," *Science*, Vol. CLXIII, January 10, 1969, pp. 124-125.

[31] Kingsley Davis, "Population Policy: Will Current Programs Succeed?", *Science*, Vol. CLVIII, November 10, 1967, pp. 730-739.

[32] Philip M. Hauser, "Population: More than Family Planning," *Journal of Medical Education*, Vol. XLIV, No. 11, Part 2, November 1969, pp. 20-29.

[33] Judith Blake, "Population Policy for Americans: Is the Government Being Misled?", *Science*, Vol CLXIV, May 2, 1969, p. 529.

[34] Oscar Harkavy, Frederick S. Jaffe, and Samuel M. Wishik, "Family Planning and Public Policy: Who Is Misleading Whom?", *Science*, Vol. CLXV, July 25, 1969, pp. 367-373.

[35] Judith Blake, "A Reply," in William Petersen (ed.), *Readings in Population* (New York: Macmillan, 1972), pp. 459-466.

[36] J. Richard Udry, Karl E. Bauman, and Charles L. Chase, "Population Growth Rates in Perfect Contraceptive Populations," *Population Studies*, Vol. XXVII, No. 2, July 1973, pp. 365-371.

[37] J. Richard Udry and Karl E. Bauman, "Effect on Unwanted Fertility of Extending Physician-Administered Birth Control in the United States," *Demography*, Vol. XI, No. 2, May 1974, pp. 189-194.

[38] Secretary of Health, Education, and Welfare, *Five-Year Plan for Family Planning Services and Population Research Programs* (Washington, D.C.: Government Printing Office, 1971), pp. 337 and 77.

[39] Arthur A. Campbell, "The Role of Family Planning in the Reduction of Poverty," *Journal of Marriage and the Family*, Vol. XXX, No. 2, May 1968, pp. 236-245.

[40] Judith Blake and Prithwis Das Gupta, "The Fallacy of the Five Million Women: A Re-Estimate," *Demography*, Vol. IX, No. 4, November 1972, pp. 569-587.

[41] Karl E. Bauman and J. Richard Udry, "Evaluation of the Five-Year Family Planning Plan," *Health Services Reports*, Vol. LXXXVIII, No. 9, pp. 814-817.

[42] Philip M. Hauser, "Population Criteria in Foreign Aid Programs," in J. Philip Wogaman (ed.), *The Population Crisis and Moral Responsibility* (Washington, D.C.: Public Affairs Press, 1973), p. 239.

[43] *Ibid.*, p. 238.

[44] Minoru Muramatsu, "Policy Measures and Social Changes for Fertility Decline in Japan," *Proceedings of the World Population Conference: 1965* (New York: United Nations, 1967), Vol. II, pp. 96-99.

Recommended Readings

If this book whets the appetite sufficiently to inspire a search for further information and analysis about population, the following books are recommended as good starting places, in addition to the sources cited in the notes. For a thorough examination of any facet of population, it is a good idea to inspect longer bibliographies plus the card catalog of a good library. Articles in periodicals are especially timely, but they are not included here in order to keep this list short and practical.

The most encyclopedic one-volume coverage of demography is offered by Donald J. Bogue, *Principles of Demography* (New York: Wiley, 1969) and the United Nations, *The Determinants and Consequents of Population Trends* (New York, 1973) — tomes that are more to be consulted than read. Readers who like the present book might want to inspect a larger one by the same author: Ralph Thomlinson, *Population Dynamics* (New York: Random House, 1976).

The classic work on population theory remains Thomas R. Malthus, *An Essay on the Principle of Population* (London: 1798, 1826). No newer theorist has replaced Malthus, although a number of contemporary books are devoted to population theory.

Methods of acquiring and analyzing demographic statistics are discussed exhaustively in Henry S. Shryock and Jacob S. Siegel, *The Methods and Materials of Demography* (Washington, D.C.: Bureau of the Census, 1971). Two shorter but highly competent books are George W. Barclay, *Techniques of Population Analysis* (New York: Wiley, 1958); and Roland Pressat, *Demographic Analysis* (Chicago: Aldine, 1969). A broader yet briefer presentation of research methods is Ralph Thomlinson, *Sociological Concepts and Research* (New York: Random House, 1965).

The three fundamental demographic variables have a huge literature, especially fertility. Modern American fertility and birth control attitudes are reported in Norman B. Ryder and Charles F. Westoff, *Reproduction in the United States: 1965* (Princeton: Princeton University, 1971). Birth control techniques are described in John Peel and Malcolm Potts, *Textbook of Contraception Practice* (London: Cambridge University, 1969).

The standard reference work on general mortality is the dated Louis I. Dublin, Alfred J. Lotka, and Mortimer Spiegelman, *Length of Life* (New York: Ronald, 1949). For a mixture of humor, history, and epidemiology, magnificently carried off, read Hans Zinsser, *Rats, Lice, and History* (Boston: Little Brown, 1935).

The history of world migration is outlined in Donald R. Taft and Richard Robbins, *International Migrations* (New York: Ronald, 1955). As moving as a novel about the trip from rural Europe to America is Oscar Handlin, *The Uprooted* (Boston: Little Brown, 1951).

Urban growth is documented in Kingsley Davis, *World Urbanization: 1950-1970* (Berkeley: University of California, 2 vols., 1969 and 1972). On urban ecology, see Ralph Thomlinson, *Urban Structure* (New York: Random House, 1969).

Characteristics are analyzed in many and varied volumes. Two examples are Peter M. Blau and Otis Dudley Duncan, *The American Occupational Structure* (New York: Wiley, 1967); and Leo Grebler, Joan W. Moore, and Ralph C. Guzman, *The Mexican-American People* (New York: Free Press, 1970).

The largest country in the world — China — should have more books written about its population than the few which exist. The most interesting is Leo A. Orleans, *Every Fifth Child* (London: Eyre Methuen, 1972). A descriptive survey of the developing nations of Africa, tropical Latin America, and most of Asia is provided in Glenn T. Trewartha, *The Less Developed Realm* (New York: Wiley, 1972).

Population history is becoming increasingly popular as demographers exploit archival sources of data. A particularly good treatment is Thomas H. Hollingsworth, *Historical Demography* (London: Hodder & Stoughton, 1969).

At the other temporal extreme is the future of world's population, for which uncertain foray one would do well to consult United Nations, *World Population Prospects as Assessed in 1968* (New York: 1974). Urban prospects and history are combined in United Nations, *Growth of the World's Urban and Rural Population: 1920-2000* (New York: 1969).

Recommendations toward a population policy for the United States were recently put forth by a Congressional Commission, whose report is most readily available as Commission on Population Growth, *Population and the American Future* (New York: New American Library, 1972). Optimum population and the problems of overpopulation in the United States are discussed in Lincoln H. Day and Alice Taylor Day, *Too Many Americans* (Boston: Houghton Mifflin, 1964).

Masses of statistical data for most of the world are presented annually in the United Nations, *Demographic Yearbook* (New York). In each nation, the census bureau usually publishes extensive tabulations.

The two leading journals in the field are *Demography* (Population Association of America, since 1964) and *Population Studies* (London School of Economics, since 1947). Citations to articles and books in many languages are supplied by topic, author, and geographic area in the magnificent quarterly bibliography, *Population Index* (Princeton: Population Association of America, since 1935).

Two dictionaries of particular relevance to population are the United Nations, *Multilingual Demographic Dictionary* (New York: 1958); and Thomas Ford Hoult, *Dictionary of Modern Sociology* (Ames, Iowa: Littlefield Adams, 1968).

236

Index of Names

Adams, Henry, 192, 214
Aird, John S., 233
Alexander, Robert C., 188
Aquinas, Thomas, 121
Aristotle, 120, 125
Asoka, Emperor, 59

Babbage, Charles, 42, 53
Back, Kurt W., 133
Barclay, George W., 235
Barrett, J. C., 150
Barth, Alan, 188
Bauman, Karl E., 130, 135, 230-1, 234
Beeson, Irene, 97
Behrens, William W., 34
Berelson, Bernard, 1, 44, 53, 123-4, 134, 232
Besant, Annie, 126
Black, Eugene R., 232
Blake, Judith (Davis), 132, 135, 229-30, 233-4
Blau, Peter M., 236
Bogue, Donald J., 105, 229, 233, 235
Bonar, James, 18, 33
Bonner, James, 53
Borlaug, Norman E., 21
Bradlaugh, Charles, 126
Brenez, Jacques, 94
Brooks, Robert R. R., 33
Brown, H. Rap, 127, 134
Brown, Harrison, 34, 53
Bumpass, Larry, 135
Byron, Lord (George Gordon), 34

Calhoun, John B., 34
Campbell, Arthur A., 116, 132, 134, 150, 234
Campbell, Ralph J., 133
Carder, Michael, 232
Carlson, A. J., 34
Carpenter, J., 33
Carr-Saunders, A. M., 44
Charret, Edouard, 118
Chase, Charles L., 234

Chasteen, Edgar R., 232
Chauvin, Rémy, 34
Chen, Ta, 80
Choldin, Harvey M., 117
Chung, Bom Mo, 116
Club of Rome, 27-8
Coale, Ansley J., 119
Collver, Andrew, 80
Commoner, Barry, 28, 34
Comstock, Anthony, 126
Cook, Robert C., 34, 41, 188
Cottrell, Fred, 33
Cox, Peter R., 116

Darity, William A., 134
Darwin, Charles, 19-20
Das Gupta, Prithwis, 234
Davis, Kingsley, 33, 80, 218, 229, 232-3, 236
Day, Alice Taylor, 27, 34, 236
Day, Lincoln H., 27, 34, 127, 134, 236
Debavalya, Nibhon, 214
de Castro, Josue, 17
Defoe, Daniel, 156, 172
de Groot, Hugo, 24
Demeny, Paul, 217, 232
Denney, Reuel, 214
Descartes, René, 97
Devereux, George, 133
Driver, Edwin D., 117
Dublin, Louis I., 235
DuBois, W. E. B., 127
Duncan, Otis Dudley, 236

Eaton, Joseph W., 116
Ehrlich, Paul, 27, 33
Eisenhower, Dwight D., 227, 233
El-Hamamsy, Laila Shukry, 116
Evans, W. Duane, 53

Fagley, Richard M., 134
Fix, Evelyn, 173
Flexner, Abraham, 158, 172
Franklin, Benjamin, 10
Freedman, Jonathan L., 29, 34

Freedman, Ronald F., 116-17, 132-4, 150
Frejka, Thomas, 53

Galen, Claudius, 158
Galilei, Galileo, 141, 157
Gardner, Martin, 172
Garreau, L., 214
Geis, Gilbert, 191
Gillin, F. J., 133
Girard, Alain, 188
Glass, H. Bentley, 226-7
Glazer, Nathan, 214
Gourgaud, Gaspard, 116
Grabill, Wilson H., 117
Grafenberg, Ernst, 120
Graunt, John, 10-11, 172
Grebler, Leo, 236
Gregg, Allen, 34
Gregory, Dick, 127, 134
Guzman, Ralph C., 236

Halley, Edmund, 156, 172
Hamilton, Walter, 183
Handlin, Oscar, 187, 236
Hardin, Garrett, 150
Harkavy, Oscar, 229-30, 233
Harris, Sara, 116
Harvey, William, 157
Hauser, Philip M., 149, 153, 170, 173, 229, 231, 233-4
Henderson, Elmer L., 173
Henshaw, Paul S., 133
Herold J. Christopher, 116
Hill, Reuben, 133
Himes, Norman E., 132
Hoebel, E. Adamson, 133
Hoffenberg, Marvin, 53
Hollingsworth, Thomas H., 15, 236
Holmes, Oliver Wendell, 158, 172
Hostetler, John A., 116
Houdaille, Jacques, 111, 116
Hoult, Thomas Ford, 236
Huxley, Aldous, 92, 95
Huxley, Julian, 41

Jaffe, Frederick S., 229-30, 233
Jaffe, Louis J., 188
John XXIII, Pope, 137
Johnson, Lyndon B., 182, 188, 227
Jones, Gavin W., 30, 33-4, 206, 214

Kelly, George A., 143, 150
Kelly, Walt, 28
Kennedy, John F., 228
Keyfitz, Nathan, 15

Khan, A. Majeed, 117
Kinsey, Alfred C., 144
Kiser, Clyde V., 117
Kitagawa, Evelyn M., 170, 173
Knowlton, Charles L., 126

Lamb, Charles, 207, 214
Lee, Everett, 174
Lee, Luke T., 133
Lee, Sang Joo, 116
Lee, Sung Jin, 116
Lewis-Fanning, E., 117
Licht, Hans (Brandt), 116
Linton, Ralph, 214
Lorenz, Konrad, 34
Lotka, Alfred J., 154, 235
Lucas, Frank Laurence, 145, 150
Luce, Clare Booth, 139
Lucretius, 125

McArthur, Norma, 94
McWhirter, Norris, 116
McWhirter, Ross, 116
Malthus, Thomas Robert, 11, 18-20, 33, 235
Martin, Dean, 217
Mayer, Albert J., 116
Meadows, Dennis L., 34
Meadows, Donella H., 34
Mearns, Hughes, 149
Mercer, Johnny, 170
Merton, Robert K., 116
Mill, James, 126
Mill, John Stuart, 125, 134
Miller, Harold A., 188
Modell, Walter, 172
Moore, Joan W., 236
Moore, Maurice J., 150
Morrison, Emily, 53
Morrison, Peter A., 53
Morrison, Philip, 53
Muramatsu, Minoru, 231, 234
Murtagh, John M., 116
Myrdal, Gunnar, 186, 188

Napoleon, 100
Nehru, Jawaharlal, 216
Nesbitt, Robert E. L. Jr., 173
Neyman, Jerzy, 173
Nixon, Richard M., 228, 233
Noonan, John T. Jr., 133, 150
Nortman, Dorothy L., 80
Notestein, Frank W., 5, 15

Ohlin, Goran, 15

238

Orleans, Leo A., 33, 116, 236
Osler, William, 159

Paddock, Paul, 22, 33
Paddock, William, 22, 33
Palmore, James A., 116
Park, Robert E., 188
Pasteur, Louis, 158
Paul VI, Pope, 137-9, 149-50
Peel, John, 235
Pepys, Samuel, 156, 172
Pericles, 214
Petersen, William, 232
Peyrefitte, Roger, 150
Pierson, George W., 174, 187
Pike, James A., 216, 232
Piotrow, Phyllis Tilson, 15, 133, 233
Pius XII, Pope, 137
Place, Francis, 126
Plato, 10, 125
Pliny, 125
Polissar, Lincoln T., 53
Pommerenke, W. T., 133
Pool, D. I., 94
Potter, Robert G. Jr., 133, 149
Potts, Malcolm, 235
Prachuabmoh, Visid, 53, 134
Pressat, Roland, 235
Priscianus, Theodorus, 108
Putkha, M. V., 80

Rabelais, Francois, 17
Rainwater, Lee, 116
Randers, Jorgen, 34
Ravenholt, R. T., 133, 233
Riesman, David, 214
Robbins, Richard, 236
Roof, Michael K., 80
Rutstein, David D., 172
Ryder, Norman B., 135, 147-8, 150-1,
  235

St. Augustine, 125-6, 144
St. John-Stevas, Norman, 150
Salaff, Janet W., 116
Saunders, Lyle, 136, 149
Sauvy, Alfred, 116
Saxbe, William B., 88
Schaff, P., 134
Schlesinger, Edward R., 173
Schultz, Theodore W., 32, 34
Seale, Patrick, 97
Semmelweis, Ignaz, 158
Shapiro, Sam, 173
Shryock, Henry S., 235

Shryock, Richard H., 172
Siegel, Jacob S., 235
Simmons, George B., 233
Simon, Julian L., 149
Sinatra, Frank, 170
Soranus of Ephesus, 125
Speidel, J. J., 133
Spencer, Baldwin, 133
Spengler, Joseph J., 1, 23, 33
Spiegelman, Mortimer, 235
Stern, Bernhard J., 157, 172
Steuart, James, 17, 33
Stewart, George R., 34
Stolnitz, George J., 117
Stycos, J. Mayonne, 117, 133, 147,
  150-1
Suenens, Leon Joseph Cardinal, 141, 146
Sulloway, Alvah W., 134, 150
Sun, T. H., 117
Sunnen, Joseph, 228
Symonds, Richard, 232

Taeuber, Conrad, 89
Taeuber, Irene B., 80, 89
Taft, Donald R., 236
Takeshita, John Y., 117
Tennyson, Alfred, 42
Tertullian, 17, 33
Theodoric, 158
Thiebaux, H. Jean, 134
Thomas, Dorothy Swaine, 89
Thomas, John L., 150
Thomlinson, Ralph, 34, 53, 80, 116,
  134, 187-8, 214
Thompson, Warren S., 5, 15, 89, 232
Tien, H. Yuan, 225, 233
Tietze, Christopher, 133-4
Trewartha, Glenn T., 24, 33, 82-3,
  87, 94, 236
Turner, Castellano B., 134
Turner, Frederick Jackson, 174

Udry, J. Richard, 130, 135, 230-1,
  234

Vesalius, Andreas, 157
von Geusau, Leo Alting, 142, 150

Wallace, Alfred R., 19, 33
Weir, John, 53
Weisbord, Robert G., 134
Wenceslaus, King, 167
Westoff, Charles F., 135, 147-8,
  150-1, 191, 235

Whelpton, Pascal K., 89, 116-17,
    132, 134, 150, 232
Whitehead, Alfred North, 18
Wishik, Samuel M., 229-30, 233

Youssef, Nadia Hoggag, 214

Zachariah, K. C., 94
Zahl, Samuel, 173
Zaidan, George C., 33
Zelnik, Melvin, 117
Zinsser, Hans, 156, 172, 235

Index of Subjects

Abortion, 118, 120-1
Abstinence, 118, 139
Adjustment of migrants, 184-5
Africa, 82-4
Aged persons, 193-5, 197-201
Age-sex pyramids, 193-4
Age structure, 56
Aggressiveness, 28-9
Agriculture, 23-4
Aliens, illegal, 178
American Medical Association, 168
Amish, 103, 106
Anglo America, 88-91
Apartments for dead, 20
Aphrodisiacs, 108
Aquaculture, 23-4
Arab countries, 84-6, 212
Arizona, 90
Asepsis, 157-8
Asia, 57-8
Australia, 81-2

Baby boom, 113
Balances, old and new, 5
Bangladesh, 60-1
Bantu, 83-4
Billionfold increases, 41
Birth control failures, 131
Birth control methods, 118-23
Birth rates, 66-79, 109-10, 114-15
Black activists, 10, 127, 140
Black Death, 156
Black population, 130, 185-6, 195-6,
  197-201
Boy preference, 99-100, 103
Brain drain, 180
Brazil, 87
Brownian movement, 184

Caldepop, 217
California, 90-1
Calories, 20-1
Canada, 88
Cannibalism, 153
Catastrophes, 17

Catholic Church, 119, 125-6, 136-45
  226-7
Catholic fertility, 111-12, 127, 130-1,
  146-8
Cemeteries, 20
Census taking, 38-9
Chicago, University of, 205, 228
Childbearing span, 59-60, 110
Childhood diseases, 160
Childlessness, 128, 132
Child-woman ratio, 110
China, 19, 24-5, 62-3, 99-100, 224-5,
  236
Civil liberties, 8, 124-5, 218
Clinics, birth control, 227
Cohort analysis, 110
Coitus interruptus, 118
Coitus obstructus, 118-19
Coitus reservatus, 119
Colleges, 205
Colorado, 121
Commission on Population Growth and
  the American Future, 12, 178, 188,
  218-19, 228-9, 232-3, 236
Completed family size, 110
Computers, 159
Comstock laws, 126
Condom, 119
Connecticut, 126
Contraception, 119-20
Contragestion, 121
Costa Rica, 193-4
Current Population Survey, 40

DDT, 28
Data, quality of, 43-5, 54-5
Death causes, 156-7, 168
Death rates, 66-79, 154-5, 161-3
Demographers, professional, 12-13
Demography defined, 2
Density, 28-9, 64, 82-3
Dependency, 193-5
Developing areas, 46-7, 222-3
Deviant behavior, 101
Disease prevention, 159-61

241

Dismal theorem, 17
Divorce, 202-3
Doubling population, 43-4, 66-79
Douche, 118
Drugs, 158-9, 167

Ecology, laws of, 28
Economics and fertility, 102-3
Education, 29-30, 197-201, 203-4
Egypt, 83
Emigration from Europe, 176-8
Emko, 228
Employment, 206-13
Encyclical on birth control, 137-9
Equation, balancing, 2-3
Esthetics, 20
Ethiopia, 16, 83
Europe, 55-6
Euthanasia, 221
Evolution theory, 19-20
Expectation of life, 155, 163-7
Expected family size, 131-2
Explosion of population, 14, 31-2

Family functions, 202
Family size preferences, 128-32
Family subsidy, 222
Fecundity, 101
Fertility, maximum, 100
Fertility determinants, 98-9
Fertility motives, 103-5
Filtering down process, 112
Florida, 90-1
Food supply, 7, 20-6
Foreign born, 179, 197-201
Foreign stock, 178-9
France, 111, 148
Freedom, 124-5, 221
French Canadians, 88
Frigidity, 101
Future expectations, 47, 91-4

Genocide, 10, 127, 140
Gerontology, 160-1
Greeks, ancient, 155-6
Green revolution, 21
Gross national product, 31, 46-7, 66-79
Gross reproduction rate, 110-11
Growth rates, national, 66-79

Haiti, 111-12
Harvard University, 205
Hawaii, 195-6
Health insurance, 168-9
Health services, 167-8

Higher education, 204-5
History of demography, 10-12
Homosexuality, 101, 153
Hong Kong, 64
Hospitals, 167-8
Household size, 197-201
Hutterites, 106-7
Hydroponics, 24

Ideal population size, 30-1
Immigration laws, 181-3
Immigration to United States, 88-9, 167-9
Impotence, 108
Income, 204, 206-11, 213
India, 6, 21, 59-60, 112, 194, 223-4
Indians, American, 196
Indonesia, 61-2
Industrialization, 26-7
Infanticide, 121
Infant mortality, 171-2
Inquisition, Spanish, 157
International Labour Office, 186
Intrauterine devices, 120
Ireland, 202, 222
Israel, 58-9

Japan, 6, 16, 20, 64, 225-6, 231
Java, 61
Jews, 59

Korea, South, 100, 225
Kuwait, 85

Labor force, 206, 208-12
Latin America, 86-8, 226
Laws, 220-1
Leisure, 206-7
Life table, 154-5
Literacy, 29-30, 205-6
Living standard, 26-7, 91-2
Longevity, 163-7
Los Angeles, 90
Luxury, 108

Malnutrition, 21-2
Manufacturing workers, 206, 208-11
Maori, 81
Markov states, 159
Marriage, 202
Marxism, 136
Massachusetts, 227
Maternal mortality, 158, 171
Mauritania, 86

Measurement techniques, 109-10,
  154-5, 174-6, 235
Medical expenses, 168-70
Medical science, 156-9
Mental illness, 161
Mexico, 86-7, 178, 196
Migration motives, 183-4
Migration rates, 174-6
Minorities, 195-7
Mortality, preindustrial, 155-6
Mortality differentials, 170-1
Moslems, 84, 100
Multiple births, 108

National power, 146
Natural increase, 89-90, 111
Natural law, 144-5
Near East, 58-9, 212
Negative population growth, 218
Net reproduction rate, 110-11
Netherlands, 56
Nevada, 90
New York, 196
New Zealand, 81
Nigeria, 83
Nomads, 85-6
Nonwhite population, 195-6
Norms, social, 99-101
North Dakota, 90
Nurses, 167
Nutrition, 20-1, 24-6

Oceania, 81-2
Optimum size and growth, 30-1
Overpopulation, 30-1, 218-19

Pakistan, 60-1
Papal commission, 137-8, 143-4
Papal infallibility, 138-9, 149
Perfect fertility control, 230-1
Pharmacological agents, 157-9
Philippines, 62
Physicians, 167
Pill, birth control, 121-2, 139
Plague, 156
Policy types, 220-1
Political arithmetic, 11
Pollution, 27-8
Population Council, 9-10, 15, 222-3, 229
  233
Population defined, 2
Population Reference Bureau, 54, 79
Poverty, 130, 206, 208-11, 213, 229-30

Prevented birth, 136-7
Preventive medicine, 159-60
Primitive birth control, 120, 125
Projection methods, 48-50
Pronatalism, 131
Prostitution, 101
Protestant ethic, 207
Protestantism, 100, 126
Puerperal fever, 158

Quotas, immigration, 181-3

Race, 83-4
Rank of country, 66-79
Regions, United States, 197-201
Registration systems, 39-40
Religion, 196-7
Replacement, generational, 110-11
Reproductive wastage, 171-2
Resources, natural, 27-8
Retirement, 195, 207
Rhythm method, 119, 138-9
Romans, ancient, 155-6

Sample surveys, 40
Sanitation, 28, 156
School enrollment, 203
Sea, law of, 24
Semitic peoples, 84
Sex ratio, 192-3
Sex roles, 192
Sexual behavior, 101-2, 144-5
Small family system, 111-12, 148
Social class, 108
Socialized medicine, 168-9
Sources of data, 38-40, 175-6
South Africa, 83-4
South Dakota, 90
Southeast Asia, 61-2
Soviet Union, 56-7, 222
Spanish origin, 196
Stabilization of growth, 218-19
Standardized rates, 109-10
Starvation, 21
Sterility, 107-8
Sterilization, 119
Subfecundity, 107-8
Surveys, 40
Sweden, 16, 193-4, 222

243

8, 212

Tokyo, 20
Transition, demographic, 5, 42
Triage, 22
Turkey, 58

Underdeveloped areas, 46-7
Unemployment, 206, 208-11
United Kingdom, 182
United States, 88-92, 226-9
Universities, 205

Value systems, 127-8

Vegetarian diet, 24-6
Vermont, 196
Violence, 28-9

Waste disposal, 28
Welfare business, 169
West Virginia, 90
White collar workers, 206, 208-11
Women's liberation, 8, 212
Working women, 212
Work week, 206-7
World growth, 66-79

Youth dependency, 193-4, 197-201

Zero population growth, 217-19, 231